# Agricultural Commodities, Trade and Sustainable Development

Edited by Thomas Lines

Based on two global strategic dialogues in 2004 and 2005 hosted by the International Centre for Trade and Sustainable Development (ICTSD) and the International Institute for Environment and Development (IIED)

International Institute for Environment and Development (IIED)
3 Endsleigh Street, London WC1H, UK
Tel: +44 (0)20 7388 2117, Fax: +44 (0)20 7388 2826
E-mail: sustainablemarkets@iied.org, Website: www.iied.org

International Centre for Trade and Sustainable Development (ICTSD)
International Environment House 2
7 chemin de Balexert, 1219 Geneva, Switzerland
Tel: +41 22 917 8492, Fax: +41 22 917 8093
E-mail: ictsd@ictsd.ch, Website: www.ictsd.org

© International Institute for Environment and Development and International Centre for Trade and Sustainable Development

Disclaimer: The views expressed in this publication are those of the authors and do not necessarily reflect the views of IIED or ICTSD.

ISBN: 1 84369 573 1

Printed by Russell Press Ltd, Nottingham, UK
Designed by Smith+Bell Design
Cover photo: Harvesting coffee, Colombia © Jeremy Horner/Panos Pictures

This publication may be purchased from:
Earthprint, PO Box 119, Stevenage, Herts SG1 4TP,
E-mail: iied@earthprint.com,
or through www.earthprint.com

# Contents

List of tables and figures ............................................................... i

List of contributors ...................................................................... iii

List of abbreviations and acronyms ........................................... v

Foreword ...................................................................................... ix

**Chapter 1**
**Introduction** ................................................................................ 1

**Chapter 2**
**Sustainable Development, Poverty and**
**Agricultural Trade Reform**
Duncan Green, Bernice Lee, Jamie Morrison and Alex Werth .......... 15

**Chapter 3**
**WTO Negotiations on Agriculture:**
**What Can Be Achieved?**
Kevin Watkins and Akhtar Mahmood ............................................. 41

**Chapter 4**
**Trade, Agriculture, the Environment and Development:**
**Reaping the Benefits of Win-Win-Win?**
Vangelis Vitalis ............................................................................... 67

Contents | **Agricultural Commodities, Trade and Sustainable Development**

**Chapter 5**
**Conspiracy of Silence:**
**Old and New Directions on Commodities**
Duncan Green ........................................................................................**93**

**Chapter 6**
**Commodity Production and Trade:**
**Public Policy Issues**
Jason W. Clay ........................................................................................**129**

**Chapter 7**
**Commodity Policy in an Era of Liberalized**
**Global Markets**
Peter Gibbon ........................................................................................**153**

**Chapter 8**
**Where There's a Will There's a Way:**
**Supply Management for Supporting the Prices**
**of Tropical Export Crops**
Niek Koning and Peter Robbins ..........................................................**181**

**Chapter 9**
**Leverage Points for Encouraging**
**Sustainable Commodities**
Jason W. Clay, Annie Dufey and James MacGregor ...........................**201**

**Chapter 10**
**Conclusions** ........................................................................................**227**

# List of tables and figures

Figure 2.1: Policy phases to support agricultural transformation ..............................21

Table 3.1: Selected Tariff Peaks in Agriculture ..........................................................47

Table 3.2: Tariff Escalation on Selected Product Groups ...........................................47

Figure 3.1: EU and US support by WTO reporting category (1999) .......................51

Figure 3.2: US direct payments to agriculture (2003) ................................................53

Figure 3.3: Application of the Swiss formula for tariff reductions .............................59

Table 4.1: Enlightened self-interest: gains from agricultural reform for developing countries and gains for the developed world ..........................................................75

Figure 4.1: State of the World's Fish Stocks...............................................................85

Annex 4.1: Estimated welfare effects of liberalization: summary of recent studies ......86

Figure 5.1: Cycles in real prices of selected primary commodities, 1957-2005 ..................................................................................................................95

Table 5.1: Environmental impact of commodity production....................................106

Figure 5.2: Monthly New York coffee futures..........................................................115

Figure 5.3: The inter-country distribution of income: percentage
share of final retail price ........................................................................................117

Table 5.2: Summary of interventions for sustainable commodities ...........................120

Table 5.3: Summary of interactions and complementarities between approaches
to the commodity problem ....................................................................................124

Figure 6.1: The Impact of a Commodity Price Shock Takes Several Years
to Dissipate ............................................................................................................132

Table 7.1: Export prices of coffee and cocoa in the wake of the
collapse of ICA and ICCA .....................................................................................155

Table 8.1: Commodity price changes since 1980 taking inflation into account........182

Table 9.1: Key sustainable development impacts associated
with selected commodities ......................................................................................202

# List of Contributors

**Jason W. Clay**, Vice-President, World Wildlife Fund-US
**Annie Dufey**, International Institute for Environment and Development, London
**Peter Gibbon**, Danish Institute for International Studies, Copenhagen.
**Duncan Green**, Head of Research, Oxfam GB; formerly at the Department for International Development, London
**Niek Koning**, Senior Lecturer, Wageningen University, the Netherlands
**Bernice Lee**, International Centre for Trade and Sustainable Development, Geneva
**Thomas Lines**, independent consultant on trade and development, Oxford, England
**James MacGregor**, International Institute for Environment and Development, London
**Akhtar Mahmood**, Independant Consultant, Former Federal Secretary to the Government of Pakistan
**Jamie Morrison**, Centre for Environmental Policy, Imperial College London, Wye, Kent, England
**Peter Robbins**, Commodity Market Information Service, London
**Vangelis Vitalis**, Ministry of Foreign Affairs and Trade, New Zealand; was Chief Adviser (Sustainable Development) at the OECD, 2001-2003
**Kevin Watkins**, Director, *Human Development Report*, UN Development Programme, New York; formerly Head of Research, Oxfam GB
**Alex Werth**, formerly of International Centre for Trade and Sustainable Development, Geneva

Contents | **Agricultural Commodities, Trade and Sustainable Development**

# List of Abbreviations and Acronyms

| | |
|---|---|
| ACDDC | Agricultural commodity-dependent developing country |
| ACP | African, Caribbean and Pacific (countries enjoying preferential access to EU markets) |
| AGOA | African Growth and Opportunity Act (in the US) |
| AMS | Aggregate Measure of Support (under the WTO's Agreement on Agriculture) |
| AoA | Agreement on Agriculture (at the WTO) |
| APEC | Asia-Pacific Economic Co-operation |
| AU | African Union |
| AVE | *Ad Valorem* Equivalent |
| BMP | Better management practice |
| BSE | Bovine spongiform encephalopathy (mad cow disease) |
| CAFTA | Central American Free Trade Agreement |
| CAP | Common Agricultural Policy (of the European Union) |
| CBD | Convention on Biological Diversity |
| CCCC | Common Code for the Coffee Community |
| CFC | Common Fund for Commodities |
| c.i.f. | cost, insurance and freight (applying to a price quotation for a cargo) |
| CQP | Coffee Quality Improvement Programme |
| CSM | Contemporary supply management |
| CSR | Corporate social responsibility |
| DC | Developing country |
| DFID | Department for International Development (in the UK government) |
| DSU | Dispute Settlement Understanding (at the WTO) |
| DTI | Department of Trade and Industry (in the UK government) |

| | | |
|---|---|---|
| EGS | Environmental goods and services | |
| EHS | Environmentally harmful subsidies | |
| EU | European Union | |
| FAO | Food and Agriculture Organization (of the UN) | |
| FIPs | Five Interested Parties (in the AoA negotiations: the US, EU, Brazil, India and Australia) | |
| FLEX | Fluctuations in Export Earnings (programme under the EU-ACP Cotonou Agreement) | |
| FNC | Federación Nacional de Cafeteros (Colombia) | |
| f.o.b. | Free on board (applying to a price quotation for a cargo) | |
| FTA | Free trade agreement | |
| FTAA | Free Trade Area of the Americas | |
| G8 | Group of Eight leading industrial countries (Canada, France, Germany, Italy, Japan, Russia, United Kingdom and United States) | |
| G10 | Group of Ten (negotiating group at the WTO: net-food importing countries such as Switzerland and Japan) | |
| G20 | Group of Twenty (negotiating group at the WTO: advanced developing countries including Brazil, India, China and South Africa) | |
| G33 | Group of Thirty-three (negotiating group at the WTO: middle-income countries such as Indonesia, concerned to retain flexibility to protect their farmers) | |
| G90 | Group of Ninety (negotiating group: all the ACP, AU and LDC members of the WTO) | |
| GATT | General Agreement on Tariffs and Trade | |
| GDP | Gross domestic product | |
| GEN | Global Eco-labelling Network | |
| GI | Geographical indication | |
| GIS | Geographic Information System | |
| GM(O) | Genetic manipulation *or* genetically manipulated (organism) | |
| GNP | Gross national product | |
| GPA | Government Procurement Agreement (at the WTO) | |
| GSP | Generalized System of Preferences | |
| GVC | Global value chain | |
| ha | hectare | |
| HIPC | Heavily Indebted Poor Country | |
| HS | Harmonized System | |
| IATP | Institute for Agriculture and Trade Policy | |
| ICA | International Coffee Agreement or International Commodity Agreement | |
| ICAC | International Cotton Advisory Committee | |
| ICTSD | International Centre for Trade and Sustainable Development | |
| ICCA | International Cocoa Agreement | |

## List of Abbreviations and Acronyms

| | |
|---|---|
| ICO | International Coffee Organization |
| IFAP | International Federation of Agricultural Producers |
| IFC | International Finance Corporation |
| IFI(s) | International financial institution(s) (the IMF, the World Bank and regional development banks) |
| IFOAM | International Federation of Organic Agriculture Movements |
| IFPRI | International Food Policy Research Institute |
| IIED | International Institute for Environment and Development |
| ILO | International Labour Organization |
| IMF | International Monetary Fund |
| IMO | Institut für Marktökologie (Institute for Market Ecology, Switzerland) |
| IPC | Integrated Programme for Commodities |
| ISO | International Organization for Standardization |
| ITF | International Task Force on Commodity Risk Management in Developing Countries |
| LDC | Least developed country (as defined by the U.N.) |
| MDG | Millennium Development Goal |
| MEA | Multilateral Environmental Agreement |
| MFN | Most favoured nation (category under GATT rules) |
| MSC | Marine Stewardship Council |
| NAFTA | North American Free Trade Agreement |
| NAMA | Non-Agricultural Market Access |
| NEIO | New Empirical Industrial Organization |
| NGO | Non-governmental organization |
| ODI | Overseas Development Institute (London) |
| OECD | Organization for Economic Cooperation and Development |
| PL480 | Public Law 480 (regulating US food aid) |
| PPM | Production and process methods |
| PPP | Public-Private Partnership |
| PRM | Price risk management |
| PRSP | Poverty Reduction Strategy Paper |
| PSD | Private sector development |
| PSE | Producer Support Estimate |
| Quad | Leading developed countries at the WTO (US, EU, Japan and Canada) |
| R&D | Research and development |
| SAP | Structural Adjustment Programme |
| SDT | Special and differential treatment |
| SMEs | Small- and medium-sized enterprises |
| SP | Special Product |
| SPS | Sanitary and phytosanitary standards |
| SSA | Sub-Saharan Africa |

| | |
|---|---|
| SSG | Special Safeguard (under the existing AoA) |
| SSM | Special Safeguard Mechanism (as proposed for the AoA under the Doha Round) |
| STABEX | Stabilization of Export Earnings (programme under the former EU-ACP Lomé Conventions) |
| TBT | Technical barriers to trade |
| TRIPS | Trade-Related Intellectual Property Rights |
| TRQ | Tariff-rate quota |
| UK | United Kingdom (of Great Britain and Northern Ireland) |
| UN | United Nations (Organization) |
| UNCTAD | UN Conference on Trade and Development |
| UNDP | UN Development Programme |
| US | United States (of America) |
| USTR | US Trade Representative |
| WCO | World Customs Organization |
| WHO | World Health Organization |
| WTO | World Trade Organization |
| WWF | World Wide Fund for Nature |

N.b. The $ sign everywhere indicates the US dollar unless otherwise stated.

# Foreword

The chronic crisis in trade in agricultural commodities is closely linked to issues of poverty and environmental degradation. Dealing with entrenched rural poverty and major impacts from agriculture on ecosystem viability requires a new look at how commodity markets work or fail. If we are to introduce fairness, justice and sustainability into these markets, we must understand better how they work, and the room for manoeuvre in public and private sector policy design. This challenging context provides the background for this book, which brings together an edited selection of think pieces and inputs prepared for two strategic dialogues. The first, on Agriculture, Trade Negotiations, and Poverty was held in Windsor, UK, in July 2004. The second, on Commodities, Trade and Sustainable Development, took place in Barcelona Spain, in June 2005. Both were jointly convened by the International Institute for Environment and Development (IIED) and the International Centre for Trade and Sustainable Development (ICTSD) with the generous support of the Rockefeller Foundation and the William and Flora Hewlett Foundation.

Talks on agricultural trade liberalization at the World Trade Organization must take into account the needs of commodity-dependent developing countries, to ensure that agricultural trade and commodity production will deliver outcomes that favour both the environment and poverty reduction. Alongside the trade negotiations, there are also hot debates amongst a range of actors and networks on ensuring functioning of domestic agricultural markets, improving governance and sustainability in bulk commodity markets among civil society groups. Environmental and conservation groups seek the application of better management practices (BMPs) organized either through segregated supply chains or through preferential access to markets and finance. This group is focused on private regulation, 'upgrading' of buyer-driven chains, and supply chain management. Elsewhere, a cluster of organizations are revisiting supply management to reduce oversupply and price volatility, focusing on learning lessons from the failures of International Commodity Agreements (ICAs). And a group of farmer and development organizations is concerned about growing corporate concentration in commodity markets and the impact of skewed market power on the small and decreasing share of wealth finding its way back to primary producers. This group is focused on competition policy and corporate accountability.

Our objective has been to bring these divergent threads together and weave them into a thorough debate, to identify leverage points for ways to achieve more sustainable commodity production and trade. The "Windsor Initiative" has been generated as a result of the dialogues as a proposal of actions in the form of an open-ended invitation to work towards pro-poor, pro-sustainable development solutions.

The book has been edited by Thomas Lines, who has worked with authors to update papers with speed and skill. The contributions of the authors and participants to the two strategic dialogues, which form the basis of this book, are gratefully acknowledged. We would particularly like to acknowledge the support of colleagues in IIED and ICTSD: Constantine Bartel, Christophe Bellmann, Annie Dufey, Sarah Henson, Bernice Lee, James MacGregor, Frances Reynolds, Bill Vorley, and Alex Werth; and also Jacob Werksman of the Rockefeller Foundation and John Audley of GMF. Many thanks are also due to Ramón Torrent for his warm hospitality at the University of Barcelona, in June 2005.

**Camilla Toulmin, Director, IIED, London**
**Ricardo Meléndez-Ortiz, Executive Director, ICTSD, Geneva**

**November 2005**

# Chapter 1

# Introduction[1]

## 1. Background

This book arises from two Strategic Dialogues that were recently organized jointly by the International Centre for Trade and Sustainable Development (ICTSD) and the International Institute for Environment and Development (IIED). The first was held in Windsor, England, in July 2004 on **Agricultural Trade Negotiations, Poverty and Sustainability**, and the second in Barcelona in June 2005 on **Commodities Trade, Poverty and Sustainable Development**.[2] Both brought together a mix of policymakers, researchers and activists.

The dialogues were not designed to generate a road map or coalition for action but to gain a broader understanding of leverage points for action and opportunities for collaboration within ongoing negotiations and other processes. Given the multi-stakeholder nature of these events, there may be strong differences of opinion, for instance around interventions in the market to manage supply. This introductory chapter seeks

---

1. This chapter is based on reports by Bernice Lee and Bill Vorley, who also drew on inputs from John Audley and Jacob Werksman, the rapporteurs during the Windsor dialogue, as well Ricardo Meléndez-Ortiz and Camilla Toulmin. It was compiled from the reports of the Windsor and Barcelona dialogue meetings by Thomas Lines.
2. Generous support for this process was received from the William and Flora Hewlett Foundation and the Rockefeller Foundation.

to capture the arguments and outputs from both dialogues.

Securing a sustainable livelihood for smallholder farmers remains the principal means for reducing poverty in many countries of the South. The multilateral trading system has yet to respond to sustainable development and poverty reduction concerns raised by developing countries. Neither have other agriculture-related concerns such as declining terms of trade, diversification and market concentration been addressed in a meaningful fashion at the global level. ICTSD and IIED sought to examine how trade rules and other processes might address some of these concerns at the Windsor Dialogue in 2004, shortly before WTO members agreed the 'July framework' that revived the Doha Round talks. The goal was to determine how the agricultural negotiations could increase benefits for poor people and nations and how to link developments in the negotiations to other areas of policy change necessary for trade liberalization to realise its potential towards improvement of the lives of the world's poor. At the Windsor meeting, questions were asked on three broad issues:

1. **Principles for pro-development outcomes.** Are the principles and assumptions that have driven agricultural trade reform conducive to pro-development outcomes? In the current WTO round's three-pillar approach, with negotiations taking place on market access, export competition and domestic support, which specific features are most likely to secure gains for poor countries and poorer people?
2. **Opportunities to help poor countries.** Are there opportunities outside the formal structure of trade negotiations, such as consumer campaigns or dispute settlement, which would help poor countries to benefit from further liberalization? How can these opportunities be realized? How do they interface with the negotiation and implementation of trade rules? What is needed at this stage to ensure that outcomes from the Doha talks support these opportunities?
3. **A vision for pro-poor policy.** Can we develop an overall vision of how trade, agriculture, and development policies need to come together to benefit the poor? What kind of information, collaboration and strategy are required to create such a vision?

The Barcelona Dialogue built on ideas and debate generated at Windsor to produce a focus on the crisis in **agricultural commodity production**, which needs to be placed at the centre of debates on poverty and environmental degradation. Dealing with both chronic rural poverty and major eco-system impacts of agriculture requires a new look at how commodity markets work, and how trade negotiations as well as public and private sector policies can introduce fairness, justice and sustainability into these markets. Despite the central role of commodity production for poor countries, the issue is largely ignored by recent initiatives to tackle poverty, such as the Millennium Development Goals (MDGs) and the G8 Summit.

Civil society proposals to improve governance of primary commodity markets for sustainability have clustered around four broad approaches:

1. Environmental groups seek the application of **commodity stewardship**, which uses markets to increase the demand for sustainably produced products, through segregated supply chains or through preferential access to markets or to finance.

2. A cluster of organizations is revisiting **supply management** to reduce oversupply and price volatility, focusing on multilateral public policy and the lessons from the collapse of International Commodity Agreements (ICAs) in the 1980s and 1990s.
3. A group of farm and development organizations is concerned about growing corporate concentration in commodity markets and supply chains, and the impact of **imbalances of market power** on the share of wealth accruing to primary producers. This group is focused on competition policy and corporate accountability.
4. Some groups argue that the elimination of trade barriers and market distortions in the context of ongoing **WTO negotiations** will increase world prices and provide new trading opportunities for developing countries. The WTO's July framework and its Annex A on agriculture address some of those issues, notably through provisions on export subsidies, domestic support, tropical products and trade preferences.

This chapter sets out the key points from the papers presented at both strategic dialogues. The dialogues helped improve understanding of where agricultural trade fits within the bigger picture of achieving a fairer, more sustainable planet. The ensuing discussions, and certain conclusions drawn by the participants, are summarized in Chapter 10 at the end of the book.

## 2. Sustainable development, poverty and agricultural trade reform

In Chapter 2 Duncan Green, Bernice Lee, Jamie Morrison and Alex Werth review the contemporary obstacles and opportunities to agricultural development, as well as other systemic factors that have stood in the way of progressive policies at the WTO. Agriculture lies at the heart of the trade and sustainable development nexus. It comprises over 50 per cent of gross domestic product (GDP) in some of the poorest countries and provides livelihoods for the large majority of people in developing countries. Besides promoting economic growth and income generation, agricultural trade has significant implications for other key public policy objectives such as food security, income distribution and poverty reduction, rural development, environmental and biodiversity protection, as well as food safety and health. Despite the importance of agriculture for many countries, and the idea that agricultural trade liberalization should be the driving force for integrating developing countries in world trade, the three-year-long agriculture negotiations under the WTO Doha mandate have yet to yield tangible results for the poor in many countries.

Exports from many developing countries are yet to achieve real access to developed countries' markets, which remain closed due to relatively high, often escalating tariffs, overly burdensome food safety and other technical requirements. Highly subsidized developed-country farm products are also often 'dumped' on the world market, creating import surges in developing countries and jeopardizing the livelihoods of many farmers. In addition, subsidized exports from OECD countries frequently displace developing countries' products in third countries' markets.

Even though developed countries have reduced their overall levels of tariffs and subsidies for agricultural products as a result of the WTO negotiations, they have retained protection for certain 'sensitive' products, which are often also products of interest to developing countries. Developed countries have been able to increase production-linked support to specific commodities so long as the aggregate reduction target is met.

The authors argue that **the state** needs to play a significant role in stimulating the early stages of transformation of agriculture. Success in India at this stage was based on state support to credit, inputs and irrigation infrastructure, which was necessary because of widespread diseconomies of scale and market failures. Yet in many LDCs, particularly in Sub-Saharan Africa, donors now insist that agricultural development should take place with very limited state support. For poor countries, the rural equivalent of **infant industry support** is necessary for the early stages of agricultural development, although it is often difficult to cut back on state support once systems have been put in place. But donors have effectively 'kicked away the ladder' of development by insisting on a minimal role for the state at just the point when state intervention is required to facilitate take-off.

Developing countries need to combine continued pressure on developed countries to improve market access with an understanding of local producers' real capacity to capitalize on new openings. Questions include how best to ensure that the benefits from better market access are retained at home and equitably distributed. Governments could usefully provide trade support services to facilitate access to international markets, thereby reducing transaction costs and providing trade knowledge.

The authors expect only a partial elimination of tariffs and trade-distorting subsidies in the current round of negotiations and such cuts are not likely to be undertaken immediately. Since taking action is perceived as too politically expensive at home, countries employing significantly distorting measures could agree to 'pay' abroad. These **compensation mechanisms** could provide a negotiating trade-off for developed countries wishing to hold on to subsidies. An example is the proposed transitional compensatory mechanism suggested by four cotton-producing West African countries. Another idea is for developed countries to contribute an amount equivalent to a certain share of their domestic agricultural subsidy bill – including the 'Aggregate Measure of Support' (AMS) and the Agreement on Agriculture (AoA)'s 'Blue' and 'Green' Boxes – to smallholder farmers in developing countries. These sums could be used to encourage them to continue preserving and improving plant genetic resources for food and agriculture. These compensation payments would be phased out in line with reductions in OECD domestic support. Such a tool could also help abate biodiversity loss, compensate farmers for the distortion caused by subsidies, and provide an incentive for subsidizing countries to phase these out.

## 3. WTO negotiations on agriculture

Chapter 3 is based on a paper by Kevin Watkins at the Windsor Dialogue, with additional material from Akhtar Mahmood's paper in Barcelona. It argues that the Doha

Round provides an opportunity to address longstanding inequalities in agricultural trade, but the encouraging words for development adopted at the start of the Doha Round in 2001 now have a hollow ring. So far, the 'development' round has delivered little more than encouraging rhetoric, punctuated by deadlock and episodic breakdown. Rich countries have not delivered the reforms needed to make the global trading system a more powerful force for development.

According to the authors, failure to change this picture will damage the legitimacy of the rules-based system represented by the WTO, with attendant implications for multilateralism. There is a broad consensus that the costs of failure will be high. Can they be avoided?

The answer will depend crucially on progress in the negotiations on agriculture. Reform of the rules governing agricultural trade is essential for both substantive and symbolic reasons. The substantive reasons are well known. Industrialized-country support programmes restrict access to Northern markets, generate large surpluses and subsidize exports. Producers in developing countries – a constituency that includes a large proportion of the world's poorest people – are excluded from market opportunities and forced to compete against heavily subsidized competition in international and even in local markets. The symbolic relevance of the agriculture negotiations relates to the legitimacy of the WTO system itself.

The chapter points to dichotomies and conflicts that affect the course of the negotiations. Some of the issues are:
- the vulnerability of developing countries to fluctuations in the prices of agricultural products;
- strong political and economic interests of the industrialized countries in maintaining their shares in production and trade in agricultural products through protection and support;
- high barriers to trade being maintained both by developed and developing countries;
- regionalism versus multilateralism;
- heterogeneity of interests among developing countries, including LDCs; and
- controversies about the relationship between trade and growth and poverty.

Watkins and Mahmood argue in particular that bringing Northern agricultural support systems under more effective multilateral rules could create new opportunities for poverty reduction. It would also strengthen the legitimacy and credibility of the rules-based multilateral system.

However, it goes without saying that major obstacles remain. The negotiating power of individual developing countries is limited – and the vested interests in industrialized countries are powerful. Consolidating and deepening the G20 and its alliances with other groups holds the key to progress. While it is impossible to disassemble the AoA framework, in the short to medium term there is a strong case for focusing political energies on a number of discrete goals. These include a prohibition on direct export subsidization, a revision of the distinction between 'distorting' and 'non-distorting' subsidies, and measures to restrict exports of all products at prices below the costs of production.

## 4. Trade, agriculture, the environment and development

Vangelis Vitalis' chapter, based on a paper presented at Windsor in 2004, argues that a meaningful attempt to tackle export subsidies, domestic support and tariff policies is vital. The implications of this are significant for both developed and developing countries. As the primary suppliers of agricultural subsidies, OECD members have a responsibility to consider the impact their agricultural policies have on other countries, particularly when those policies have a negative effect on the poor. This responsibility coincides with self-interest, since subsidization and protecting domestic markets imposes costs on importers, exporters and on consumers and taxpayers. Reductions in agricultural support have win-win effects for both developed and developing countries. Notwithstanding this, while global reform of agricultural policies is a good start, it is not in and of itself a sufficient condition for poverty alleviation. Reform needs to be supplemented by better strategies for development assistance.

Above all, fundamental reform of agriculture must be pursued with the vigour, and indeed the rigour, it requires. It should not be derailed by spurious environmental considerations. Rather, while trade negotiators should bear such issues in mind when negotiating liberalization, there should be sufficient flexibility to address genuine and well supported public good-type initiatives that relate to the environment. Where support is provided, this needs to be contestably and transparently dealt with. Specifically, the focus on non-production-related support for agreed public goods needs to be matched with a rapid diminution of product-related support for public goods like the environment. The potential to reap considerable further win-win-win gains is therefore significant.

This chapter suggests that the WTO is the right place to tackle subsidies that have 'double whammy' effects. The way it handles fish subsidies will be a test case, but there are some important points to bear in mind. These include an assurance that the disciplines applied to constrain and eliminate environmentally harmful subsidies (EHS) are consistent with WTO agreements and that the recourse to dispute settlement procedures is both clear and explicit. That said, nothing can conceal the fact that the complicated relationships between EHS and trade, and the use of WTO disciplines to address them, throws into sharp relief a number of intriguing questions that go to the heart of the future of the WTO. These are urgent issues and, in the interests of sustainable development, negotiators should not shy away from them.

## 5. Conspiracy of silence

Chapter 5 is based on Duncan Green's overview paper at the Barcelona dialogue. It summarizes the main aspects of the crisis affecting agricultural commodities, both those that compete with Northern agriculture (e.g. sugar, maize) and the non-competing commodities such as coffee and tea, also known as tropical commodities. It examines and compares the main approaches taken both within the mainstream policy community and among a wider range of thinkers and advocates.

Green argues that for rich countries, the recent steady fall in commodity prices has been good for consumers, while attempts to re-establish the commodity stabilization schemes of the 1960s and 1970s have been firmly set aside, given the current pro-market paradigm. However, in the last couple of years a new impetus has developed to address the various dimensions of tropical commodity production and its links with poverty, environment and power. The chapter identifies six main currents of thought:

1. **'Mainstream macro'**, which emphasizes the WTO agriculture negotiations, and compensation and aid schemes. Green makes a distinction here between 'competing commodities' (produced by both developed and developing countries, such as sugar, rice and cotton) and 'tropical commodities,' such as cocoa and coffee. In the first case, a major area of debate concerns subsidies paid to agricultural producers in rich countries, especially the EU and the US. Such subsidies generate overproduction, downward pressure on world market prices, and dumping on third markets including those in developing countries.

   For tropical commodities, improved market access is seen as one means to improve incomes, such as in reducing tariff escalation on processed commodities so that more value can be generated in developing countries. Some also point to South-South trade as a direction to take. Various schemes have been run to compensate for fluctuations in tropical commodity prices, such as the EU's former STABEX mechanism. However, the eligibility criteria tend to be very tight, and payment delayed. Voluntary schemes such as for cotton and sugar have also been proposed, but with little progress to date.

2. **'Mainstream micro'** includes proposals for diversification and market-based price risk management. The focus is mainly on encouraging diversification out of commodity production, through switching to new crops, increased processing of existing crops and spreading into a range of non-agricultural activities. However, this is not without risks. For instance, several countries may decide to invest in the same 'new' commodities. Diversification into non-agricultural activity has been a successful option for many Asian and Latin American countries but would be more of a challenge for smaller, poorer African economies. Market-based price risk management is an option being explored, focusing on schemes to insure against price volatility.

3. **'Sustainable commodities'** approaches advocate improved environmental management, fair trade, organics and corporate social responsibility. Schemes of this sort channel a price premium from socially and environmentally conscious consumers towards producers. They depend on establishing, monitoring, certifying and labelling particular standards sought in production processes, which include, for example, improved soil management, strengthened natural eco-system functions on-farm, and reduced waste. But many small-scale producers find it hard to demonstrate their conformity with better practices and face high fixed costs in getting their farms certified, so they are unable to access certification schemes and the opportunity for higher prices. Fair-trade schemes are another option for producers to receive higher prices,

but are usually offered only to farmers' cooperatives. To date these schemes constitute only a tiny proportion of the overall global market, while the proliferation of standards can lead to confusion amongst consumers.

4. **'National coordination'** relates to state marketing boards, producer organizations, and increased attention to quality and product differentiation. Most systems of state-led marketing boards were abolished in the 1980s and 1990s. This led to reduced access to inputs, credit and assured markets for millions of smallholders. However, a new generation of producer organizations is now starting to emerge in the form of farmers' cooperatives, which aim to exploit economies of scale, increase their bargaining power through bulk sales, provide market information and improve access to extension advice, credit and inputs. Promotion of such farmer-based schemes appears more promising than the re-establishment of state-led initiatives.

5. **'International coordination'** concerns proposals to revive supply management and proposals to harmonize standards. Various ICAs were set up in the 1970s and 1980s to provide for market stabilization through the use of buffer stocks and the management of national supplies. They faced a number of difficulties, such as rapid expansion of supply from many new producing countries, and 'free-rider' problems. The shift in political paradigm from the mid-1980s onwards led to the abandonment of such supply mechanisms in favour of relying on market forces alone. Today, despite renewed interest in supply management, there seems limited political and financial will to back up such an approach. At national level, the state-led market coordination mechanisms upon which such a global system would be built have often been dismantled.

6. **'Corporate concentration'** emphasizes competition law, and monitoring and transparency. All farmers, whether in the developed or developing world, are capturing a smaller and smaller share of consumer prices. Some believe concentration in commodity chains is a major contributing factor to this. For some commodities, a handful of vertically integrated companies now dominate the purchase, processing and distribution system, and the greatest profits are gained by those who control critical points along the supply chain. This concentration has led to lower returns and diminished power amongst smallholders. Those who cannot demonstrate adherence to ever-rising standards are excluded from the supply system. Attempts to deal with anti-competitive behaviour at global level have yet to make progress. Some progress might be achieved through publicizing information on corporate power and concentration, and on the prices paid to producers relative to the final price paid by consumers.

## 6. Commodity production and trade: public policy issues

Chapter 6 is based on a paper by Jason Clay at the Windsor dialogue. It argues that food production and poverty alleviation, although related, need to be de-linked. Producing more food will not necessarily feed more people. The focus now needs to be on creating more jobs, income and equity. Over the past 35 years, the production of food has increased faster than the population, yet the number of hungry people on the planet has increased.

Clay also pointed out that commodity trade liberalization and cutbacks in OECD farm subsidies will produce a range of winners and losers throughout the supply chain. In order to understand the impacts, a clear understanding of these questions is needed:
- Which commodities will be most affected by liberalization?
- What possibilities for substitution between commodities exist (for producers, manufacturers, or consumers)?
- Which producers will be particularly affected (by country, size of farm, gender)?
- How will impacts be distributed along the supply chain?
- What interest do consumers exhibit in the commodity price issue?

Trade liberalization is only one of the factors, though an important one, that affect trade. It is important also to identify likely changes to demand for commodities. Most studies to date suggest that overall consumption in developed countries will increase only slightly, if at all, for many commodities. This is true for soya in Europe, as well as bananas, coffee, rubber and fish protein, among others, in Europe and North America.

Significant increases in consumption are likely to result from dynamic economic growth in the South. China's growth of 8 per cent or more per year over the past decade has boosted demand for many raw materials; it has also increased demand for more calories and higher protein-based diets. Much of the expansion of soya in South America is directly linked to rising consumption of animal protein amongst the Chinese population. China does not depend entirely on imports to satisfy this rise in consumption; since 2003 it has been the largest agricultural producer globally, and now surpasses the US. These trends in higher consumption and stimulation of local food production are likely be mirrored in many developing countries when they achieve a sustained level of economic growth.

It is also important to note that some crops may be particularly well suited to improving the livelihoods of poor smallholder farmers. These include perennial crops in the tropics that are labour-intensive and do not lend themselves to mechanization such as coffee, cocoa, fruit crops, palm oil, or rubber; labour-intensive horticultural crops, such as fruit and vegetables; and organic farming where labour is substituted for other inputs. In general, perennial crops tend to have fewer adverse environmental impacts, are less easily mechanized, and have longer investment payback periods that discourage larger, more capital-sensitive investors. For all these reasons they tend to be ideal for long-term poverty-reduction strategies.

## 7. Commodity policy in an era of liberalized global markets

Chapter 7 combines two papers written by Peter Gibbon, for both the Windsor and Barcelona dialogues. Gibbon points out that a third element – oligopolistic market structures on the demand side – has been added to the classic 'commodity questions' of price volatility and relative price decline. Using coffee as the main example, he discusses what evidence there is of market concentration and monopsonistic behaviour in commodity markets, and what this means for policy.

The current mainstream donor agenda is replete with problems and limitations. *Compensatory financing* mechanisms, while still relevant, would have to be increased sharply to have any impact. The difficulties involved in *assistance for diversification* are often underestimated. *Price risk management* instruments are only likely to be much use to very large-scale, volume-secure, creditworthy producers. And private or public-private commodity-specific initiatives directed at *promoting 'fairer' or more responsible trade* are questionable, because they fall as obligations on producers and are skewed heavily toward estate production.

The issue of oligopoly, once seen as a problem *of* producing countries (and their marketing boards) is now seen increasingly as a problem *for* them. There are high and growing levels of oligopoly at the downstream end of agro-commodity chains, perhaps with the exception of cotton. The largest five coffee roasters control 69 per cent of the world market, and the largest eight international coffee-trading companies control 56 per cent. There are even higher levels of concentration at national level. There is a declining share of final prices going to producing countries and producers. A particularly sharp decline occurred between the 1990s and the present decade, with international prices as a share of final retail prices down from 35 per cent in 1989-98 to 19 per cent since 1999. Gross mark-ups of coffee roasters are 81-89 per cent of the ex-roaster price, of retailers 20-25 per cent of the retail price, and of coffee houses 70-80 per cent of the coffee house price.

Gibbon sees the regulation of oligopoly as problematic. For example, *renewed* ICAs rely on the re-establishment of national market coordination mechanisms. And global *competition law* to regulate oligopolistic behaviour lacks economic criteria for identifying the exercise of monopsony power or types of legal reasoning that could serve as a basis for action. The asymmetry of power between suppliers and processors, based on opportunistic behaviour by processors rather than collusion, is difficult to frame as an antitrust issue.

New ways of regulating and balancing market power must be found. These can include interventions that (a) scale-up smallholders' competitiveness and bargaining power; (b) target the market distortions that bolster the position of large-scale (including Northern) producers; or (c) impose new obligations of transparency on global oligopolists, such as labelling the final blended product with its precise varietal composition.

## 8. Where there's a will there's a way

This chapter attempts to develop a solution to the economic problems that have occurred in producer countries in the wake of the collapse of ICAs since the 1980s. ICAs are essentially a multilateral organization of markets. Since they collapsed, no new paradigms for ensuring sustainable and equitable supply have emerged.

## Introduction | Chapter 1

The authors, Niek Koning and Peter Robbins, suggest that although ICAs were not perfect, they delivered some outcomes that remain desirable but are often unattained by producers today. The collapse of ICAs owed more to the influence of non-producer countries than that of producers. Industry and government lobbying in the US and the EU – where consumers benefit from lower prices – helped undermine the ICAs. Since 1980 real prices of tropical export crops have more than halved, leading to increased poverty, ecological damage and urban population flows.

The ICAs were not designed to raise commodity prices but to stabilize them at levels, which were 'equitable' for both producers and consumers. Other examples from history, such as quota systems in developed countries during the 1930s, show that intervention can work.

The authors aim to refine past ICA approaches, proposing a new model, which they term 'contemporary supply management' (CSM), to achieve price rises, reduce opportunities for rent seeking and break the cycle of dependence of developing countries on consumer countries. While most ICAs in the past included both producing and consuming countries, CSM is aimed at producers only, in order to lift prices to a level agreed by the parties to the agreement. The authors argue that this more market-based approach avoids the inefficient incentives and outcomes that damaged the original ICAs. Producers could form a cartel, choose a desired price range and limit their production to match demand, through transferable production quotas. An intergovernmental secretariat would manage and enforce these new-style ICAs, ensuring that prices were kept within acceptable ranges for countries by purchasing and destroying excess stock. It would use peer pressure to enforce producer and retailer compliance. An interim export tax would be used to finance the endeavour.

Problems with such arrangements would include free-riding, rent-seeking, abuse and evasion. However, the chapter argues that opponents of ICAs exaggerate these problems. It suggests that the problems could be mitigated by mobilizing broad support, linking the schemes to product quality, environmental sustainability and improved conditions for workers.

The reality of commodity production means that surpluses will always arise and mechanisms are needed to ensure that countries and individual farmers have some flexibility in their production strategies, such as the use of buffer stocks. Achieving cooperation between producer countries would require considerable political will. Production is often spread over tens of countries, and a cartel can only operate with the most significant countries involved. While all producer countries would benefit from cooperation within a cartel, the biggest threat stems from 'cheating.' Cooperation between companies could greatly facilitate supply management: they could agree to cease trading with free-rider countries or quota-busting producers, and help monitor supply flows and destroy short-term low-quality surpluses. One proposal is for the international secretariat to establish its own trading company to develop 'guerrilla' tactics and intervene in the market to stop 'free-riding'. Further issues concern government behaviour, such as taxation of farmers and manipulation of exchange rates.

The introduction of a well-designed CSM scheme could increase the power of farmers to negotiate, access information and finance and counteract market dominance of buyers and processors. But there is still a risk that processors will find alternative ways of 'taxing' the farmer. The authors recognize that flexibility is required: it may be easier for some commodities to be covered by CSM, while for others significant modification of the model will be required.

## 9. Leverage points for encouraging sustainable commodity production

Agriculture is the world's largest industry, employing 1.3 billion people and producing $1.3 trillion worth of goods at the farm gate. In this chapter, Jason Clay, Annie Dufey and James MacGregor argue that a key challenge is how to expand production while minimizing adverse social and environmental impacts: what incentives can be provided to produce commodities in a sustainable way; which ones are better under which circumstances; and what can be done to encourage them?

The authors contend that 'business as usual' will not eliminate poverty, and propose exploring the potential for fostering production and trade in 'sustainable commodities' (SCs) – defined as providing greater positive or reduced negative social, environmental and economic impacts along the value chain. This definition goes beyond labelled products, such as fair trade, to include a number of private sector initiatives where individual companies are attempting to reduce the most important environmental and social impacts associated with specific commodities. These do not necessarily have any link to a third-party certification programme, and may be termed 'best management practice' approaches. Benefits are realized at a macro level through the production, consumption or disposal processes, or accrue to the people involved in production. As with any definition, there are exceptions and caveats – for instance, smallholder production for export of agricultural crops to developed countries can generate social benefits but imply greater transport emissions.

The authors identify a number of potential leverage points:

**Incentives for adoption of best management practices**: BMP approaches help prove there is a business case for sustainability. BMPs present an opportunity to limit adverse impacts of commodity production, allowing producers to maintain or improve their on-farm assets (e.g. soil, water, biodiversity), innovating (including optimized resource-use efficiency, creation of marketable by-products, waste reduction, increases in employees' skills and incomes), assuring market access and reducing risk of adverse relations with local stakeholders. Being largely market-driven, BMPs work best where buyers and investors have incentives to reduce risk. Investors are increasingly interested in using BMP criteria as financing screens. These mechanisms offer potential to shift *entire* commodity chains towards sustainability.

**Labelling of SC:** Labelled goods that emphasize sustainability appear unable to expand beyond niche markets owing to growth barriers including high costs, complex procedures, small volumes, high transaction costs and lack of harmonization or mutual recognition. Problems appear most pronounced for small producers. While future growth is expected throughout emerging and developing markets, there is doubt this will exceed 10 per cent market share for any commodity. Labelling schemes themselves present some barriers to expanding sustainability throughout agricultural commodity supply chains. The products do not always meet their claims or deliver consistent quality, producers do not always benefit and there is insufficient measurement of impact. Side-by-side comparisons of claims are needed.

**Trade policy preferences to SC-labelled products:** Trade preferences based on production and process methods (PPMs) may offer an opportunity to foster SC. It is not clear how the WTO would regard this issue and several challenges remain. Trade in Sustainable Commodities is generally insignificant in terms of overall commodity flows, and as a consequence, preferences may have little impact. Developing countries oppose trade differentiation based on PPMs because of fears of discrimination. Poorer countries have little to gain and might see their current preferential access eroded. Subsidies or market protection used by developed countries to shield domestic sustainable production might undermine the competitiveness of SC producers in developing countries. More research is needed to ensure the distribution of benefits from trade preferences does not accrue solely to developed countries, and to identify which trade arenas represent the best opportunities for SC.

**Supply chain collaboration:** Partnerships and strategic alliances offer great opportunities for SC. In fact, some of the most significant progress on understanding and promoting more sustainable commodity production has occurred when transparent processes were created, involving a wide range of stakeholders such as producers, private sector players, NGOs and governments. While the innovations in market structures linking production and consumption were not examined fully in this chapter, they suggest equally promising avenues for further work. Coordinated action needs to be undertaken commodity by commodity as well as across commodities. The IFC, WWF and others are showing some success in such initiatives for a number of commodities by combining BMP screens, market demand and government regulatory and permit systems. Government action in developing countries is crucial. Aid is needed in the forms of technical assistance, capacity building for certification procedures and health and safety issues, and market intelligence and information.

The authors accept that the concept of SC contains weaknesses. There is a tendency to burden SC systems with too many objectives. Too many BMPs are prescriptive, telling people what to do, rather than requiring on-the-ground results. Specific impacts are difficult to forecast, especially given the importance of trade-offs in defining outcomes. It seems none of the proposed leverage points can address the environmental impacts caused by agricultural expansion at the frontier or the cumulative impacts of changing production systems on those not involved in commodity production, but nonetheless affected by it.

# Chapter 2

# Sustainable Development, Poverty and Agricultural Trade Reform

Duncan Green, Bernice Lee, Jamie Morrison and Alex Werth[1]

## 1. Context

Agriculture lies at the heart of the trade and sustainable development nexus. It comprises over 50 per cent of GDP in some of the poorest countries and provides livelihoods for the large majority of people in developing countries. Agricultural trade has implications for public policy objectives such as economic growth, income generation, food security, poverty reduction, rural development, and environment and biodiversity protec-

---

1. This chapter is a combined edited version of these papers from the Windsor dialogue in 2004: 'Embedding a Pro-poor Approach in Agriculture Trade Reform' by Alex Werth and Bernice Lee, and 'Fostering Pro-sustainable Development Agriculture Trade Reform: Strategic Options Facing Developing Countries' by Duncan Green and Jamie Morrison. Alex Werth and Bernice Lee wish to thank Ricardo Meléndez-Ortiz, Christophe Bellmann, Malena Sell, Mahesh Sugathan, Chantal Line Carpentier, Charles Krakoff and Heike Baumuller for their assistance with the original paper.

## Chapter 2 | Agricultural Commodities, Trade and Sustainable Development

tion. This chapter begins from the premise that in many poor countries, agricultural production[2] offers greater prospects for broad-based economic growth and poverty reduction than non-farm opportunities do. However, the source of agricultural growth, and the mechanisms by which it is transmitted to broader economic growth, will differ across countries at different stages of development and these differences need to be factored into trade policy.

The agriculture negotiations under the WTO's Doha mandate have yet to yield tangible results. There is a widely shared perception that they have not responded adequately to poverty and sustainability concerns raised by developing countries. Many rich countries continue to conceive their 'development policies' in terms of official development aid alone. Policies in other arenas – such as agriculture, trade, investment, intellectual property, the environment and security – are usually crafted with little concern for developing countries.

In the following section, we will outline a number of systemic factors that have stood in the way of progressive policies at the WTO. In the section after that, we first briefly review the contemporary obstacles and opportunities to agricultural development, many of which differ from those facing countries that have successfully developed in the past. We then develop an argument for differentiating the policy instruments that might be appropriate at different stages of development. In section 4, we look first at export-led growth which often calls for an 'offensive' policy stance to be taken in trade negotiations, and then at import substitution as an approach that may require a more 'defensive' stance. Sections 5 and 6 discuss some elements of a pro-poor agriculture trade reform agenda, followed by some complementary mechanisms to support them.

## 2. Limitations of the negotiating system and its setting

The reasons for the slowness of the agriculture trade negotiations to deliver pro-poor outcomes are well documented. A number of systemic elements stand out as contributors to the problem.

### 2.1 Failure to embrace poverty concerns

One of the precepts of the multilateral trading system is that agricultural trade liberalization should be the main driving force integrating developing countries into world trade. Multilateral agricultural trade negotiations have focused on trade barriers at the aggregate level, based on the three 'pillars' of market access, export competition and domestic support. However, the objective of reducing distortions in agricultural trade has not been realized.

The WTO's Agreement on Agriculture contains many exemptions, such as the '*de*

---
2. The chapter focuses primarily on opportunities for agricultural development and not implicitly on non-trade concerns such as food security. Whilst it is assumed that agricultural development will contribute to such objectives in the long term, strategies in pursuit of agricultural development may not be consistent with them in the short term.

*minimis*' threshold for AMS reduction (which allows developed countries to maintain support of up to 5 per cent of the production value of a commodity), the Blue Box (partly decoupled payments under production-limitation programmes) and the Green Box (decoupled support with minimally trade-distorting effects). These enabled developed countries to formally redesign support programmes – in the form of 'decoupling' for example – and shift the modified subsidies into one of the exempt boxes, without caps or reduction commitments, so long as aggregate reduction targets were met. Because of this legal loophole, the spending on agricultural support by major subsidizing WTO members has not significantly decreased since the AoA was implemented in January 1995.[3] This also reflects the power of agricultural lobbies in developed countries.

## 2.2 Shortcomings of Special and Differential Treatment

Special and Differential Treatment in multilateral trade rules has yet to bring about significant pro-poor agricultural outcomes. The traditional SDT approach has many shortcomings. At the WTO, developing-country status is determined by self-selection, while the status of least developed country is determined by a list compiled by the United Nations. The unit is the country. This does not distinguish among sub-regions or vulnerable populations within states or among different sectors in an economy. For example, Mexico could be a competitive economy taken as a whole but it continues to have many marginalized rural communities. Similarly, an LDC like Mali could be very competitive in cotton production, despite the persistence of poverty in most of the country.

The SDT toolbox in the AoA is also limited. It only offers lower levels of commitments, softer disciplines and – in the area of some tropical products, for example – increased access to developed countries' markets. SDT is often toothless in dealing with more systemic impacts of trade liberalization, such as the erosion of trade preferences and the so-called 'crisis situation'[4] resulting from gradually falling and volatile commodity prices. Developing countries paid a high price for incorporating SDT in the WTO by accepting, in return, very modest liberalization in OECD countries, which also retained the ability to carve out certain commodities from liberalization. Many developing countries appear to have gained flexibility in areas not that relevant to their needs, such as the ability to provide certain input or investment subsidies.[5] But many of them cannot retain very high bound tariff ceilings, due to regional, bilateral or unilateral liberalization, or commitments made under World Bank or IMF loan programmes.

## 2.3 Failure to provide for 'adjustment'

Liberalization fuels social and economic changes that require a reallocation of labour and capital – adjustment. Poor farmers are often hurt by economic changes even though liber-

---

3. OECD (2004).
4. World Trade Organization (2003B).
5. See Article 6.2 of the WTO Agreement on Agriculture.

alization policies may bring benefits elsewhere. To assuage the concerns, many difficult questions need to be explored. In developed countries, for example, how will agricultural liberalization affect the livelihoods of EU cotton growers and sugar beet producers or Japanese rice farmers? In the event of subsidy removal, who are the structural losers in the OECD – agribusinesses or poor farmers? How could structural losers be encouraged to move into new areas? How could longer-term opportunities associated with opening markets be magnified? Similarly, developing countries will have to adjust to new production structures – and build supply-side capacity with scant resources – as a result of trade liberalization, even in sectors where they have comparative advantages.

A move towards identifying adjustment solutions may be a necessary condition for further progress in agriculture trade reform in the WTO. These elements will be explored later on in this chapter.

## 2.4 Failure to address market concentration and competition

Low commodity prices and high costs of moving up the value chain are marginalizing agricultural producers. Disparities in bargaining power, information and access to credit may entrench an anti-poor and anti-rural bias in markets even if trade rules could be reformed. Coffee growers, for example, face a global market in which three companies account for 45 per cent of roasting. Four companies control 40 per cent of cocoa grinding, while in soya and livestock the same three companies have the lion's share of crushing and feed production along the entire chain from South America to Europe. In the supermarket sector, the top 30 companies account for around a third of global grocery sales. Nationally, the top five supermarkets often account for 70 per cent or more of grocery sales.[6] These supermarket chains are rapidly penetrating middle- and low-income countries.

To ensure that trade policy reform is supported rather than undermined by private-sector actions, changes in public- and private-sector policy outside the multilateral negotiations are needed. In particular, national competition policies need to be rethought to take account of buyer power. Small and family farmers' access to buyer-driven chains could also be improved, for example, by involving producers in standard-setting and ensuring the development of non-discriminatory standards.

## 3. Pro-development agricultural strategies

### 3.1 Agriculture as the driver of development and poverty reduction

Agriculture's importance, in both its contribution to growth and its share of employment, declines as an economy develops. But seeing agriculture as something developing countries need to leave behind can obscure the critical role that it plays, particularly in the early stages of development. The evidence of this role is multi-faceted. Dorward

---

6. Vorley, Werth and Jacobsen (2003).

et al[7] note the high degree of correspondence between patterns of agricultural growth and patterns of poverty reduction across developing country regions. There is strong econometric evidence for the poverty-reducing impact of agricultural growth.[8] There is also a well-developed theoretical literature explaining why agricultural growth has disproportionately positive impacts. For example, Johnston and Mellor[9] demonstrate the important contribution that agriculture can make, perhaps most importantly to stimulating increased domestic demand, via increased rural incomes, that can support growth in other sectors. Additionally, when the alternatives to agriculture are examined, there are few obvious candidates as drivers of broadly-based growth in the early stages of development.

However, agricultural growth and subsequent benefits are by no means guaranteed. The transformation of agriculture from low-intensity, low-volume production to the creation of the sustained surplus needed to generate growth will only happen under certain conditions. Before discussing further how changes in trade rules might affect agriculture's ability to fulfil its potential, we need to understand where the potential for growth might lie and the conditions for it to happen.

## 3.2 An enabling environment for (pro-poor) agricultural growth

The conditions facing agricultural producers (primarily African) seeking to modernize their agriculture today are in many respects more problematic than during the Asian Green Revolutions, upon which much of the evidence referred to above is based. Dorward et al[10] divide them into (a) local conditions which include (i) more heterogeneous agro-climatic conditions in Africa (more erratic water supply, more fragile soils) and (ii) the fact that lower population densities generally mean smaller domestic markets and greater communication problems; (b) global conditions, which include the long-term decline in commodity prices and shifts in the power structures of supply chains away from producers; and (c) changes in policy environments resulting from the emphasis on market liberalization, state withdrawal and reduced fiscal expenditure, and the influence of urbanization in shifting policy priorities away from agricultural production towards cheaper food.

We take it as given that the local conditions will inevitably require greater levels of, and more sophisticated investments in, for example infrastructure and research and development. Of more concern to the current chapter are the global conditions and the policy environment.

### 3.2.1 Global conditions

Compounding falls in real commodity prices, a key change in global conditions has

---

7. Dorward *et al* (2004).
8. See for example Thirtle et al (2001) for a review.
9. Johnston and Mellor (1961).
10. Dorward *et al* (2004).

been the increasing vertical integration of agricultural supply chains with power concentrated at or near the retailer end. In addition to the constant downward pressure that this imposes on farmgate prices, decisions on market access and on safety and quality standards are increasingly determined by large multinational corporations, rather than by either national or international public bodies. In modern supply chains the effective setting of standards is slipping rapidly out of the public domain, with the public standards representing minima for many commodities. Reardon[11] shows that standards are generally set at levels required by developed countries because it is not cost-effective to segregate products destined for the local and international markets.

For these reasons, small-scale farmers are increasingly excluded from a growing sector comprising large farmers and some of the more prosperous smallholders contracting into modern supply chains, given the difficulty in meeting quality requirements which require major investments and the ability to obtain and respond to timely market information. Facing such difficulties, smallholders may be better advised to concentrate on the shrinking portion of developed countries' markets where traditional marketing chains continue to play a role. Research by Reardon and others suggests that in developed countries, supermarket penetration appears to plateau at about 75 per cent of the food market with the remainder consisting of less diverse, inferior and lower-priced products, which may offer lower margins for producers. Even those smallholders that opt to concentrate on domestic markets are not safe from the onward march of the supermarkets. Supermarket penetration in developing countries is expanding rapidly, often bringing in its wake 'Northern' quality standards.

### 3.2.2 Policy environment

Whilst the dynamics of the shift in market structures will be critical for allowing a smooth transition in rural economies, they can be influenced by domestic policy. The policy environment in many countries has been changing in two inter-related dimensions: increased opening of markets and a reduced role for the state, both driven by the liberalization agenda.
- **Opening markets**. In theory at least, opening local markets to trade will cause a shift from the production of non-tradables/semi-tradables[12] to the tradables in which a country has a comparative advantage. In practice, however, developed countries use a range of instruments (e.g. subsidies and non-tariff barriers) to safeguard their farm industries, so that even if they reduce tariffs, developing countries may not benefit. The result of greater openness in the context of a still distorted international market has often been falling and more volatile local food prices.
- **Government withdrawal**. Associated with policy to open/liberalize markets have been

---
11. Reardon (2002).
12. Non-tradables are defined here as products traded exclusively on local markets (generally due to their low unit value). Semi-tradables are mainly traded on local markets due for example to poor transport infrastructure or policy constraints such as pan-territorial pricing, but can be readily traded outside the local market if these constraints are alleviated.

reduced regulation of input and output markets, reduced use of subsidies, and reforms (generally elimination) of parastatals. Often, there have been good reasons for such reforms due to fiscal unsustainability of existing interventions, rent seeking and corruption.

However, as Dorward[13] et al argue, reforms towards greater openness and a reduced role for governments may have damaged the prospects for growth in the agricultural sector of many countries. This is because countries go through phases of agricultural modernization and growth (see figure 1) and in different phases, different policy interventions will be required, many of which have been precluded by changes in policy options.

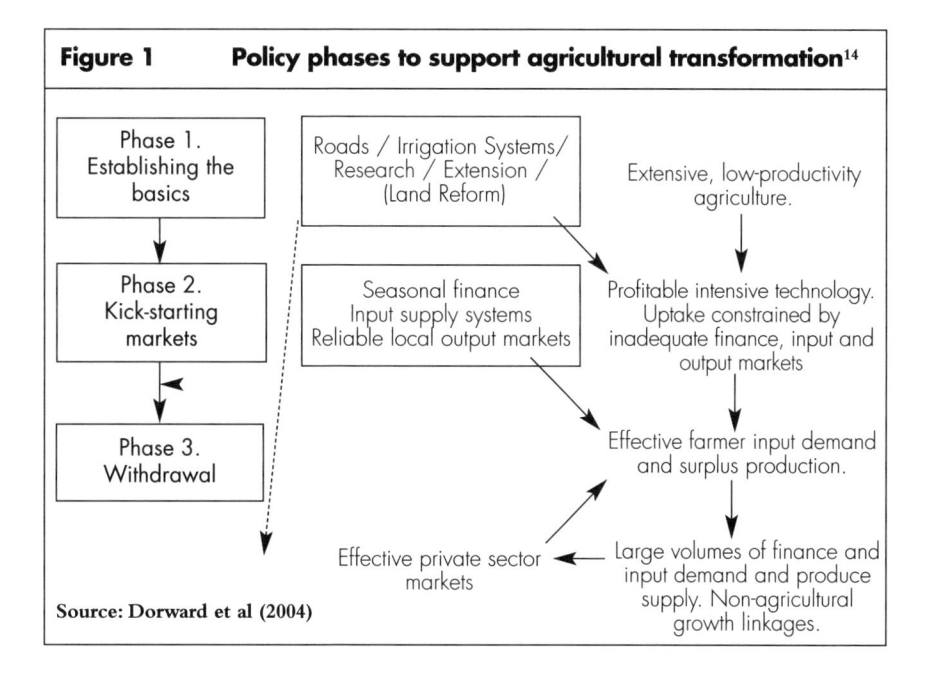

**Figure 1    Policy phases to support agricultural transformation**[14]

- Phase 1. Establishing the basics
  - Roads / Irrigation Systems / Research / Extension / (Land Reform)
  - Extensive, low-productivity agriculture.
- Phase 2. Kick-starting markets
  - Seasonal finance / Input supply systems / Reliable local output markets
  - Profitable intensive technology. Uptake constrained by inadequate finance, input and output markets
- Phase 3. Withdrawal
  - Effective private sector markets
  - Effective farmer input demand and surplus production.
  - Large volumes of finance and input demand and produce supply. Non-agricultural growth linkages.

Source: Dorward et al (2004)

Essentially, Dorward et al make an infant-industry argument for agriculture: state intervention is necessary to achieve agricultural take-off, but should then be progressively reduced to ensure market disciplines maintain producer competitiveness. The following paragraphs outline how this happens.

In the first phase, the basic conditions for a transformation from low-intensity, semi-subsistence agriculture are put in place. However, an intermediate phase is required in order to move to the situation of surplus generation (Phase 3), a necessary condition for agriculture to fulfil its growth-enhancing potential. In this second phase, the process of transformation is 'kick-started' with the assistance of government interventions aimed at reducing

---
13. Dorward *et al* (2004)
14. The central column of the figure provides examples of required government interventions (boxed) with the private sector filling the role when the state withdraws in later stages. The third column characterizes the level of agricultural development.

risks to producers that seek to invest in improved technologies, and enabling access to seasonal credit and to input and output markets on more favourable terms. Without such intervention, necessary investments will not be made by producers or the private sector.

However, for many countries, the chance to progress through Phase 2 has been removed as donors have effectively (if inadvertently) 'kicked away the ladder' of development[15] by insisting on a minimal role for the state at just the point when state intervention is required to facilitate take-off.

Evidence shows that the state needs to play a role in stimulating the transformation of agriculture. The successful agricultural transformation in India was based on state support to credit, inputs and irrigation infrastructure. These were necessary because initial conditions were characterized by widespread diseconomies of scale and market failures. State action was critical in overcoming these in India yet in contemporary LDCs, particularly in Sub-Saharan Africa, where episodes of transformation have been at best limited, donors now insist that agricultural development occurs best with very limited state support. History suggests that they are mistaken.

Under the current orthodoxy, the absence of direct state support is believed to provide a better environment for development based around private-sector activity. Whilst there is some evidence that this may have worked for some cash crops, which were often taxed under previous regimes (e.g. cocoa in Ghana, tobacco in Uganda[16]), it did remove some critical functions needed for the transformation of cereal/food sub-sectors that are central to take-off.

It is important to recognize that once Phase 2 has been successfully negotiated, the benefits of this type of state intervention fall off rapidly, because investment will generally arise once a critical level of market activity has been reached. The policy challenges then become very different and relate to issues such as the adverse environmental consequences of intensification. At this stage, withdrawing government agricultural supports that were critical at the early stages but now redundant is vitally important. As Imber et al[17] comment, most *temporary* policies tend to become permanent as lobbies grow in power, making the measures hard to remove. India's protection of edible oilseeds contributed to the 'yellow revolution' of the 1980s and 1990s, but is viewed as having been implemented for too long. Indeed the fact that many redundant and increasingly damaging policy interventions have been maintained (generally at the behest of agriculture lobbies) is one of the reasons for the current lack of enthusiasm for a role for the state in the sector.

### 3.3 Opportunities for agriculture-led growth

From the discussion relating to global conditions, it is clear that strategies based on export-led growth will face significant obstacles, particularly where transport costs are

---
15. Chang (2002).
16. Although this success may equally be attributed to exchange-rate devaluations.
17. Imber *et al* (2003).

high. Whilst there may be greater opportunities for export-led growth where OECD markets are opening, the poorer developing countries with their infrastructural and institutional constraints will undoubtedly struggle to compete with more developed non-OECD economies such as Brazil and China. Where export-led growth is feasible, it may be characterized by enclave development[18] restricted to commercial farms able to meet required standards and delivery contracts, and thus have more limited poverty-reducing impact. Moreover, successful examples of export-led growth have generally depended on good external conditions, where periods of high world prices have allowed exporters to accumulate the surplus necessary to move on from commodity exports before the customary bust. That is hardly a description that fits most world markets today.

But an export-led strategy is only one strategy for agricultural growth. In many situations, local and global market conditions are such that cereal-based intensification, often implying a strategy of import substitution, is likely to be more promising. This finds support in a review of successful cases of agricultural growth during the 1990s.[19] But why might policies that facilitate import substitution be more promising? The linkages literature argues that the growth-enhancing effects of increased production will depend on local demand characteristics of goods affected by policy change, their tradability and local production characteristics (for example, supply elasticity and input intensity). It has been demonstrated that where a good is less than fully tradable, i.e. essentially sold on the local market, and is widely consumed, then the multiplier effects can be significant. Cereals, with their high household budget share and often limited tradability, meet these criteria.

## 4. Challenges in relation to trade rules, policies and negotiations

Having made the case that agriculture has an important role to play, but that the potential will differ in different countries at different stages of development and will require strategies that reflect these differences, we now consider the trade rules and obstacles to (i) an export-led and (ii) an import-substitution development strategy. Although not entirely clear-cut, the export-led strategy will call for an offensive stance, and import substitution a more defensive posture in trade negotiations.

### 4.1 Opportunities and constraints to export-led growth

The focus of trade debates is often on the protection of agriculture in OECD countries, which has remained massive despite a commitment to liberalization, and moves towards what, at least in theory, are less trade-distorting mechanisms of agricultural support. OECD countries' use of domestic support in association with high tariffs stimulates domestic supply, resulting in increased net exports (often facilitated by export

---
18. UNCTAD (2004B).
19. Dorward and Morrison (2000).

subsidy payments) and consequently lower world prices.[20] This constrains export-led growth and is damaging for developing countries' farmers, especially for low-cost producers of 'competing' commodities such as cotton, sugar and tobacco.

Developed countries damage developing countries' export potential by restricting the opportunity to exploit their comparative advantages through selling into developed countries' markets (limited market access); by discouraging the growth of processed, higher value-added products (tariff escalation, preference rules) and by undercutting them in their own and other countries' markets (dumping as the result of excessive domestic and export subsidies).

### 4.1.1 Market access

Developed countries' tariffs are on average lower than those of developing countries, but they are characterized by very high tariffs (peaks) on specific lines, often in labour-intensive products such as agriculture and textiles. These tariff peaks are often criticized for diminishing the scope for diversification in developing countries' exports. Ingco et al[21] give examples of high tariffs for tobacco in the US (350 per cent), groundnuts in Japan (555 per cent) and maize in the EU (84 per cent).

Tariff peaks are often found in combination with tariff escalation on processed products, which is a problem for countries trying to increase the returns they can make on exports. Protection tends to be lower for primary products but increases sharply for labour-intensive food processing, whilst falling off at the upper end of the technology spectrum. Tariffs facing poor countries engaged in labour-intensive production are often four to five times those facing countries using more capital-intensive technology. A good illustration is the fact that the US collected $331 million in tariffs on imports (mainly garments) of $2.4 billion from Bangladesh in 2001, almost the same as it collected from $30 billion of imports from France.[22] Similar patterns of differential protection are found in a number of processing chains. Ingco et al calculate the tariff on raw agricultural imports to the EU to be about 1.7 per cent, rising to 21.3 per cent at higher stages of processing. Stern[23] points out that the US tariff on fresh tomatoes is 2.2 per cent, on dried tomatoes 8.7 per cent and on tomatoes in sauce 11.6 per cent.

It is often suggested that elimination of escalation and tariff peaks could help developing countries diversify their agriculture. This raises several questions. The first relates to the extent to which tariff escalation really acts as a barrier to trade. A number of studies address this issue and differ in their conclusions, depending on the methods of calculation used.[24] A second, less tangible point is that the benefits of reducing tariffs on

---

20. OECD countries' agricultural support amounts to about $300 billion annually, while aid flows are only a sixth of this, and it exceeds the total incomes of the 1.2 billion poorest people (Watkins 2003).
21. Ingco et al (2002).
22. Finance & Development (2002).
23. Stern (2002).
24. Gallezot (2003) argues that the overall level of EU protection of all agricultural and agri-food products is about 10 per cent, whilst others, using different methods, suggest protection of about 40 per cent (Messerlin 2001).

more processed goods depend on how important it is for processors to source material locally. If, for reasons of quality control, speed of response etc, they prefer to source locally, close to final manufacture and packaging (as in oil palm products), then removal of these tariffs may not make much difference. A third reason is that many countries are 'stuck' in Phase 1, unable to generate the consistent surplus required for the shift to higher value-added production.

It is often argued that poorer developing countries are not as constrained in their access to developed countries' markets, due to their access to preference schemes, and that reductions in tariffs that erode these preferences could in fact be damaging. There are likely to be losers from erosion, but in a number of cases preferential access has had very limited benefits for the exporting country anyway. Imber et al note that these schemes are not as effective as they might seem for a number of reasons:
- preference margins are smaller for products that the importing country deems to be sensitive,
- they offer little relief from tariff peaks,
- they could act as a deterrent to moving into higher-valued production,
- as a large number of countries with similar export structures tend to benefit from them, any advantage to an individual country is low,
- often, goods must pass certain tests on origin to be eligible for the tariff cut (e.g. US African Growth and Opportunities Act).

In practice, developing countries have largely failed to make full use of the preferences on offer. Utilization rates have been low for reasons that include restrictive rules of origin, uncertainty of renewal and the fact that preferences can be too low to cover the costs of compliance. To the extent that they are used, the schemes effectively shield countries from competition; and when MFN tariffs are cut, countries that had enjoyed preferential access are likely to find it hard to face competition.[25]

### 4.1.2 Export subsidies and export credit

Currently, the EU is by far the largest user of export subsidies, accounting for about 90 per cent of use. Many other countries have eliminated or suspended export subsidies. This may be due to a greater use of direct subsidies to farmers in developed countries, meaning that they can survive on lower market prices. An alternative policy is the use of export credits, which provide access to subsidized finance that lowers the total cost of exports. There is a debate, prompted by the EU's demand for 'parallelism' between export subsidies and export credits, over the extent to which there is an unsubsidized element in export credits, or whether by providing greater certainty, they should be deemed 100 per cent trade-distorting. In any case, it is likely that the majority of beneficiaries of reduced export competition will be other OECD countries (e.g. New Zealand, which dominates the world dairy market) and more advanced developing countries (e.g. Brazil in cotton, oilseeds etc).

---

25. Ruffer and Swinbank (2003).

### 4.1.3 Domestic support

Domestic support in developed countries effectively acts as an export subsidy by reducing producer costs, increasing production and lowering the cost at which they are able to export. The debate here centres on the extent to which different forms of support are trade-distorting, and therefore the extent to which developed countries should be allowed to shift their subsidies between the Amber, Blue and Green Boxes, without cutting overall subsidy levels.

OECD agricultural policy is only one contributor to the obstacles facing developing countries. During the 1980s and 1990s, the developing world's share of world agricultural exports was certainly affected, being essentially unchanged (36.4 to 37.5 per cent) against an increase from 17.7 to 28.8 per cent in all merchandise trade. There was actually a sharp fall in net exports from Sub-Saharan Africa, where the share of global agricultural export value fell from 8.4 per cent in 1965 to 2 per cent in 2000. Moreover, in this region the share of primary commodities in exports did not change, whereas it did in South America and South-east Asia, indicating that some countries have been able to move into higher value-added goods despite distorted world markets. SSA has become marginalized in world markets, with much of the diversification into higher-value products occurring elsewhere. The composition of exports is important in view of the weakness of most primary commodity markets.

### 4.1.4 Strategies in support of export-led growth

There is a broad consensus that improved access for developing countries' exports is necessary, but not sufficient, to engender sustained growth. IMF/World Bank[26] state that improved access needs to be part of a broader strategy aimed at improving price transmission and promoting supply response within developing countries. Similarly, Rodrik[27] argues that trade reform is only one element of successful development policy and that many other institutional reforms are also needed.

Whilst developing countries need to keep the pressure on developed countries to improve their access, government policy to take advantage of increasing export opportunities needs to be based on an understanding of local producers' real capacity to take advantage and of the policy instruments necessary to ensure that the benefits of this integration are retained at home and get back to all those who contribute to final production. The roles of the state may include services to facilitate access to international markets, reduce transaction costs and provide trade knowledge. Negotiations to reduce tariff levels and tariff escalation in developed countries need to be combined with measures to encourage investment in domestic processing, with competition laws to prevent restrictive business practices and a macro-economic policy encouraging the domestic reinvestment of profits.

---

26. IMF/World Bank (2002).
27. Rodrik (2002).

Whilst there is a general push for duty-free access for LDCs and for some product lines for other developing countries, it may be important to agree these on a non-reciprocal basis, for reasons outlined below. The benefits from tariff reduction will also be greater if the formulae for their reduction significantly reduce tariff peaks in OECD countries. However, developing countries need to remain realistic about the actual impacts of reductions in tariff escalation. Equally, the negative effects of preference erosion may not be as severe as is sometimes contended.

Similarly, whilst the reduction in the use of export subsidies will be unambiguously positive for most developing-country exporters, this impact may be limited (given that they are not as prevalent as they have been), and for some net food importers it could even be negative (by increasing world prices for their food imports). The prospective impacts of changes in domestic support policies are also likely to be limited. The emphasis on decoupling as a mechanism for making policy less trade-distorting may be overplayed. The EU cotton regime, with 65 per cent decoupling, is implicitly designed such that production is not significantly reduced. Developing countries pursuing an export-led strategy should continue to argue for reductions in, rather than reallocations of, support.

## 4.2 Opportunities and constraints to a strategy of import substitution

It is notable that the emphasis in current dialogue has shifted away from import substitution as a policy approach: 'in most countries, import substitution strategies of the past have been replaced by development policies that emphasize the gains from integration with the global economy.'[28] The emphasis is thus on gaining international market access and reducing unfair competition. Safeguards against low import prices and import surges tend to be justified on the basis of the persistence of distorted international markets. But this only goes part of the way to promoting the role of cereal-based intensification in growth processes. For example, it may be necessary to use border protection in order for price-stabilization mechanisms to be established, but equally important to facilitate access to domestic input and output markets through state intervention. A key question is how policies that allow protection and support of domestic producers should be configured.

### 4.2.1 Market access

Partly as a result of the dominant orthodoxy, developing countries have been under pressure to cut their own import taxes and remove restrictions on import volumes. The literature is divided over the merits of this. A number of World Bank publications suggest there is a positive relationship between the degree of openness in developing countries and their economic growth rates. Others question this relationship. For

---

28. FAO (2003).
29. Rodrik (2002).

example, Rodrik[29] points out that almost all successful cases, notably East Asia, China and India, have had a strategy involving the *partial* and *gradual* opening to imports.

### 4.2.2 Tariff levels

Not all developing countries have high bound tariffs despite the opportunity provided in the Uruguay Round. In a series of case studies, FAO[30] found that 13 out of 21 countries had average bound tariffs of greater than 40 per cent and the remaining eight countries had tariffs less than 40 per cent. Of the latter, four were net food importers. In most cases the applied tariffs were significantly less than the bound tariffs (18 per cent vs. 84 per cent), implying some degree of flexibility. The reasons for lower applied tariffs include the pressure to reduce barriers as part of structural adjustment programmes and the effect of regional integration. In many cases, the downward pressure on domestic prices resulting from tariff reduction has been offset by devaluations of the exchange rate, meaning that real farmgate prices have not necessarily fallen.[31]

Tariffs on sensitive products, notably food, are however generally higher and much closer to the bound rates, and there is some debate as to whether they should be included in general tariff reduction. This has been recognized in the concept of Special Products, now a part of the agriculture negotiations within the WTO, which recognizes that developing countries should have greater tariff flexibility on a limited number of products of particular importance to food security and rural development. However, there is still a wide range of views on criteria for the definition of SPs.

### 4.2.3 Safeguard mechanisms

Given the primacy of tariffs as the (only) trade instrument available to developing countries aiming to stabilize prices and safeguard against import surges, there is debate as to whether mechanisms such as surcharges and price bands should be allowed. Safeguards are currently built into the AoA, but are only available to countries that 'tariffied' their non-tariff barriers. Even these countries have made limited use of them. In an attempt to allow general tariff reduction, but at the same time alleviate the potential difficulty of countries which have recourse only to tariffs, a new Special Safeguard Mechanism (SSM) for import-sensitive tariff lines in developing countries has been proposed. SPs and the SSM are discussed in Section 5 below.

### 4.2.4 Domestic support

It is not just international market distortions that justify policy instruments to stabilize prices. Take, for example, semi-tradable cereal production (e.g. maize) in a landlocked country (e.g. Malawi) with high transport costs that create a wedge between import

---

30. FAO (2003).
31. FAO (2004).

and export prices. Wide fluctuations in production due to *climatic factors* will cause fluctuation in prices. The risks of low returns in some years will reduce investment and therefore the scope to expand production. An intervention policy to help stabilize output prices may be required to reduce these risks and stimulate intensification.

The fact that existing agreements place constraints on developing countries wishing to use domestic support is generally 'brushed under the carpet' by suggestions that most of them do not have the financial resources to subsidize and so will not be constrained. But a shift in policy that recognizes the potential for import substitution may bring these limits into sharper focus. Expenditure on supporting Phase 2 of agricultural transformation can be more cost-effective in promoting development than current expenditure in other sectors such as 'decoupled' safety nets.

## 4.2.5 Strategies in support of import substitution

The potential for cereal-based import-substitution strategies is not an argument for a shift to a more protectionist stance for all developing countries. Indeed the general strategy of openness and state withdrawal may well be appropriate for middle-income developing countries, but for some LDCs import substitution may be a better way forward. Developing countries need to determine how far they should agree to reform, in both reduced border protection and commitments on domestic support. In the current negotiations, how and how much to differentiate is the key question. On the basis of the discussion in this chapter, SDT with respect to tariffs and domestic support should be based on the stage of agricultural transformation. However, this raises further issues:

- **What is the definition of a country in Phase 2 of agricultural transformation?**
Given the diversity of country situations and commodity chains it is necessary to conduct analysis at a greater level of detail. Policy analysis needs to be much more disaggregated in order to determine whether a country or commodity is a likely 'winner' in pursuit of development goals. For example, some poor countries might benefit from improved access to markets for traditional exports, but also need to protect domestic food production which can offer greater scope for broad-based growth. Other countries, at a more advanced stage of development, could benefit from cheaper food imports.

- **What types of policy are critical?**
Strategists need to consider how the producers in Phase 2 situations might be protected from exposure to greater openness to (low-cost, subsidized) imports whilst improvements in productivity are being achieved. There is also a potential role for regional markets with common external tariffs and no restrictions to internal trade, as a substitute for the larger domestic internal markets often found prerequisite to growth in Asian economies, since they facilitate the shifting of the commodity from surplus to deficit areas, thus smoothing prices. At the same time, governments need to think about how to provide incentives for raising productivity at reasonable fiscal cost (e.g. price inter-

vention for smallholders only), without damaging the food security of net consumers.

## 5. Preliminary elements of a pro-poor agriculture trade reform agenda

Notwithstanding the distortions of agricultural trade caused by developed countries' policies, new developments have appeared in the current negotiations. These in part relate to the formation of new or strengthened alliances that are stepping up pressure to discuss trade rules that better respond to developing countries' interests. These new alliances include:

- The **G-20** of advanced developing countries grouped around Brazil, India, China and South Africa. The main element of G-20's agenda is to push for the elimination of agricultural export subsidies and substantial reductions in trade-distorting domestic support.
- The **G-33** led by Indonesia. This group mainly comprises middle-income developing countries with specific vulnerabilities. Concerned that their agricultural populations' livelihoods could be endangered by further liberalization – especially if subsidies continued and their farmers had to compete with artificially cheap imports – the G-33's main objective is to retain flexibility to protect their farmers through higher tariffs on SPs and a new SSM for developing countries.
- The **G-90** consisting of all ACP, African Union and LDC members of the WTO. Comprising the world's poorest and most vulnerable countries, this grouping is mainly interested in effective market access while preserving trade preferences; supply-side support to enhance competitiveness; and food security. These countries do not see themselves as being in a position to undertake further significant liberalization.
- The **G-10** grouped around Switzerland and Japan. This grouping consists of net-food importing countries concerned that deep tariff cuts could place the livelihoods of their farmers at risk. They are seeking flexibility not to provide effective new market access on a number of products.

These new alliances have generated some new impetus in trade negotiations towards pro-poor outcomes. Other developments have also contributed. A WTO panel ruled in favour of Brazil against US cotton subsidies while a similar challenge against EU sugar subsidies is under way. Against this background, it may be worth considering a number of elements that help formulate a pro-poor agriculture trade reform agenda. Preliminary ideas include: a commodity-specific focus in the agriculture negotiations; new approaches on differentiation; opportunities elsewhere in the Doha agenda; new strategic alliances; and complementary approaches outside the WTO negotiations.

### 5.1 The emerging commodity focus at the WTO

The prices of many primary commodities – such as coffee, cocoa and palm oil –

declined by nearly 70 per cent between 1980 and 2000.[32] Over 50 developing countries depend on three or fewer commodities for most of their exports,[33] and the decline in prices has led to a steep fall in their foreign exchange earnings and pushed their farmers' incomes below poverty levels. Many of the poorest countries also appear to have lost their comparative advantage in the production of certain commodities, such as coffee and cocoa, to richer developing countries. Many developing countries have been unable to diversify away from commodity dependence or capture significant gains in other forms, such as value-added processing. Africa, for example, has hardly benefited at all from the global boom in manufactured exports. At around 30 per cent in 2000, the share of manufactures in Africa's total merchandise exports has increased by only ten percentage points since 1980.[34]

Countries specializing in the production and export of primary commodities are unlikely to gain as much from WTO reforms, or may even lose in comparison with countries with a more diverse product base. But as the Cotton Initiative illustrates, the agriculture negotiations have generally failed to guarantee the reduction of subsidies on commodities of interest to poor countries.[35] Benin, Burkina Faso, Chad and Mali launched the initiative because they found no guarantee that cotton support measures would be significantly reduced. Commodity-specific commitments could help ensure predictability and certainty for poor countries, and hence poverty-relevant outcomes of the trade round. Several commodity-specific elements emerged in the modalities negotiations, and the emerging commodity focus could be a means to disaggregate the agriculture trade debate.

Every developing country has products of particular importance to it, but their interest in other commodities may be limited or non-existent. If negotiations increasingly were to take place on a commodity basis, negotiators could better utilize their limited negotiating capital and focus on the most relevant aspects of the negotiations to them. Within the narrower framework of commodity-specific negotiations, developing countries could better analyze the gains and losses to expect.

The Cotton Initiative provides useful lessons – both positive and negative – for poor countries with respect to other strategic products. Measures could include financial compensation of vulnerable producers against loss of revenues as long as dumping continues. (See 'Compensatory Mechanisms' in the section below.) Richer countries could be required to accord more favourable market access to other products of particular importance to poor countries, such as tropical products. Governments could also consider starting negotiations within the WTO on ten key products for developing countries – for example, sugar, rice, dairy, livestock, poultry, vegetables, fruit, soya, maize, wheat and oilseeds. Such initiatives could take into account a broader set of sustainable development considerations including, for example, environment protection and biodiversity conservation.

---

32. World Trade Organization (2003B).
33. Ibid.
34. UNCTAD (2004A), pp. 2-3.
35. World Trade Organization (2003A).

## 5.2 New approaches on differentiation

The Doha mandate on agriculture states that 'special and differential treatment for developing countries shall be an integral part of all elements of the negotiations..., so as to be operationally effective and to enable developing countries to effectively take into account their development needs, including food security and rural development.' As discussed above, the traditional approach to SDT has failed to protect the rural poor. It has not provided countries with 'policy space' to safeguard their agricultural populations and respond to challenges arising from liberalized markets, nor did it provide sufficient market access and fairer trade rules for particular commodities. There is a need to rethink SDT away from the one-size-fits-all approach towards targeted, context- and needs-specific flexibility and incentives – with a sub-national focus, for example, on the needs of the rural poor.

Additional differentiation approaches have emerged. Members have considered, for example, granting special treatment to recently acceded countries to the WTO that are yet to implement liberalization commitments under their terms of accession. It has also been discussed whether weak or vulnerable developing countries, facing similar problems to the LDCs, should be subject to more favourable terms under SDT.

An important new approach is that of **special products**. This seeks to enable developing countries to address food security, rural development and livelihood security needs. These would be achieved by granting poor countries the flexibility to designate a number of SPs to be excluded from new tariff reduction commitments, or included only minimally. While the SP concept is widely accepted as a tool for SDT, governments are divided over the question of how far developing countries should be able to designate SPs for themselves, or whether the selection should be based on objective criteria. The challenge is to establish objective and verifiable criteria that respond to the situations of each country and its sub-national entities.

Closely linked to the concept of SPs is the call by many developing countries to replace the existing special agricultural safeguard (SSG)[36] with a new SSM for developing countries only. Many developing countries do not have access to SSG, which many countries – developing and developed alike – want to abolish. The current debate is about when, and on which products, the SSM should be applied. Countries are faced with determining what kinds of import surge would justify border measures; how this new mechanism could be designed to be effective for poor countries; and whether it could be applied to all products (including SPs), or only in cases where countries have undertaken significant tariff reductions, for example.

Whilst there are strong arguments for allowing some developing countries flexibility on some aspects of the rules, their negotiating partners will not look favourably on an approach which tries to provide flexibility to all developing countries in all aspects. It is important not to confuse definitions of 'special' products and the SSM for developing countries with developed countries' demands for their own 'sensitive products' to

---

36. World Trade Organization, Agreement on Agriculture, Article 5.

be granted flexibility. The development case for the first is entirely different to the case for the second. However, developed countries are more likely to assert the need to protect their own 'sensitive products' if more flexibility is granted to developing countries. The latter will have to pay a negotiating price for any SDT they win, so they need to be sure that it is both necessary and effective in meeting their development needs.

In designing new SDT tools, governments have to strike a balance between general liberalization and the preservation of individual countries' 'policy space.' However, preserving policy space for developing countries can limit opportunities, for example in South-South trade. In the long term, it may also limit Southern producers' response to new food demands in developing countries. For SDT to meet the needs of the poor, links should be established with poverty reduction agendas such as the Poverty Reduction Strategy Papers. Transparency and monitoring will be required to ensure that SDT tools target vulnerable agricultural populations, and not merely protect traditional agro-lobbies.

### 5.3 Other potential opportunities in the Doha Agenda for the rural poor

Based on the assumption that liberalization can generate a 'win-win' situation both for trade and the environment, WTO members entered into a commitment at Doha to reduce or eliminate tariff and non-tariff barriers to **environmental goods and services**.[37] Governments have yet to agree on a definition of what constitutes an environmental good. This could provide a venue for negotiating more favourable market access for agricultural niche products such as organic or other sustainably produced agriculture products (which are not currently part of the negotiations). The agriculture-related aspects of the EGS negotiations could provide an incentive for agricultural producers to expand production that supports both poverty reduction and environmental sustainability.

In addition, under the TRIPS Agreement, WTO members have explored the possibility of granting higher levels of protection for **geographical indications** – currently applicable only to wines and spirits – to other agricultural goods. The assumptions are that GIs can protect smaller producer groups utilizing long-standing production techniques against agro-industries producing standard products. Within the agriculture negotiations, governments could extend GI protection to create new pro-poor incentives, replace dismantled or reduced public intervention, and provide new means to promote local markets. Poor countries could also be encouraged to take full advantage of GI protection already available under the TRIPS Agreement.

### 5.4 Generating strategic alliances and partnerships

As discussed earlier, small farmers in many countries lack organization and political representation, in contrast to the agricultural lobbies in developed countries (and in a

---

37. World Trade Organization (2001), paragraph 31(iii).

number of more advanced developing countries). As a result, their concerns are frequently not reflected in trade negotiations. In addition, negotiations tend to be dominated by mercantilist rather than sustainability or poverty concerns. To counter these problems, new alliances could be established to give voice to the rural poor and those championing poverty reduction and sustainability. For example, global alliances of stakeholders in commodity chains could be generated through inclusive dialogues. Stakeholders to include in these alliances are producers, traders, consumers, governments, development agencies, IFIs and civil society groups.

## 6. Complementary approaches

Agricultural trade liberalization cannot be expected to provide all the answers to poverty reduction and sustainable development. SDT and more needs- and context-specific flexibilities can play a part but they need to be complemented by other mechanisms such as targeted development assistance, infrastructural support, technical assistance and measures to attract foreign investment. These approaches are needed to help countries adapt to changes associated with liberalization, enhance supply capacity, realize comparative advantages and build competitiveness. The following are some initial thoughts on such mechanisms that could promote pro-poor outcomes in agriculture trade.

### 6.1 Adjustment mechanisms

Trade liberalization can bring about unanticipated economic, social and environmental changes. Carefully crafted adjustment policies can be used to help populations adjust to these changes. Many adjustments – to generate pro-poor, pro-sustainability outcomes – are likely to take place within countries, be they changes in economic policy, incentive structures, institutional arrangements or regulatory systems. Poorer countries, and poor farmers in better-off countries, often lack the resources to adjust on their own. In addition, small farmers seldom have access to their own governments – due to their lack of organization at the national level or the absence of accountable political processes. As a result, they rarely have access to targeted assistance.

Trade liberalization can bring direct negative impacts on countries, as illustrated by the Marrakech Decision which was adopted with the overall WTO accord.[38] The Decision addressed the concerns of food-importing countries that food price rises due to the removal of subsidies could limit the availability of foodstuffs. This decision has not been effectively implemented, and members are now considering the creation of a 'revolving fund' for vulnerable countries in need of affordable foods.

In order to deal with adjustment, a number of organizations have suggested some form of global adjustment fund which would cater for developing countries' adjustment needs during liberalization. Some countries suggest a multilateral fund to support preference-receiving countries adjusting to preference erosion. The fund could also

---

38. World Trade Organization (1993).

service multilateral price-support mechanisms to help abate price decline and volatility. It could help poor commodity producers to diversify or to enter new markets by shifting to value-added production. Taking the concept forward, the fund might emulate the Global Environmental Facility: starting with an assessment of adjustment costs, governments could pool financial resources and establish a multi-stakeholder process to adjudicate the fund. This could involve the IFIs as well as bilateral development agencies.

### 6.2 Compensatory mechanisms

Tariffs and trade-distorting subsidies can only be expected to be partially eliminated in the current round of negotiations and reductions and cuts are not likely to be undertaken immediately. Countries employing significantly distorting measures may continue to make the case for maintaining relatively high levels of protection and support for 'sensitive products' and 'non-trade concerns' such as food security, rural development and the environment. These countries could agree to 'pay' for this. This would entail channelling money directly to those countries or constituencies that suffer from any lack of developed-country action on agriculture. As opposed to the adjustment mechanisms described above – which should be undertaken on a voluntary basis by countries in need of easing the changes induced by liberalization – compensation mechanisms could be seen as a negotiating trade-off for developed countries wishing to hold on to tariffs or subsidies.

The Cotton Initiative provides an example. The Initiative proposed the establishment of a transitional compensatory mechanism, under which countries subsidizing cotton production and exports would compensate LDC cotton producers. The amount of compensation would depend on the level of cotton-related support. The compensation would be limited to the subsidy elimination period, and its amount would decline as cotton subsidies were reduced.[39] This idea could be applied to market access. Developed countries wishing to protect sensitive products could compensate producers or exporters of these products in poor countries which would be deprived of market access. The compensation could match the continuing distortion, on one hand, and the importance of the respective product for specific developing countries, on the other.

The Clean Development Mechanism of the Kyoto Protocol under the UN Framework Convention on Climate Change is an example of an instrument set up to allow developed countries to funnel resources into developing countries in exchange for domestic action. Developed countries committed to reducing greenhouse gas emissions can offset part of their obligation at home by sponsoring targeted emissions reduction projects in developing countries. The projects are expected to transfer technology and build local capacity. These projects are carried out under the oversight of an executive board. A similar instrument could be envisioned in the area of agricul-

---

39. See U.N. Conference on Trade and Development (2004A).

ture, with projects targeting small-scale, low-income farmers and regions of developing countries.

Developed countries could also contribute an amount equivalent to a share of their agricultural subsidies – including AMS, Blue and Green box support – to small farmers in developing countries, for the preservation and improvement of plant genetic resources. Compensation would be phased out as internal support is reduced and eliminated. This could abate biodiversity loss, compensate farmers for the distortion caused by subsidies and provide an incentive to phase out subsidies.[40]

### 6.3 Standards and technical regulations

Consumer demands regarding food quality, process and production methods, as well as health and environmental standards, are increasing. This has led to a proliferation of sanitary and phytosanitary standards (SPS) and technical barriers to trade (TBT), with which producers must comply if they want to enter foreign markets. These non-tariff import regulations constitute significant market entry barriers, especially for poor and vulnerable producers in the South.

Both the SPS and TBT Agreements at the WTO require developed countries imposing new non-tariff barriers to take exporters' concerns into account by negotiating an agreed equivalence between domestic standards and those of exporting countries. Both agreements also call on standard-using countries to provide technical assistance to exporting countries – especially developing countries – to enable these countries to comply with new standards. These provisions are, however, either non-binding or have not been effective. Therefore clear and binding commitments are needed for standard users to enter into mutual recognition agreements with exporting countries or provide assistance to producers in poor countries to offset incremental costs. In addition, these producers and exporters could participate in standard setting to ensure that their constraints are taken into account.

### 6.4 Competition policy

Missing in the debate on agriculture trade liberalization are issues related to the concentration of buying power and the control of agrifood markets by few companies. There is need for governments to implement appropriate antitrust laws, but only one in three developing countries has competition laws. Countries could be provided with technical and financial support to put competition policies in place. However, disciplining international companies at the domestic level can be insufficient to discourage anti-competitive behaviour and abuses of market power. A well-designed multilateral framework for competition policy – outside the WTO perhaps – could serve as a complementary tool to alleviate power imbalances in agrifood markets.[41]

---

40. See Perry (2003).
41. See for example CUTS (2003).

### 6.5 Supply-side responses

Fairer trade rules and adjustment mechanisms are crucial in helping poor countries capitalize on agricultural trade liberalization. However, few poor countries are able to realize their comparative advantages. They often cannot provide stable supplies of quality products and they lack access to (affordable) international transport, market information, capital and know-how. They also find it difficult to attract agriculture-related foreign investment and credit. Donors' assistance is yet to bring about tangible improvements in supply-side capacity in many poor countries. One suggestion is to focus their efforts on specific commodities, in order to promote international competitiveness through the development of infrastructure and regulatory frameworks, moves up the value chains, strengthening of SMEs and promotion of investment.

## 7. Final remarks

After the collapse of the Seattle ministerial, WTO members agreed in Doha to launch a new round of trade negotiations. This was made possible by putting development at the centre of the new round – at least in rhetoric. By giving a prominent role to agriculture, the Doha declaration constitutes an attempt to integrate sustainable development in trade negotiations. To ensure that the multilateral trading system delivers in this area, we need to move away from conceptions of it as a platform for arbitration among conflicting national interests. In an alternative conception, WTO members could promote the provision of global public goods as the goal of the multilateral trading system. Under this approach, trade rules would not be seen as an end in themselves but as tools to achieve objectives such as poverty reduction, sustainability and development.

It is clear that pro-poor outcomes in agriculture, including SDT, are necessary for the successful conclusion of the round. Despite the many limitations of the system, serious concerns confronting the poor in the area of agriculture trade can only be addressed multilaterally. Harmful domestic support in OECD countries and export subsidies cannot be addressed at the bilateral or regional levels. Bilateral trade agreements in agriculture have failed to address poverty concerns adequately. Instead they seem to have exacerbated imbalances among poor countries. Bilateral free trade agreements could also limit the flexibilities offered by multilateral negotiations.

Ensuring a pro-poor agenda throughout all branches of governments – in rich and poor countries alike – remains one of the most important but difficult challenges. This chapter has suggested elements of a pro-poor approach to agricultural trade negotiations as well as a number of complementary mechanisms. These include exploring a commodity-specific approach, rethinking SDT, exploring other potential opportunities to further the interests of the rural poor in the Doha Round, and building new alliances around commodity chains. It would also be important to place more emphasis on complementary mechanisms for adjustment and compensation.

## References

Chang, H-J, *Kicking Away the Ladder: Development Strategy in Historical Perspective* (London: Anthem Press, 2002).

CUTS Centre for International Trade, Economics and Environment, *Multilateral Competition Agreement* (2003).

Dorward, A., Kydd, J., Morrison, J. and Urey I (2004) A Policy Agenda for Pro-Poor Agricultural Growth, *World Development* 32 (1) 73 – 90.

Dorward, A and J.A Morrison (2000). The Agricultural Development Experience of the Past 30 Years: Lessons for LDC's. Background paper prepared for FAO ESCP.

FAO (2003), WTO Agreement on Agriculture: The Implementation Experience. Rome: FAO.

FAO (2003a) Trade Reforms and Food Security: Conceptualising the Linkages. Rome: FAO.

FAO (2004) Trade Reforms and Food Security: Conceptualising the Linkages. Case Studies. Rome: FAO.

*Finance and Development* (2002) Trading Up. September 2002. Volume 39, Number 3. IMF, Washington DC.

Gallezot, J (2003) Real access to the EU's agricultural market. INRA http://tradeinfo.cec.eu.int/doclib/docs/2003/july/tradoc_113490.pdf.

Imber, V, J. Morrison and A. Thomson et al 2003 Food Security, Trade and Livelihoods Linkages. Report prepared for DFID. www.passlivelihoods.org.uk/site_files/files/reports/project_id_52/ Food per cent20Security, per cent20Trade per cent20and per cent20Livelihoods per cent20Linkages per cent20Report__FS0079.pdf.

IMF and World Bank (2002), Market Access for Developing Country Exports: Selected Issues. Washington DC: IMF and World Bank.

Ingco, M, T Kandiero, and J Nash (2002), Liberalizing Agricultural Trade: Issues and Options for Sub-Saharan Africa in the Doha "Development" Round. Washington DC: World Bank.

Johnston and Mellor (1961) Johnston, B. F., & Mellor, J. W. (1961). The role of agriculture in economic development. The American Economic Review, 51(4), 566–593.

Mattoo, A, D Roy, and A. Subramanian (2002), "The Africa Growth and Opportunity Act and its Rules of Origin: Generosity Undermined?" Washington DC: World Bank.

Messerlin, P (2001) Measuring the costs of protection in Europe: European Commercial Policy in the 2000s. Institute for International Economics. Washington DC.

Morrison, J.A. and R. Pearce (2000). Interrelationships between economic policy and agrienvironmental indicators: an investigative framework with examples from South Africa. *Ecological Economics*. 34 (3) 363 – 377.

OECD, Agricultural Policies at a Glance (2004).

Perry, S., "Agriculture Negotiations: Compensation to Small Farmers for Biodiversity Protection," BRIDGES Vol. 7 No. 2 (2003).

Reardon, T., Berdegué, J. and J. Farrington (2002) Supermarkets and Farming in Latin America: Pointing Directions for Elsewhere? ODI Natural Resource Perspectives Number 81, December 2002.

Rodrik, (2002), Trade Policy Reform as Institutional Reform, in Trade Policy, Economic Development and Multilateral Negotiations: A Sourcebook, B Hoekman and P English and A Mattoo, Eds. Washington DC: World Bank.

Ruffer, T and A Swinbank (2003), Stock-Take of the WTO Agriculture Negotiations: Implications for Developing Countries. Oxford: Oxford Policy Management.

Stern, N (2002) Making Trade Work for Poor People," in Speech delivered at: National Council of Applied Economic Research. New Delhi.

Thirtle, C., Irz, X., Wiggins, Lin Lin, S., & McKenzie-Hill, V., (2001). Relationship between changes in agricultural productivity and the incidence of poverty in developing countries. Paper prepared for DFID. London: Imperial College.

U.N. Conference on Trade and Development, *Economic Development in Africa: Trade Performance and Commodity Dependence* (New York and Geneva, 2004A).

U.N. Conference on Trade and Development, *The Least Developed Countries Report 2004: Linking International Trade with Poverty Reduction* (New York and Geneva, 2004B).

Vorley, W., A. Werth and M. Jacobsen, *International Agricultural Reform and Power Balance in Agrifood Chains,* ICTSD-IIED Policy Views on Trade and Natural Resource Management (2003).

Watkins, K., 'Northern Agricultural Policies and World Poverty: Will the Doha "Development Round" make a difference?', Annual Bank Conference on Development Economics (2003).

World Trade Organization, 'Agreement on Agriculture.'

World Trade Organization, Doha Declaration (2001).

World Trade Organization, 'Ministerial Decision on Measures Concerning the Possible Negative Effects of the Reform Programme on Least-Developed and Net Food-Importing Developing Countries' (1993).

World Trade Organization, 'Submission by Benin, Burkina Faso, Chad and Mali,' document no. TN/AG/GEN/4 (2003A).

World Trade Organization, 'Submission by Kenya, Uganda and Tanzania,' document no. WT/COMTD/W/113 (2003B).

## Chapter 2 | Agricultural Commodities, Trade and Sustainable Development

# Chapter 3

# WTO Negotiations on Agriculture: What Can Be Achieved?

Kevin Watkins and Akhtar Mahmood[1]

## 1. Introduction

*'We recognize the need for all peoples to benefit from the increased opportunities and welfare gains that the multilateral trading system generates.'*
Ministerial Declaration, WTO, 14 November 2001

Four years on, the encouraging words adopted at the start of the Doha Round have a hollow ring. So far, the 'development' round has delivered little more than encouraging

---

1. This chapter is a combined and edited version of Kevin Watkins' paper, 'WTO Negotiations on Agriculture: Problems and Ways Ahead,' from the Windsor dialogue in 2004, and Akhtar Mahmood's paper, 'Commodities, Poverty Eradication and Sustainable Development: What can be achieved in the Doha Round of Trade Negotiations?,' from the Barcelona dialogue in 2005. Kevin Watkins' paper was prepared for a dialogue at Oxford's Global Economic Governance Programme in June 2004. The author kindly contributed it as a background paper for these Strategic Dialogues.

rhetoric, punctuated by deadlock and episodic breakdown. Rich countries have not delivered the reforms needed to make the global trading system a more powerful force for development. Failure to change this picture will inevitably damage the legitimacy of the rules-based system represented by the WTO, with attendant implications for multilateralism. There is a broad consensus that the costs of failure will be high. Can they be avoided?

The answer to this question will depend crucially on progress in the negotiations on agriculture. Reform of the rules governing agricultural trade is essential for both substantive and symbolic reasons. The substantive reasons are well known. Industrialized-country support programmes restrict access to Northern markets, generate large surpluses and subsidize exports. Producers in developing countries – a constituency that includes a large proportion of the world's poorest people – are excluded from market opportunities and forced to compete against heavily subsidized competition in international and even in local markets.

The symbolic relevance of the agriculture negotiations relates to the legitimacy of the WTO system itself. Most developing countries see a change in the rules on agriculture as a litmus test for the commitment of rich countries to a fairer international trading system. Notions of fairness may be disputed, but current agricultural rules and trade practices enshrine what can only be described as a set of double standards. Northern governments seldom miss an opportunity to preach the virtues of openness to developing countries, but remain resolutely protectionist themselves. Rules in the WTO perpetuate a system under which the distribution of opportunity in agricultural trade is shaped not by comparative advantage but by comparative access to subsidies – an area in which rich countries have an unrivalled advantage. Failure to change this picture will inevitably reinforce a perception that WTO rules skew the benefits of trade and globalization towards the industrialized world.

In an optimistic scenario, the Doha Round could still produce real change. In the previous Uruguay Round, which set up the WTO, agricultural trade negotiations were essentially a bilateral EU–US affair. Developing countries – the vast majority of WTO members, with the biggest stake in agricultural trade rules – were bystanders. Negotiating outcomes reflected inequalities in negotiating power. Thus the Agreement on Agriculture provided a multilateral façade for what was a bilateral arrangement designed to accommodate, rather than constrain, EU and US subsidies. The arrival of the G20 and the increased voice of African governments during the Cancún ministerial meeting shifted the terms of engagement on agriculture, making a repetition of the Uruguay Round unlikely.

Prospects for a positive outcome have been strengthened by wider developments. Dispute-panel rulings have directly challenged EU and US agricultural support systems, creating precedents for future action and, by extension, incentives for Northern governments to seek a rules-based resolution. With the expiry of the Peace Clause, Northern governments must now weigh consideration of WTO legality in the balance of domestic reform considerations.

This paper looks at some of the issues at stake in the Doha Round negotiations on agriculture, and at strategies for achieving tangible outcomes that benefit developing countries. Agricultural tariffs have been higher than manufacturing tariffs in both rich and poor countries. For instance, in 2001, average agricultural MFN rates of Quad countries (Canada, EU, Japan and US) were 10.7 per cent compared with 4 per cent for manufactured products, while, on average, agricultural tariffs of large middle-income countries (Brazil, China, India, South Korea, Mexico, Russia, South Africa and Turkey) were 26.6 per cent for agriculture and 13.1 per cent for manufactures.[2] Average MFN tariffs of the EU were 19 per cent for agriculture compared with 4.2 per cent for manufactures. But an agreement on agriculture is not an end in itself. It should be viewed as one of the means to remove the causes of global poverty.

In strategic terms, we argue that stringent disciplines on direct and indirect export subsidies, and on the support systems that generate surpluses, should be the immediate priority. Such disciplines will require a fundamental departure from the current negotiating framework – itself a product of the Uruguay Round. The distinction between 'distorting' and 'non-distorting' subsidies at the centre of this framework is unworkable and unwarranted. It has allowed the EU and the US, the architects of the framework, to evade disciplines on support and continue subsidizing overproduction. Subsidy segmentation is another problem. Domestic support and export subsidies are currently treated as separate categories, whereas their market effects clearly overlap. All payments to sectors in structural surplus clearly incorporate an export subsidy component.

Special and differential treatment is another theme in this paper. Failure to allow developing countries the policy space to protect their agricultural systems in the interests of food security would compromise efforts to combat rural poverty. Yet proposals tabled by Northern governments advocate a restriction of this space through import liberalization – and liberalization in agriculture has the potential to inflict grave human development costs. The key requirement for SDT is an acceptance that there should be limits to the reach of multilateral rules.

Such an outcome will be difficult to achieve. Increased access to developing countries' markets is one of the central pillars of agricultural policy in the US – and for reasons that are readily apparent. In contrast to manufacturing, agriculture generates a large balance of payments surplus: overall, exports account for one-quarter of agricultural sales. Recent trade deals negotiated with the five countries of CAFTA, the Andean pact countries and Australia served to highlight the mercantilist underpinning of US strategy, with a twin emphasis on aggressive market opening overseas and limited market access at home (witness sugar under CAFTA). Strong SDT applied to a large group of developing countries would rest uneasily with the commercial imperatives driving US policy.

Meanwhile, differences over preferences, the pace and scope of liberalization, and over SDT could all cause conflict among developing countries and weaken their bargaining power. However, the WTO is a vehicle through which developing countries can build pressure for the reform of policies that are detrimental to their interests, not to mention the interests of most people in industrialized countries.

---

2. World Bank (2004).

This paper is organized as follows. Part 2 summarizes the problems associated with Northern agricultural policies. Part 3 turns to issues raised by the measurement of agricultural support, focusing on the distinction between 'distorting' and 'non-distorting' subsidies. Part 4 considers the implications of some recent dispute-panel rulings. Part 5 examines issues at the heart of the debate on SDT. Part 6 concludes by reviewing some of the strategic choices facing developing countries.

## 2. Subsidizing poverty: the impact of Northern agricultural policies on developing countries

Agricultural trade negotiations at the WTO are shrouded in a complex legal and technical discourse that sometimes obscures the importance of the issues at stake. The outcome of these negotiations matters, because it will have a bearing on the future distribution of benefits in international trade – and hence on patterns of globalization. More immediately, changes in WTO rules will define the terms of competition between the highly capitalized, large-scale agricultural systems of industrialized countries on one side, and the smallholder agriculture of poor countries on the other.

For developing countries, the structure of this competition matters a great deal. Two-thirds of all people living on less than $1 a day – around 800 million in total – live in rural areas, most of them working as smallholder farmers and agricultural labourers. The profile of international poverty may be increasingly urban, but on current trends, more than 50 per cent of poverty will still be rural for the next 30 years. While the rural poor have diverse livelihoods, they depend critically on income generated by the sale of farm products and on agricultural wages. Agricultural income growth also generates multiplier effects beyond agriculture. Research by IFPRI in Sub-Saharan Africa suggests that every $1 generated in the agricultural sector can produce $3 through linkages to other sectors. Such facts explain why, for a large group of developing countries, growth in agriculture – especially the smallholder sector – will continue to have a disproportionate effect on poverty reduction.

It goes without saying that trade is not the most important factor shaping prospects for rural poverty reduction. Export activity can benefit smallholder farmers under the right conditions, but those conditions – such as access to land, credit and marketing infrastructure – are often lacking. Domestic policies, not WTO rules, hold the key to a wider distribution of benefits from global integration. But it is WTO rules that define the space in which domestic policies are formulated.

### 2.1 Agricultural support and price vulnerabilities

Competition between Southern and Northern agricultural systems has a bearing on the markets in which many smallholders operate. The terms of that competition are largely dictated by the support systems operating in Northern agriculture. Measurement of this support is a controversial exercise – and as we show below, one that has a direct bearing on WTO negotiations.

Using the OECD's Producer Support Estimate, overall support for agriculture in industrialized countries amounted to $230 billion in 2001, with the EU and the US accounting for two-thirds of the total. Support levels, as measured by the PSE, are equivalent to one-third of the value of output in the EU, and to one-fifth in the US. Beyond these headlines, there is ample scope for interpretation. Policymakers in the US point out that the EU has a higher overall level of support, and that this support represents a higher share of the value of output. In retaliation, the EU likes to highlight the higher per capita support provided to US farmers. More importantly, US support is more heavily concentrated on a narrow range of products, of which the US is a major exporter. As a result, US subsidies may distort key international markets more than is indicated by simple PSE comparisons.

Agricultural support in industrialized countries takes a bewildering variety of forms. Market-price support accounts for around two-thirds of the total, albeit with large variations between countries (the US is lower than the EU on this count). From an international trade perspective, OECD support is important for a number of reasons. The US is a major exporter of crops such as cereals and cotton. International markets absorb a large share of its production for basic commodities such as wheat (45 per cent), soya beans (34 per cent) and rice (40 per cent). For its part, the EU is a major exporter of cereals, dairy and sugar products. It follows that the terms on which the EU and the US produce and export have implications for the global market. At the same time, OECD support systems restrict the entry of imports through a complex array of tariff and quota arrangements.

The main products produced and traded by industrial countries are cereals, timber, dairy products, fish and vegetables while developing countries are dominant in exports of tropical beverages, sugar, tobacco and rubber.[3] The products that OECD countries protect the most through support measures are grains, oilseeds, sugar, milk, meat, wool, eggs etc.[4] These products are produced and traded both by developed and developing countries. In other words, developing countries have a strong interest, both as exporters and importers, in the protected products traded by industrial countries.

The rich countries also trade in a broader range of commodities, which enables them to cope with disturbances in one or two commodity markets without much difficulty. It was estimated recently that there are 43 developing countries for which more than 20 per cent of total merchandise export revenue and more than 50 per cent of total agricultural export revenue come from one agricultural commodity.[5] Twenty-one of these countries are in Sub-Saharan Africa while 32 are LDCs and/or small island developing states. It has also been observed that dependence on a single commodity is more pronounced in tropical countries. Consequently, even a slight movement in the markets for agricultural commodities, particularly tropical products, exerts a disproportionately strong influence on the economies of a large number of developing countries. Now, individual commodity price indices displayed a great deal of divergence in 2004.

---

3. Overseas Development Institute (1995).
4. OECD (2004).
5. FAO (105).

For example, cotton prices fell 34 per cent from the end-2003 level, soya bean prices declined by 21 per cent, while the prices of sugar, rice and coffee rose by at least 30 per cent. In other words, for the time being at least, the AoA has not led to any perceptible reduction in agricultural price volatility.

An important characteristic of trade in agriculture is the secular downward tendency of commodity prices, and their high variability. Both sharp fluctuations and long-run trends in commodity prices have a large impact on the output, balance of payments and budgetary positions of many commodity-exporting developing countries. A recent study of the behaviour of real commodity prices over the period 1862-1999 found that there has been a downward trend in commodity prices of one per cent annually over the last 140 years.[6] The short-term behaviour of prices can be seen in the Indices of Primary Commodity Prices issued by the IMF. These series reveal how the Food Index as a whole (indices of cereals, vegetable oils, meat, seafood, sugar and bananas) dipped from 100 in 1995 to 77.8 in 1999 and then rose to 99.2 in 2004. The movement of beverages (coffee, cocoa and tea) slid down from 100 in 1995 to 68.5 in 2004. Agricultural raw materials (timber, cotton, wool, rubber and hides) showed a similar tendency and their overall index now stands at 85.6.

Policymakers in the EU and the US regularly seek to justify agricultural support by reference to social equity objectives. In passing the 2002 Farm Act, President Bush appealed to a tradition of independent family farming, while a recent French agriculture minister described the CAP as part of the EU's social model. Back in the real world, agricultural subsidies are directed overwhelmingly towards large producers and agribusiness interests. Second-round subsidy effects inflate land rents and prices for inputs. Current support patterns are bad not only for the poor in developing countries and for global income distribution, but also for income distribution in subsidizing countries.

## 2.2 Transmission effects

Taken overall, Northern agricultural support restricts imports, expands output and generates large surpluses for export, usually with the help of a range of direct and indirect subsidies. Developing countries and their agricultural producers suffer the costs of this through four transmission channels:

- **Restricted market access.** Tariffs and quotas limit imports and favour producers in rich countries. Average tariffs understate real levels of protection for various reasons, including the large variance in tariff rates, the incidence of tariff peaks and prevalence of specific duties. Even so, they are two to four times the level of tariffs in manufacturing, with peaks up to 500 per cent. For the Quad group, around one-third of tariff lines in agriculture carry applied rates above 30 per cent. Table 1 shows some of the tariff peaks of advanced countries on agricultural products.

Table 2 gives some examples of the escalation of tariffs with the degree of processing of agricultural products.

---

6. IMF (2002).

## Table 1: Selected Tariff Peaks in Agriculture

| Commodity Market | Bound Tariff % |
|---|---|
| EU–Sugar | 228 |
| EU—Milk Powder | 119 |
| Norway—Beef | 474 |
| Switzerland —Butter | 771 |
| US—Sugar | 181 |
| US—Butter | 96 |
| Japan—Rice | 778 |
| Japan—Butter | 546 |
| Korea —Milk powder | 194 |

Source: Australian Bureau of Agriculture and Resource Economics

## Table 2: Tariff Escalation on Selected Product Groups (per cent)

| Commodity | EU | US | Commodity | EU | US |
|---|---|---|---|---|---|
| *Tropical Products* | | | *Expanding Commodities* | | |
| Coffee | | | Fruits | | |
| Raw | 7.3 | 0.1 | Raw | 9.2 | 4.6 |
| Final | 12.1 | 10..1 | Intermediate | 13.3 | 5.5 |
| Cocoa | | | Final | 22.5 | 10.2 |
| Raw | 0.5 | 0.0 | Vegetables | | |
| Intermediate | 9.7 | 0.2 | Raw | 9.9 | 4.4 |
| Final | 30.6 | 15.3 | Intermediate | 18.5 | 4.4 |
| Sugar | | | Final | 18.0 | 6.5 |
| Raw | 18.9 | 2.0 | Seafood | | |
| Intermediate | 30.4 | 13.8 | Raw | 11.5 | 0.6 |
| Final | 36.4 | 20.1 | Intermediate | 5.1 | 3.2 |
| | | | Final | 16.2 | 3.5 |

Source: World Bank (2004)

Northern market-access restrictions affect developing countries in various ways. Most obviously, they restrict imports: South–South agricultural trade has been growing at three times the rate of Southern exports to industrial countries. Growth rates in the latter have been falling. Northern import restrictions also slow the rate of world trade growth in agriculture. Agricultural trade is growing at half the rate of manufacturing trade, and it is decelerating.

- **Lower world prices and increased price volatility.** The scale of these effects is the subject of considerable controversy, partly because of the speculative nature of econometric modelling. For what they are worth, the most widely cited models point to price increases in the range of 1 to 10 per cent for grains if Northern agricultural support was removed, with higher levels for sugar and cotton. The IMF has estimated that a move to free trade in sugar would raise world prices by close to 40 per cent, while cotton subsidies depressed world prices by about 20 per cent.[7] Other models contest these figures, calculating limited price effects of Northern support. However, Northern protection and support tend to increase international price volatility because producers in OECD countries are in large measure insulated from price signals on world markets. For example, when world cotton prices fell sharply in the second half of the 1990s, US producers continued to expand output and exports, transferring adjustment pressures to other suppliers.
- **Lost shares in world markets.** Exports facilitated by subsidies artificially expand OECD market shares. In some sectors of concern to developing countries – including cotton, sugar, rice and dairy products – subsidized exporters are a major presence in the international market. Moreover, intra-industrial country trade still accounts for almost half of world agricultural trade, roughly the same as two decades ago.
- **Lower prices and displacement in domestic markets.** Subsidized OECD exports can produce negative consequences for rural producers in the importing countries, both through displacement effects and as a result of lower prices. These market effects have in turn impacted on rural investment and wages. At a national level, subsidized imports can have the effect of converting consumer tastes and creating a dependence on foreign products.

Economic models have been widely used to measure the potential benefits of liberalization. Most predict that rich-country liberalization would generate welfare gains for developing countries, ranging from $8 billion in an IMF variant to $40 billion in IFPRI's general equilibrium model. This reflects adjustments in international prices and world market shares. Inevitably, global models obscure regional and national differences, as well as distinctions between short- and long-run effects. Major exporters stand to gain from the higher prices and market share changes associated with liberalization, but food importers would face higher import costs. Models tend to predict the largest gains for Latin America, with Sub-Saharan Africa experiencing small gains or losses. Indeed, most modelling exercises point to relatively small aggregate gains for developing countries

---

7. Cited by Anne O. Krueger, First Deputy Managing Director of IMF, in a speech on 3 November 2005 at Canberra.

resulting from sweeping, and arguably implausible, liberalization scenarios in industrial countries. For example, the IMF predicts that full agricultural policy liberalization in industrial countries would raise developing countries' GDP by 0.1 per cent – not a scenario likely to prompt urgent action by G8 leaders.

None of this deflects from the real problems caused by industrial countries' policies. Some countries and groups of producers face very large losses indeed. OECD support systems inflict the highest foreign-exchange costs on major exporters. For example, Argentina loses heavily in the cereals sector, and EU sugar policies cost Brazil in excess of $400 million annually. Countries such as Vietnam and Thailand suffer losses in exports of rice – a crop grown predominantly by small farmers.

African countries are not immune to the effects of OECD policies. In the case of cotton, the continent suffers both market displacement and price-reduction effects. The background is well known, but bears repetition. US support for its cotton producers in 2000/01 amounted to nearly $4 billion – an amount comparable to the market value of its output, and exceeding the GDP of countries like Burkina Faso and Mali. Because the US accounts for around one-quarter of world exports of cotton, its domestic support has global consequences. According to the International Cotton Advisory Committee, that support has lowered world prices by around one-quarter. For countries such as Burkina Faso, Benin and Mali, where cotton accounts for around one-third of exports, the implied foreign-exchange losses are very high, and estimated at $200 million for 2001. The impact on the 10 to 11 million smallholders involved in growing cotton there is harder to establish. Household income data for Benin suggests that the decline in world price caused by US subsidies is correlated with a 12 per cent increase in poverty, pushing 250,000 more people below the national poverty line.

Several case studies have highlighted the impact of subsidized Northern agricultural exports on local markets. During the 1990s, import liberalization exposed a growing number of developing countries to competition from subsidized agricultural imports. This was the case for smallholder maize farmers in Mexico under NAFTA, the rice sector in Haiti in 1995 (facilitated by IMF loan conditions requiring rapid import liberalization) and the Indian dairy sector in 1997. For a larger group of developing countries, imports have climbed steadily over time. The FAO estimates that food imports now account for 10 to 12 per cent of the calorific intake of LDCs, and that the food import bill represents over 3 per cent of their GDP. While the underlying causes of are complex and varied, the disincentives for local investment created by export subsidies are an important factor.

**2.3 Trade preferences**

Trade preferences add further complexity to North–South agricultural trade relations. In principle, preferential schemes allow suppliers in beneficiary countries to access part of the price premium provided by tariffs and quotas. In practice, these benefits are diminished through complex entry systems and eligibility requirements. Some of the problems are well known. Under many schemes – such as AGOA – preferences can be withdrawn at any time. For its part, the EU prefers to concentrate its preferences on products that it does not produce – or on countries that lack the capacity to take advantage of market opportunities. Regulations concerning the origin of items eligible for preferences limit the ability to fill quotas. An additional problem is that preferences can lock countries into production in areas where they have limited comparative advantage.

Such considerations have prompted the World Bank and others to take a dim view of preferential trade. Not surprisingly, the beneficiaries take a different view. African and Caribbean exporters of sugar to the EU receive a price some three times above the world market price for a fixed quota of sugar. In the absence of these preferences, many sugar industries would either contract or collapse. Similarly, governments in Africa see tariff preferences under the EU Cotonou Agreement as vital to protection against competition from Latin America. For negotiators representing countries with preferences at the WTO, preference erosion can pose a real and immediate threat to export markets.

## 3. Measuring support under the Agreement on Agriculture

Prior to the Uruguay Round, multilateral rules were of limited relevance to agricultural trade. The AoA started to change this picture, introducing for the first time a framework of rules and disciplines to limit support. The Doha Round negotiations operate within the parameters of the AoA. Unfortunately, this starting point severely disadvantages developing countries.

The AoA suffers from two fundamental flaws. First, it enshrines an arbitrary distinction between 'distorting' and 'non-distorting' support. Initially developed under the Blair House accord between the EU and the US, this distinction has enabled the subsidy superpowers to evade disciplines on supports that damage developing countries' interests. The second, more fundamental, problem can be traced to the tripartite structure of the AoA framework. Under this framework, domestic support, export subsidies and market access are treated as segmented units. This is unfortunate, because the distinction between export subsidies and domestic supports is increasingly blurred.

### 3.1 When is a subsidy not a subsidy?

The subsidy 'box' system is supposed to reflect the differentiation of subsidies. Under the AoA, all domestic support measures deemed to distort production and trade fall into the 'Amber Box'. These subsidies have to be cut, subject to a provision known as the '*de minimis*' arrangement. Under the terms of the latter, Northern governments can provide financing up to the equivalent of 5 per cent of the value of production (the figure is 10 per cent for developing countries). Export subsidies also fit into the Aggregate Measure of Support, which is subject to limits and reductions. The EU and the US are required to keep the AMS below a specified ceiling. The rate at which the ceiling is lowered in the years ahead will depend on the outcome of the Doha Round negotiations.

The 'Blue Box' can be thought of as the Amber Box with conditions. Support that would normally be placed in the Amber Box can be placed in the Blue Box if it is linked to a programme designed to limit production. An example of such a programme is the EU's set-aside arrangement, introduced under the 1992 CAP reform. There are currently no limits on the amount of support that can be provided under the Blue Box – an issue that figures prominently in current negotiations.

The 'Green Box' is defined in Annex 2 of the AoA. In order to qualify for this category, subsidies should either not distort trade at all, or cause minimal distortion. Green Box subsidies can be provided without limit.

What is the relevance of all this for negotiations to change Northern agricultural policies that cause overproduction and facilitate export subsidization? Figure 1 offers a partial answer. It provides a breakdown of support categories for the EU and the US for the marketing year 1999.

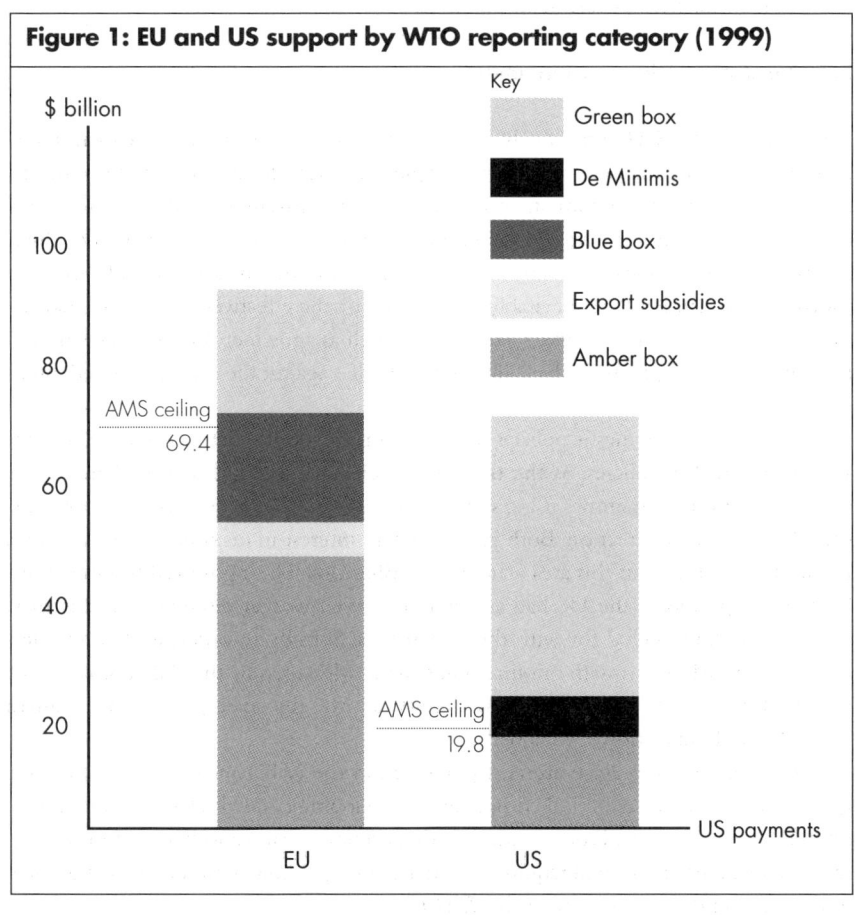

**Figure 1: EU and US support by WTO reporting category (1999)**

Key:
- Green box
- De Minimis
- Blue box
- Export subsidies
- Amber box

EU: AMS ceiling 69.4
US: AMS ceiling 19.8

Source: WTO

What emerges from the data is that the EU and the US have complied with the letter of the AoA. In 1999, both were operating well below their AMS ceilings. For the EU, combined Amber Box and export subsidies represented 76 per cent of the AMS ceiling, rising to 84 per cent for the US. Figure 1 also demonstrates that compliance with the AoA was achieved through a process of subsidy shifting, or the transfer of support into the Green Box and the Blue Box. In the case of the US, supports subject to WTO disciplines represented only 22 per cent of overall support, rising to 69 per cent for the EU. For developing countries concerned with the trade-distorting effects of agricultural support, this raises an obvious question: namely, are the non-disciplined supports genuinely non-distorting?

The present state of research does not allow this question to be answered with any accuracy. Unfortunately, the current system of categories, delays in EU and US reporting to the WTO, and the limited relevance of either the AMS or the PSE as indicators, leaves developing countries with little leverage beyond the dispute settlement system for challenging Northern government practices.

### 3.2 Domestic policy reform agendas

Agreements at the WTO reflect a dynamic interaction between domestic reform strategies and trade negotiations. There are complex feedback loops connecting positions adopted at the WTO and domestic policies. Nowhere is this more evident than in agriculture. Domestic policies are contested by powerful interest groups, many of which operate through political associations structured around the maintenance of subsidies. Northern governments are inevitably constrained by the effectiveness of these associations. They have to balance wider objectives – such as agreements in non-agricultural areas and the development of the WTO system itself – against the claims of vested interest groups.

The imprint of domestic policies on WTO agreements is much in evidence, notably with regard to US policies. At the time of the Uruguay Round, a large share of US support went on programmes using supply management. The 1992 CAP reforms took the EU in the same direction. Both parties had an interest in maximum flexibility and minimum constraints in this area – hence the Blue Box. Having moved towards more 'decoupled' payments, the US had an interest in even weaker disciplines in this area, which were duly catered for with the Green Box. Subsidy re-ordering then enabled deep cuts in AMS levels with minimal adjustment. Measured by the PSE, both the EU and the US *increased* support between 1986-1988 (the reference period for Uruguay Round subsidy reduction) and 2000.

When it comes to agricultural negotiations in the WTO, measurement matters a great deal. Beyond the technical complexities, developing countries have a strong interest in preventing a Doha Round outcome that accommodates another bout of subsidy repackaging. This in turn will require an understanding of how domestic reform debates in the EU and the US play out at the WTO.

## WTO Negotiations on Agriculture: What Can Be Achieved? | Chapter 3

The current direction of reform poses both threats and opportunities. In the case of the US, the 2002 Farm Act accelerates a move back from the decoupling model adopted in 1996. The move started with the expansion of 'emergency payments' and an increase in market-price support payments in response to low world prices at the end of the 1990s. Non-decoupled output-based payments increased from $1.6 billion annually for 1996–98 to $9 billion in 1999–2001. The 2002 Farm Act legislation increased loan rates (in effect, minimum guaranteed prices), updated the acreage and yields on which direct payments are based, and institutionalized a system of counter-cyclical payments. One upshot is that the US is now almost certainly pushing close to its AMS ceiling, creating strong incentives to limit ceiling reductions and weaken disciplines on direct payments.

Just how close the US is to the ceiling is uncertain, since the status of many of these payments remains uncertain. The structure of payments for 2003 in summarized in Figure 2. An immediate problem for US policymakers is that the 2002 Farm Act may have pushed previously Green Box support into the Amber Box, in which case their ceiling has already been exceeded. US negotiators at the WTO are likely to seek a high level of flexibility in the definition of the Green Box and to keep open the possibility of recourse to the Blue Box, possibly with reference to counter-cyclical payments.

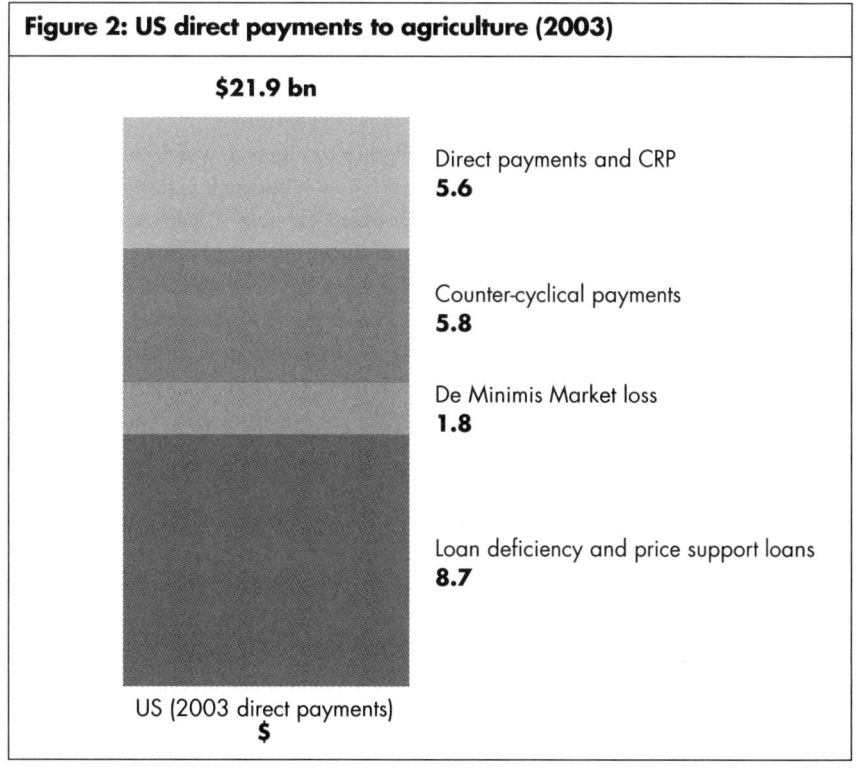

**Figure 2: US direct payments to agriculture (2003)**

$21.9 bn

- Direct payments and CRP: **5.6**
- Counter-cyclical payments: **5.8**
- De Minimis Market loss: **1.8**
- Loan deficiency and price support loans: **8.7**

US (2003 direct payments) $

Source: USDA, commodity credit corporation

In the EU, the ambition of CAP reformers has been to shift support into the Green Box through full decoupling. Differences between member states have limited progress, resulting in a (very) partial decoupling in the June 2003 reforms. One major sector – sugar – is as yet unreformed. Translated into WTO strategy, the parameters of CAP reform dictate that the EU is likely to drive a hard bargain in seeking to maintain the Blue Box and a residual right to subsidize exports directly in key sectors.

Any agreement in the Doha Round will incorporate provisions for 'decoupled' support – and rightly so. It would be politically unrealistic and socially undesirable to argue for the elimination of Northern government support in an area where there is a clear public policy interest. For developing countries the key question is what constitutes 'decoupled' support and, by extension, what is eligible for the Green Box. This is an area in which more research and a better understanding of the market effects of policies is vital. What is clear, however, is that much of the support currently directed into the Green Box does damage the interests of developing countries.

## 3.3 Export subsidies and export dumping

From the perspective of developing countries, and – more importantly – their agricultural producers, the classification of subsidies at the WTO is of less relevance than their effects on markets. Export subsidies represent a major source of concern, since they are widely regarded as being among the most damaging. With the shift in structure of Northern support, the distinction between export subsidies and domestic support is becoming increasingly artificial.

This problem can be demonstrated by reference to Figure 1, which shows that, for the purposes of WTO classification, the US was a non-subsidizing exporter at the end of the 1990s – and it remains so. The EU accounted for over 90 per cent of OECD export subsidies in 1999. However, even then its direct export subsidies represented a relatively small share of overall support; and that share has been shrinking since 1999. The word 'direct' is operative here. Both the US and the EU provide very high levels of support to sectors that are in structural surplus. In many sectors, these surpluses would not exist in the absence of direct payments to farmers. It follows that direct payments include a *de facto* export subsidy, even though they are not reported as such *de jure* for WTO purposes.

The problem can best be demonstrated by reference to specific commodities. Mention has already been made of the $4 billion in direct payments allocated to cotton producers. For WTO purposes, only around 2 per cent of these payments are categorized as export subsidies. Yet in the absence of direct payments, US exports of cotton would be much diminished for an obvious reason: in most years average production costs considerably exceed world prices. Without subsidies, cotton would not be a profitable crop for the vast majority of US producers. Cotton is not unique. In the case of rice, the OECD estimates US support to be equivalent to just under half of the value of output. Around one-third of production is exported, again without the help of export subsidies. Similar conditions prevail in maize and wheat. The point in all of these cases is that direct payments clearly serve to subsidize exports, though they are treated purely as domestic supports for WTO purposes.

In the interests of balance, it has to be acknowledged that the hidden export subsidies at work in the EU are on a larger scale than those applied in the US. In 2001, the EU provided subsidies of around $610 million on produce that it exported. However, no official export subsidies were recorded in this year, underlining the limited nature of the current reporting regime.

The IATP and others have helped to highlight the problem by focusing on the gap between export prices and cost of production. Under WTO rules, dumping is broadly defined as the sale overseas of a product at prices below the normal price prevailing on the domestic market. However, in cases where 'normal price' is impossible to establish, importers can construct value on the basis of cost-of-production criteria. Using these criteria, it is clear that the US is dumping on a large scale without export subsidies: export prices for cotton and wheat in 2003 were respectively around 50 per cent and 20 per cent of average production costs. In the case of EU sugar, the dumping margin measured as the gap between production costs and export price would be in the range 300–350 per cent. Were the Indian textiles industry to attempt exporting to the EU or the US on similar terms, it could confidently predict a barrage of anti-dumping actions. Yet when it comes to agriculture, WTO rules allow the EU and the US to dump with something close to impunity.

Existing rules on export subsidies suffer from limitations in two further areas. First, they do not cover export credit programmes – the principle form of direct export subsidization in the US. While the EU accounts for the bulk of direct export subsidies, the US accounts for the lion's share of export credits. The 'GSM102' and the 'GSM103' programmes and the Supplier Credit Programme provide for financing of around $5.5 billion. These programmes are explicitly aimed at creating and maintaining market outlets for US surpluses. They are extensively deployed in countries ranging from the Philippines to Mexico and West Africa. Depending on the method used to calculate concessionality, their subsidy component is between $500 million and $700 million annually. The only international rules in operation are a set of largely unobserved best-endeavour clauses in OECD guidelines.

The second gap in WTO rules relates to food aid. US food aid programmes have developed in large measure as a surplus-disposal policy. This remains one of the objectives of Title 1 of Public Law 480, under which countries eligible for food aid must 'demonstrate the potential to become commercial markets for US agricultural commodities'. The commercial nature of Title 1 is apparent at several levels. Countries facing real food emergencies in Southern and Eastern Africa consistently receive less than do commercial market outlets. Moreover, US food aid transfers fall when world prices rise – the opposite of what might be expected under a demand-driven programme. Current budget authorizations for Title 1 amount to $176 million annually, much of which could be categorized as export subsidies. For example, in 2001

Archer Daniels Midland, one of the world's largest grain traders, was awarded $35 million under Title 1 to supply maize and rice to the Philippines.

### 3.4 Market access

Market access is the third pillar of negotiations. Once again, the shadow of the Uruguay Round looms large. That agreement was designed to facilitate evasion and limit adjustment costs on the part of industrial countries. A central concern for developing countries is to avoid a repeat performance.

Under the AoA, governments were required to reduce average tariffs on a linear basis – the so-called Uruguay Round formula. Industrialized countries had to reduce tariffs on agricultural products by 36 per cent between 1995-2000, and developing countries by 24 per cent from 1995-2004. The aggregate nature of the tariff-cutting formula gave countries a great deal of flexibility. Large tariff reductions for commodities representing a small share of trade could be used to facilitate far shallower tariff cuts for commodities representing a larger share of trade. In fact, the high tariffs in operation during the reference years enabled most countries to meet their AoA commitments without difficulty.

In the Doha Round, debate has centred on the formula to be used for cutting tariffs. The 'Friends of the Uruguay Round Formula' group, which includes the EU, prefers a linear approach. Most developing countries – backed, with some reservations, by the US – want to have tariff cuts that escalate with the size of the initial tariff: the Swiss formula approach, as it is known. The aim is to create tariff convergence at a relatively low level and to eliminate tariff peaks. Most formulae envisaged for the Doha Round are a blend of the two approaches.

## 4. WTO dispute-panel rulings

WTO case law has become an increasingly important factor in shaping the negotiating environment. With the expiry of the Peace Clause, principles established in dispute-panel rulings now constrain the options open to Northern policymakers in agriculture – and they could strengthen the hands of developing countries' negotiators. Three cases merit special attention. They make a definitive critique of the subsidy and protection policies of the two economic superpowers, the EU and the US.

**The Brazil–US cotton ruling.** The Dispute Settlement Body ruled on US subsidies on upland cotton on 21 March 2005. Perhaps the most important decision is that Production Flexibility Contract support and, by extension, Direct Payments are non-Green Box, and therefore not exempt from subsidy reductions. It may well be that, if applied to other sectors, the ruling would place the US in breach of its AMS ceiling. Whether or not this is the case, the US is now highly vulnerable to dispute cases in other areas, even for periods covered by the Peace Clause. The Panel decided that US subsidies could not benefit from Peace Clause protection on the grounds that the level of support exceeded the amount provided in the base year. With regard to export subsidies, the Panel found against the US on two counts. First, it ruled that a cotton-specific credit programme – the Step 2 programme – constitutes a prohibited subsidy. Second, and more importantly, it ruled that the GSM and other export credit programmes circumvent US export subsidy commitments not just in cotton, but also in soya beans, fruit and vegetables, and rice. Finally, the Panel ruled that US cotton subsidies cause significant price depression in world markets and in the Brazilian market.

**The Brazil, Thailand, Australia–EU sugar dispute.** The WTO's Appellate Body ruled against EU sugar export subsidies on 19 May 2005. The EU claimed that two categories of its sugar exports were not subsidized. Under the first category are 1.2 million tonnes exported through a levy on guaranteed prices paid to processors. In the EU's view, the levy makes the exports 'self-financing'. Viewed from a different perspective, the levy is a mechanism for turning part of a consumer transfer to the industry into a disguised export subsidy. Such arrangements are prohibited under Article 9 of the AoA. The second category of exports concerns non-quota sugar, or production that is not subject to price support. In effect, these exports are financed through a cross-subsidy from quota sugar. Support prices for quota sugar make it possible for producers to cover their fixed costs, with world prices covering marginal costs. The EU's loss of the case at the WTO recasts the entire CAP reform debate as it relates to sugar, and raises questions about cross-subsidies in other sectors.

**Canadian dairy dispute.** The Dispute Panel ruled that domestic support applied to products in surplus can have the same effects as export subsidies. To cite part of the report, 'We consider that the distinction between domestic support and export subsidy disciplines would be eroded if WTO members were entitled to use domestic support without limit to provide support for exports.' This would appear to create a precedent for the EU sugar case. As with the Brazil–US cotton rulings, it also, in effect, challenges some of the central assumptions underpinning the AoA.

## 5. Special and differential treatment

The Doha mandate clearly establishes SDT as a priority for the WTO trade round. Generally, this has been interpreted on the model established in the Uruguay Round, namely, 'same direction, different speed'. Developing countries are broadly expected to follow the same reform path as industrialized countries, but over a longer period, with shallower tariff cuts and exemptions from reduction commitments for some forms of support. However, the critical importance of agriculture to food security and poverty reduction raises important questions about the role and scope of WTO rules.

### 5.1 Market access

Much of the debate on SDT in agriculture has focused on market access. The approaches adopted by different governments serve to illustrate the complexities of the issues, not least for the G20 group.

In the strategic vision of US negotiators, the aim of the Doha Round is to advance an aggressive movement towards trade liberalization beyond the borders of developed countries. Robert Zoellick, US Trade Representative, wrote to trade ministers in January 2004:'For the United States, the degree of ambition is linked to ... a substantial increase in real market access opportunities both in developed and major developing country markets.'The emphasis on market opening at the WTO is an extension of a wider strategy for agriculture. Mention has already been made of the acute dependence of US farm incomes on access to overseas markets. Agricultural exports also play a critical macro-economic role. The $10-20 billion annual surplus on agricultural trade helps to offset deficits elsewhere. Policymakers regard increased access to developing countries' markets as vital.

This has direct implications for SDT. Implicit in the USTR's formulation is a distinction between countries that represent major commercial markets and the rest. It might be reasonably assumed that the 'major market' group extends from low-income countries (including India and China) to middle-income countries (including Brazil and other Latin American countries, much of North Africa, and South-east Asia) and a large group of food-importing developing countries. This is the constituency that the US Department of Agriculture is anxious to cultivate commercially. The World Bank argues for greater differentiation between countries. Middle-income countries, it argues, need to accept less protection and weaker SDT provisions. With two major exceptions, low-income countries would enjoy a higher order of SDT. The exceptions are India and China.

With regard to market access, the application of the Swiss formula to developing countries, as envisaged by the US, would entail very deep tariff cuts, implying potentially large shifts in relative prices between imports and domestically produced goods. The aim of the Swiss formula is to produce a narrow range of final tariffs from a wide set of initial tariffs, and to arrive at a tariff ceiling. The rate of convergence is decided by the coefficient used in the formula – a subject of intense controversy.[8] Figure 3 provides one possible scenario, using a Swiss-formula coefficient of 25. It shows that countries such as India would be faced with considerable adjustments.

Figure 3 draws attention to another important aspect of the debate on market access as it relates to SDT: the gap between bound tariffs (the legally binding ceiling in WTO schedules) and applied tariffs (the tariffs that governments actually charge). For some developing countries, this gap is quite large. If the benchmark for tariff cuts is the bound rate, this offers some flexibility – especially if countries have bound at high levels. However, the US has argued that negotiations to lower tariffs should start from applied tariffs, breaking with the tradition of all previous rounds.

Wherever the benchmark is set, some countries will face acute problems. This includes those (such as Brazil, Peru, the Philippines and Egypt) that have bound tariffs

---

8. The Swiss formula is as follows: $Z = CX/C+X$, where Z equals the final tariff, X the initial tariff and C the coefficient.

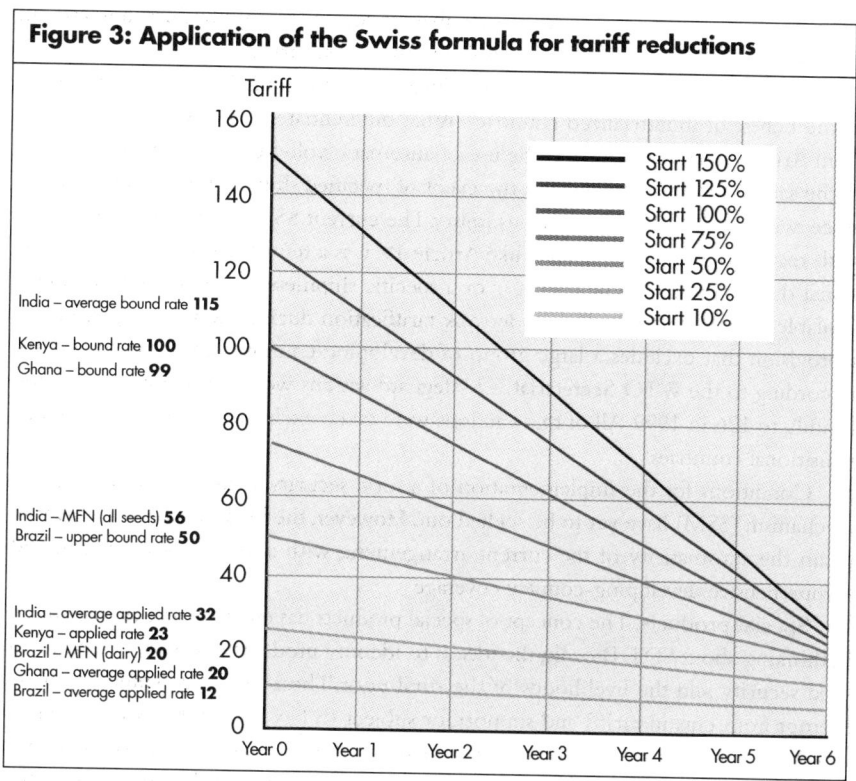

**Figure 3: Application of the Swiss formula for tariff reductions**

[Tariff reduction chart showing application of Swiss formula over Year 0 to Year 6, with starting tariff rates of 150%, 125%, 100%, 75%, 50%, 25%, and 10%. Reference values marked on the vertical axis:
- India – average bound rate **115**
- Kenya – bound rate **100**
- Ghana – bound rate **99**
- India – MFN (all seeds) **56**
- Brazil – upper bound rate **50**
- India – average applied rate **32**
- Kenya – applied rate **23**
- Brazil – MFN (dairy) **20**
- Ghana – average applied rate **20**
- Brazil – average applied rate **12**]

Source: WTO

relatively low, especially where bound rates are close to applied rates. South-South trade has become an important factor in developing countries' trade. A recent study[9] reported that in 2001, South-South trade in agricultural products was 10.5 per cent of the South's merchandize exports, 8.6 per cent as food and 1.8 per cent as agricultural raw materials. South-South trade in agricultural products as a whole grew at a 6 per cent annual average during 1990-2001. Impediments to this trade should be examined carefully.

### 5.2 Special safeguards and special products

Various options have been advanced by developing countries, NGOs and others concerned about the implications of import liberalization in agriculture. The aim is to reverse the erosion of SDT and address a broader set of concerns about food security.

**Special safeguards.** Under Article 19 of the GATT, safeguards can be introduced as a temporary measure following cuts in tariffs, in response to import surges. Importantly, tariff reductions can only be reversed if it can be established that imports cause, or threaten to cause, injury to domestic producers. The use of a safeguard is restricted

---

9. Government of Australia (2004).

to four years. Recourse to Article 19 is feasible for commercial agribusiness interests but is of limited use in support of public policies on food security.

The Uruguay Round did in fact introduce a special safeguard on agriculture, largely at the behest of industrialized countries. What differentiates this SSG under the AoA from Article 19 of the GATT is the use of automatic volume and price triggers. That is, the safeguard can be invoked in the event of specified shifts in import quantity and price, without demonstrating serious injury. The current SSG suffers from two defects with regard to food security. First, like Article 19, it is a temporary arrangement: additional duties apply for only one year or a specific shipment. Second, the provision is available only to countries that undertook tariffication during the Uruguay Round – a provision that excludes a large group of developing countries and product groups. According to the WTO Secretariat, 42 safeguard actions were notified in 1995, rising steadily to 126 in 1999. All of these actions were taken exclusively by industrialized or transitional countries.

Conditions for the implementation of a food security-focused special safeguard mechanism (SSM) have yet to be spelled out. However, the broad idea is that it would retain the automaticity of the current arrangement, with a longer time horizon and comprehensive developing-country coverage.

**Special products.** The concept of special products has emerged as a second strand of thinking about SDT. Broadly, the idea is to identify products of critical relevance to food security and the livelihoods of the rural poor. These products would either be exempt from cuts in tariffs and support, or subject to less stringent disciplines. They would be automatically eligible for coverage under the SSM. Several governments and NGOs have also set out broader proposals for a 'Development Box' in agriculture. This would allow countries to raise tariffs on food-security crops for which tariff bindings are deemed too low, regardless of tariff-cutting formulae.

Neither the US nor the EU have ruled out SP or SSM arrangements. However, their current negotiating strategies would aim to achieve a trade-off between coverage and provision: that is, the wider the coverage, the weaker the provision. In other words, it is unlikely that they will be in favour if it was requested to extend to Brazil the same treatment as provided for Africa.

### 5.3 Food security implications

The issues raised in the debate on SDT are of fundamental importance for rural development policies, poverty reduction and food security. Unfortunately, the debate itself has been driven by a perverse logic. This is an area in multilateral obligations which should be tailored to national poverty-reduction plans. Instead, negotiations over WTO rules, driven by the concerns of industrial countries to expand market access, are defining what is possible in national poverty planning.

International trade rules are only one factor affecting food security and the interaction between the two is complex. Food security is not the same as food self-sufficiency

– as witnessed by the prevalence of malnutrition in India and Brazil. However, national self-sufficiency can be an important factor, especially in low-income countries. At a household level, food security is related to the sustained ability to command access to nutrition, either through production or exchange. Agricultural protection is not inherently good for food security, either at a national or at a household level; as in the EU and the US, the benefits can be captured by the wealthy at the expense of the poor. By the same token, open markets and import liberalization can undermine food security.

In other words, there is no trade-policy blueprint for advancing food security. Demands tabled by industrialized countries may cite a food-security rationale, but this is invariably a smokescreen for the interests of commercial agricultural exporters. Consider the rationale advanced by the US and the World Bank for greater differentiation between developing countries. Headline distinctions between, say, India and Brazil on one side and Burkina Faso on the other, have an intuitive appeal. India is a large country, and Brazil is the world's fourth largest agricultural exporter. Viewed from a food-security perspective, the distinctions appear less well grounded. According to the World Bank, around 16 million Brazilians are affected by malnutrition, and there is a high incidence of poverty among smallholder farmers producing basic grains and other food crops. In the case of India, market size is not an antidote for rural poverty. More than three-quarters of India's poor – some 200 million people – live in rural areas, many of which do not figure in the 'India shining' growth model. The food-security rationale for excluding India and Brazil from SDT in agriculture is not obvious.

Developing countries have responded to US and EU demands with an essentially defensive strategy focused on SSMs and SPs. There are problems with this approach. Special safeguards are geared towards dealing with import surges, not with a sustained and regular increase in imports. Bound tariff systems lack the flexibility to respond to surges caused by fluctuations in exchange rates, gyrations in global prices and, of course, Northern subsidies. For countries seeking to reverse long-run, structural losses of food self-reliance, the problem goes beyond anti-surge mechanisms. While protection is manifestly not a guaranteed route to food security, there may be strong infant-industry grounds for border protection to create incentives for local production and investment.

Some commentators argue that an SP provision could address this problem. The argument is that products with a direct bearing on food security would be accorded a different status. However, this also has problems. There is an obvious sense in which, say, Cambodian rice or Ghanaian cassava might be construed as food-security crops, meriting differential treatment. But as the Indian government has pointed out, palm oil, rubber and cotton are also food-security crops. Markets for these crops play a pivotal role in the lives of millions of small farmers and rural labourers. In most developing countries, the poor are involved in the production of a wide range of crops and a combination of on-farm and off-farm employment. Simple distinctions between 'subsistence food crops' on one side and 'cash crops' on the other do not help. As is now widely recognized, successful rural development and poverty-reduction policies have to reflect the realities of these livelihoods.

## Chapter 3 | Agricultural Commodities, Trade and Sustainable Development

It is also noteworthy that 58 out of 63 low-income countries[10] are food-deficit countries, while two-thirds (105) of the 148 developing countries are net food importers; yet two-fifths (63) of them, including 33 low-income countries, are net *agricultural* exporters.[11] The danger is that a compartmentalized SP negotiating strategy at the WTO will leave a large gap between the behind-the-border dictates of multilateral rules and the policies required for rural development. Developing countries risk being locked into a negotiating framework under which they have to wring concessions product by product from the EU and the US. The outcome is unlikely to be favourable.

This is especially true from the perspective of the rural poor. Trade negotiations inevitably involve trade-offs and hard bargains. The terms on which these bargains are struck are shaped partly by power relations at the WTO, and partly by power relations at a national level. Take the case of Brazil. In agriculture, the emphasis of Brazilian trade policy is on expanding markets. Some of the country's most powerful political lobbies – in sugar, fruit and soya beans – are active in shaping this policy. Smallholder farmers and agricultural labourers vulnerable to import competition have a far weaker voice in influencing trade policy. The danger is that any trade-off at the WTO will reflect the priorities of powerful commercial interests, and not more marginalized groups.

## 6. Paths ahead for developing countries

The outcome of the agricultural trade negotiations – and, by extension, of the Doha Round itself – remains in the balance. Almost any scenario is plausible. One thing can be predicted with some certainty, however: in the absence of sustained pressure from developing countries, a WTO agreement will fail to address the problems caused by Northern agricultural policies.

### 6.1 EU–US rapprochement thwarted

Some notable successes have already been registered by the G20. In the run-up to the Cancún ministerial, EU–US agricultural trade relations followed the Uruguay Round trajectory. Several months of trans-Atlantic sabre-rattling gave way in August 2003 to a joint proposal reflecting a Blair House-style bilateral accommodation of interest. Efforts to advance this agenda were derailed at Cancún, principally by the G20. In retrospect, it is clear that the EU and the US underestimated both the resolve and the sophistication of the G20. Not only did its strategy include the development of an alternative to the EU–US proposal – no mean feat for a coalition spanning major food importers and exporters – but it also encompassed a broader coalition-building exercise, including a sustained dialogue with the Africa Group and the LDCs.

African governments played a critical role at Cancún. Questions have been raised about the legality, in narrow WTO terms, of the demands tabled in the Cotton Initia-

---

10. World Bank Classification
11. Valdes and McCalla (1999

tive by four West and Central African governments. However, the initiative articulated a powerful demand for stronger action on export subsidies, while at the same time forcing the SPs approach on to the agenda. At a political level, both the pro-active nature of the proposal and the refusal of the four countries to withdraw in the face of considerable pressure from the US marked a departure from the standard WTO script.

Some important lessons can be drawn from this. Perhaps the most important concerns developing-country coalitions. As negotiations move into a more substantive phase, differences will emerge. African, ACP and LDC governments remain deeply concerned over the erosion of tariff and quota preferences. Many see the case brought by Brazil and Thailand against EU sugar policy as a statement of hostile intent. Several G20 members – including Brazil and the Philippines – are in the Cairns Group of major commercial exporters. Other members – notably India – have viewed the demands of the Cairns Group in the area of import liberalization as a major threat. Both the EU and the US have highly developed divide-and-rule strategies that will seek to exploit these tensions.

### 6.2 Beyond the July framework

Governments of the G20 and other developing countries are involved in a complex negotiating process. Developments in agriculture will be affected by bargains struck in other areas – on services, for example. Moreover, WTO negotiations cannot be viewed in isolation from agricultural policy debates in the EU and the US. In the EU, advocates of CAP reform use the WTO negotiations to lever change, while the same negotiations are opposed by CAP beneficiaries bent on the status quo.

Developing countries need to assess carefully the interaction between forces driving domestic agricultural policies and the WTO negotiating strategies of industrialized countries. Issues of time horizon matter. The AoA of the Uruguay Round clearly constrains what can be achieved in the current negotiations. Beyond any concrete gains that developing countries might achieve in the Doha Round, it is important that any agreement expands rather than restricts potential gains in future rounds. How might these principles be translated into practice? That question can best be addressed by reference to the four key areas that will ultimately make – or break – a deal in agriculture.

### 6.3 Domestic support

The immediate aim here should be that of restricting the scope for support that generates export surpluses. Deep cuts in Amber Box support on a product-specific basis and early removal of the Blue Box should be immediate priorities, as proposed in the G20 proposals. Divisions between the EU and the US over the Blue Box create scope in this area for divide-and-rule in a different direction.

Turning to the Green Box, the cotton dispute panel has effectively demolished the myth that current payments in this area are decoupled, opening the door to a fundamental review of existing disciplines. There is need for an agreement on the criteria that would determine the eligibility of national measures for inclusion in either the Blue or the Green Boxes. The present vagueness about criteria can prove fatal to efforts to cap the massive subsidy programmes of industrialized countries.

### 6.4 Export subsidies

In this area developing countries have the chance to bank major gains. There are two layers to the debate on export subsidies. The first concerns direct export subsidies – now concentrated in just EU sugar and dairy – and the use of export credits and food aid by the US. Achievable aims include:
- an export subsidy prohibition across all product groups within five years;
- the elimination of the subsidy component of export credit programmes in a similar timeframe;
- a prohibition on the use of food aid for commercial market development.

Here too, there is scope for divide-and-rule. As a 'non-subsidizing' exporter, the US will strongly support moves to cut direct export subsidies, while the EU insists that any action on export subsidies is contingent on improved disciplines on US export credits and food aid.

The second layer of the export subsidy debate is more challenging. Both the cotton and sugar disputes have highlighted the role of direct payments, consumer transfers and other arrangements in cross-subsidizing exports. As shown earlier, one of the problems with the AoA is that many subsidies, which lower the export price of commodities, are not treated as export subsidies. What is needed is a new measure of support to capture this effect – perhaps an OECD Export Support Estimate. Once again, the dispute-panel process has strengthened the G20's hand in this area.

### 6.5 Market access

Here, we restrict ourselves to two strategic questions raised by tariff-cutting formulae and preferences. The current G20 approach is to argue for (i) a strict application of the Swiss formula applied by tariff line, to address the twin problems of tariff peaks and tariff escalation, and (ii) the expansion of tariff-rate quotas. From a negotiating perspective, this raises a dilemma. It is difficult to envisage either the EU or the US conceding the application of a Swiss formula for themselves without reciprocal measures on the part of a large group of developing countries.

Turning to preferences, the challenge is to avoid division. Some preference erosion is inevitable, whatever the terms of a final agreement: as MFN rates come down, preference margins will fall. However, conflict can be avoided if major exporters do not challenge preferential access in key areas, notably EU sugar. This will entail financial costs for commercial exporters in the G20, but the political benefits of avoiding divisions with LDCs and the Africa group outweigh the costs.

### 6.6 Special and differential treatment

The most pressing concerns in this area revolve around market access and differentiation. Application of the Swiss formula would create unacceptable adjustment costs. Many developing-country governments may have the flexibility to lower tariffs without fundamentally shifting relative prices, eroding self-reliance or damaging rural livelihoods. But liberalization in this area should reflect national policy choices, not WTO imperatives. Food security is one area in which a one-size-fits-all model is doomed to failure. Distinctions based on country size, export status, average income, dependence on food imports and so on may be of relevance in many areas, but they are at best weak and at worst irrelevant proxies for food-security status.

Developing countries could make a far more powerful case for a WTO regime that allows for flexibility. Far more should be done to highlight the potential threats posed by inappropriate forms of liberalization. Northern governments themselves face an issue of credibility. It is one thing to advocate open markets in areas where they have some claim to lead by example. It makes less sense to erode the right of poor countries to protect their producers when the EU and the US remain the superpowers of the subsidizing world. Diluting SDT in this context will inevitably be seen as another case of double standards – which will erode the legitimacy of the WTO itself in the eyes of many.

## 7. Conclusion

The Doha Round provides an opportunity to address longstanding inequalities in agricultural trade. This chapter has pointed to dichotomies and conflicts that are affecting the course of the Doha Round negotiations. Some of the issues are:
- the vulnerability of developing countries to fluctuations in the prices of agricultural products;
- strong political and economic interests of the industrialized countries in maintaining their shares in production and trade in agricultural products through protection and support;
- high barriers to trade being maintained both by developed and developing countries;
- regionalism versus multilateralism;
- heterogeneity of interests among developing countries, including LDCs; and
- controversies about the relationship between trade, growth and poverty.

Bringing Northern agricultural support systems under more effective multilateral rules could create new opportunities for poverty reduction. It would also strengthen the legitimacy and credibility of the rules-based multilateral system.

It goes without saying that major obstacles remain. The negotiating power of individual developing countries is limited – and the vested interests in industrialized countries are powerful. Consolidating and deepening the G20 and its alliances with other groups holds the key to progress. While it is impossible to disassemble the AoA framework, in the short to medium term there is a strong case for focusing political energies on a number of discrete goals. These include a prohibition on direct export subsidization, a revision of the distinction between 'distorting' and 'non-distorting' subsidies, and measures to restrict exports of all products at prices below the costs of production.

**References**

Cashin, P. and C.J. Mcdermott, 'The Long-Run Behavior of Commodity prices: Small Trends and Big Variability,' IMF Staff Papers Vol. 49, No. 2 (Washington: International Monetary Fund, 2002).

Food & Agriculture Organization, 'Dependence on single agricultural commodity exports in developing countries: Magnitude and Trends,' (Rome: 105).

Government of Australia, 'South-South Trade' (Canberra: Department of Foreign Affairs and Trade, 2004).

Organization for Economic Cooperation and Development, 'Agricultural Policies 2004, At a glance' (Paris: 2004).

Overseas Development Institute, 'Commodity Markets: Options for Developing Countries' (London: November 1995).

Valdes and McCalla: 'Issues, Interests and Options of Developing Countries' (1999).

World Bank, Global *Economic Prospects* 2004 (Washington, 2004).

# Chapter 4

# Trade, Agriculture, the Environment and Development: Reaping the Benefits of Win-Win-Win?

Vangelis Vitalis

## 1. Introduction

Agriculture is a key sector for most developing countries. In the LDCs it contributes nearly one-third of GDP, compared with less than 3 per cent in developed countries. The poor in most developing countries are heavily engaged in subsistence farming, and food accounts for a significant proportion of all poor people's expenditure. Moreover, a high proportion of the poor live in rural areas – more than 60 per cent worldwide,

---

1. This chapter is an edited version of a paper presented at the Windsor dialogue in 2004. Vangelis Vitalis is currently a Senior Negotiator with the New Zealand Ministry of Foreign Affairs and Trade. The views expressed here are his own and do not necessarily represent the views of the New Zealand Ministry of Foreign Affairs and Trade.

nearly 90 per cent in China and Bangladesh, and between 65 per cent and 90 per cent in Sub-Saharan Africa.[2] Concerning the link between agriculture, the environment and development, more than half of the world's poorest people live in ecologically vulnerable areas.[3] And those developing countries that have enjoyed the fastest agricultural export growth have also tended to achieve faster GDP growth, with accompanying increases in rural incomes and poverty reduction.[4] In short, for these people what happens to agriculture in the Doha Development Round is not simply an abstract policy question.

Despite the obvious interlinkages between trade, agriculture and poverty alleviation, the international trade in agricultural products continues to be heavily distorted by the developed world's policies. This chapter briefly delineates the relationship between trade and economic growth and then reviews developed countries'[5] agricultural protection policies with a focus on export subsidies, domestic support and tariff policies. The chapter makes the specific point, however, that we need to be realistic about what the reform of developed-world agricultural policies can and cannot do. Such reform cannot deliver development by itself.

The second part of the paper examines the way in which the environment is increasingly being used by some countries to justify the retention of subsidies. While one should acknowledge that subsidies can have both positive and negative effects on the environment, the important point will be how subsidies might support agreed (contestable and transparent) public-good initiatives in a non-trade distorting manner. In this regard, trade negotiators need to be clear on the issues and, in particular, decide how to deal with them. The paper argues that the WTO may be the obvious place to develop disciplines on this, but that it is fraught with complications and sensitivities.

## 2. Trade and economic growth

Trade and macro-economic variables do not operate in a vacuum. They are strongly interrelated and indeed interdependent. These relationships may be considered in two ways. First, macro-economic variables such as national income, consumption, employment, aggregate investment and price levels are all affected by trade. Specifically, trade affects macro-economic performance in terms of the dynamics of the economy's growth, its stability and indeed its distribution. Second, the reverse causality – from macro-economic variables to trade – also holds true. Domestic growth can, for instance, raise the demand for imports and divert resources from the production of exportables to production for domestic markets. Other things being equal, the trade balance will

---

2. Khan, M.H. (2000).
3. OECD (2001B).
4. See, for instance, IMF (2002).
5. For the purposes of this paper and the data-related references, developed countries have been defined as the members of the OECD. It is important to note, however, that the OECD and non-OECD distinction is not a neat contrast of rich and poor: three OECD members have developing-country status at the WTO (South Korea, Mexico and Turkey).

tend to deteriorate. The theory is clear: trade matters.

### ... So much for the theory, is trade really important for growth?

The linkage between trade and growth is well established.[6] Econometric analyses have demonstrated that there is a positive correlation between the role of exports in economic growth over time and this positive effect is further correlated with openness to trade. Moreover, trade is one of the more statistically significant variables in explaining differences in the economic growth of countries.[7] Even critics of the mainstream literature[8] agree that there is a link between trade and growth though there is still disagreement about the direction of causality between trade and growth.[9] Numerous cross-sectional analyses have, however, demonstrated the positive effect of trade on per capita income growth.[10] At least one econometric analysis is explicit on the point, noting that a rise of 1 per cent in the ratio of trade to GDP can be linked directly to an increase of 0.5 per cent in income per capita.[11]

There are a number of mechanisms which account for the positive effect of trade on economic growth over time. These include comparative advantage-related specialization; the exploitation of increasing returns from larger markets; knowledge and innovation flows; and the diffusion of technology.[12]

### ... and what about developing countries?

Numerous cross-sectional analyses have also shown the positive effect of trade on income growth per capita in developing countries.[13] It is estimated, for instance, that those developing countries that have experienced the fastest growth in exports of non-energy products have experienced annual growth in real GDP 1 per cent higher than countries with slower export growth.[14]

Developing countries receive considerably more foreign exchange revenue from trade than from almost any other source. One study concluded that, on a per capita annual basis, developing countries' exports generate more than 30 times as much revenue ($322 per capita) as aid disbursements ($10). Similarly, the LDCs generate 12 times as much from exports ($113 per capita) as from aid ($9).[15] Moreover, a 1 per cent rise in

---

6. World Bank (2001).
7. See for instance E. S. Prassad and J. R. Gable (1997).
8. Rodriguez, F. and D. Rodrik (1999).
9. DFID (2002).
10. See, for instance, D. Dollar and A. Kray (2001) and J. A. Frenkel and D. Romer (1999).
11. See in particular J. A. Frenkel and D. Romer (1999), pp. 379-399.
12. Baldwin, R. E. (2002). See also F. Rodriguez a nd D. Rodrik (1999).
13. See, for instance, D. Dollar and A. Kray (2001) and J. A. Frenkel and D. Romer (1999).
14. World Bank (2001).
15 The counter to these figures is that this is a comparison of apples and oranges, i.e. that revenue (from trade) is offset by costs, while aid disbursements are in effect pure profit. More important perhaps is the question of allocation within countries and among them.

world export market shares of the developing-country group has the capacity to raise annual income per capita in South Asia by 12 per cent, 4 per cent in Latin America and East Asia, and up to 20 per cent in Sub-Saharan Africa.[16] This could reduce the number of people living in poverty by nearly 130 million, or 12 per cent of the world total, with the greatest gains likely in Sub-Saharan Africa.[17] In short, even relatively modest improvements in developing countries' levels of access to developed-world markets are likely to generate expanded exports and thus improved revenues.[18]

Barriers to trade raise the prices of both imports and domestic goods. Aside from limiting consumer choices in developed countries, protection also implies higher consumer prices, because it eases competitive pressures. More specifically, the developed world's protection fragments markets, limiting incentives to lower production costs due to specialization and access to cheaper inputs. By raising prices, higher trade barriers act like a tax hike with attendant income effects. The burden of these kinds of policy falls particularly heavily on developing countries and has a negative impact on economic growth and poverty reduction.

There is a growing consensus that freer access to international markets would in most cases benefit both developed and developing countries. Depending on the models used, estimates of the annual static welfare gains from the elimination of all barriers to goods and services trade (in all markets, including developing countries) range from $250 billion to $620 billion, of which one-third to one-half (depending on the model one favours) would accrue to developing countries.[19] The table in section 12 summarizes the estimated welfare effects of liberalization.

It is important to acknowledge that in the poorest economies, it is impossible to have poverty reduction without growth. If per capita income is less than $1 per day, then redistribution alone will not alleviate poverty. That said, the structure of growth matters as well. Concentrated growth will not necessarily raise people out of poverty as swiftly as a broader-based growth trajectory. Indeed, although there is broad agreement about the wider welfare effects of trade liberalization, there is still disagreement about the direction of causality between trade and growth. The evidence is such that one should not assume that any single economic policy tool (such as the lowering of trade barriers) will accelerate economic development or poverty reduction.[20] If a country is to reduce poverty, numerous domestic reforms[21] are required in tandem with interna-

---

16. Oxfam (2002), pp. 47-48.
17. See, for instance, L. Hanmer et al (2000).
18. It is worth emphasizing that the distortions affecting 'South-South' trade are both significant and important. Notwithstanding this, the current chapter focuses on OECD member policies, not least because a separate chapter of this book fully explores the South-South dimension in considerable detail.
19. For the range of results see World Bank (2002), pp.166-173; K. Anderson (2001); P. Dee and K. Hanslow (2000); S. K. Dessus et al (1999). See also Table 27 in OECD (2002), which is reproduced as Annex Table 1 to this chapter.
20. Baldwin, R. E. (2002). See also F. Rodriguez and D. Rodrik (1999).
21. For a good outline of the kinds of policy measures and reforms that could be considered by developing countries, see N. McCulloch et al (2001).

## 3. Agricultural protection

The case for multilateral trade reform rests on a simple but persuasive principle, that of comparative advantage. This holds that a country can gain from specialization in those goods (or services) in which its relative costs of production are lower than in other countries and exporting them in return for products in which it has a comparative disadvantage. This ideal can only emerge, however, if countries avoid distortionary and protectionist policies that may affect the allocation of resources in tradable sectors. Many developing countries have a comparative advantage in some aspect of agricultural production and a reduction in protection by potential trading partners should enhance export opportunities in these activities. In principle, the efficiency gains from agricultural trade reform should also translate into more rapid economic growth and help alleviate poverty.[23]

The key international commitment on agricultural trade is contained in the Doha WTO Ministerial Declaration, which identifies a shortlist of areas for negotiation in agriculture. The Declaration notes that countries will work towards 'reductions of, with a view to phasing out, all forms of export subsidies; and substantial reductions in trade-distorting domestic support.'[24] The following outlines the current situation in these areas.

## 4. Export subsidies

Export subsidies have a significant impact on world markets, through their ability to increase exports from subsidizing countries and to depress world prices. In this way, they depress the returns to non-subsidized exporters. It is interesting to note that only 25 of the current WTO members have export subsidy reduction commitments, and that only 14 of these members are actually using export subsidies. The overwhelming majority of the export-subsidy commitments are concentrated in the EU countries (including recently acceded members), Switzerland and the United States.

Modelling work suggests that a complete elimination of export subsidies would raise global incomes by $3.6 billion a year by 2010.[25] The greatest beneficiaries would be taxpayers in the European Union. Developing countries would benefit too: world market prices for agricultural products would rise and lead to higher returns for producers. In theory, this should benefit net exporters and farmers in importing countries, though it may add to import costs for economies that are net importers of agricultural goods.

There are encouraging signs that the provision of export subsidies not only in their traditional form, but also provided through subsidized export credits, food aid and so on

---

22. For a good overview of the main issues, see H. Nordstrom *et al* (2001).
23. OECD (2003).
24. Paragraph 13 of the Doha Declaration (WTO 2001).
25. ABARE (2001).

will be addressed in the coming months. All of the significant providers of such support have indicated a willingness to consider reductions in current levels of assistance. Export subsidies, however, are only part of the problem.

## 5. Domestic support

Since the Uruguay Round concluded, domestic support policies in developed economies have barely been dented and in some cases they have worsened.[26] The net effect of domestic support policies in developed countries is to increase production and, by inflating consumer prices, to discourage demand. The surpluses that result have to be sold (or 'given away') on world markets, often with the assistance of export subsidies or via food aid with an attendant depressing effect on prices. Moreover, the range of mechanisms used to deliver support to the sector prevents consumers and farmers from responding to realistic price information. In this way, a larger share of the burden of adjusting to shocks is passed on to other participants in the market, widening the fluctuations in world prices.

Farm support in OECD member countries absorbs more than $229 billion a year, or about 1 per cent of those countries' GNP, and more than four times what these countries spend collectively on development assistance to developing countries. This figure accounts for 32 per cent of farm income in the OECD.[27] The individual statistics are sobering. Annually, for instance, the EU spends nearly €2 billion on subsidizing its sugar farmers to produce something that can be produced more efficiently and cheaply in the developing world. In the United States, oilseed farmers receive nearly $12,000 a year each in income support. Compare this to the modest aim of achieving the Millennium Development Goal of raising the developing world's incomes above $1 a day.

The costs to consumers of such assistance are similarly significant. The CAP has been estimated to cost an average family of four around €1,450 a year in artificially supported prices and direct costs of €100 per head as taxpayers to subsidize farmers directly.[28] More lightheartedly, the New Zealand Government has estimated that EU consumers and taxpayers transferred sufficient funds, through a variety of border measures and domestic price-support policies, to pay for each of the OECD's 41 million dairy cows to fly first class around the world one and a half times.[29] A similar, more up-to-date calculation concluded that, not only could the cows fly around the world, they would have nearly €1,000 spending money as well![30]

Perhaps the most significant shift globally relates to the EU's reform of the CAP. On the face of it, the deal agreed in 2003 looks very promising. Many of the subsidies linked to specific farm products are, at last, to be decoupled – the idea is to replace them with a direct payment to farmers, unconnected to particular products. In this way, the

---

26. OECD (2000).
27. OECD (2004).
28. Spicer (1997).
29. Cited in OECD (1998).
30. See the amusing but educational film at www.cafod.org.uk/moostersmillions.

principle of decoupling of rural income support from agricultural production is now firmly established in the minds of EU policymakers. This lays the groundwork for the eventual evolution of a liberalized internal agricultural market. Not surprisingly, Commissioner Franz Fischler described this reform as 'the beginning of a new era' and suggested that 'European agricultural policy will change fundamentally'.[31]

The devil is in the details and a closer look suggests that the EU put off real reform of the CAP for at least another five years – by which time the full impact of operating the still expensive and bureaucratically contorted policy in a 25-country EU will become apparent. Despite this 'new era' and apparent qualitative shift in support, the EU remains the world's largest subsidizer of farmers. There will actually be no reduction in the overall level of subvention to agriculture as a result of the decision. CAP expenditure is likely to remain at €40-42 billion a year. On the basis of current information on the likely pattern of application of the new arrangements, it is likely that of the current €28-30 billion a year of direct subsidies, some €15 billion will be converted into single income payments – principally because of the predominance of the arable sector in the direct subsidy bill and because the cuts in production-linked subsidy will be greatest in this sector. In short, most of the major market-distorting features of the policy – production-linked subsidies, market intervention, quotas and export subsidies – remain in place.

In France, most remarkably, there will be no change in the structure or form of support until 2007. Only in the UK, Denmark and Sweden will the principle of decoupling be fully applied. In the other 11 countries and in France after 2007, direct production-coupled subsidies will remain to be only partially replaced by the decoupled income subsidy. What will create the most obvious distortions in the internal market will be not only the disparity between the three decoupling countries and the other 12, but the differences in linked subsidy levels in the twelve countries determined to retain the subsidization of production.

## 6. OECD countries' tariff policies

Tariffs in developed countries disproportionately affect exports from developing and least developed countries. Between one-sixth and one-third of the tariff peaks extant in Quad economies, for instance, exceed 30 percent, and some tariffs exceed 200 per cent.[32] Tariff peaks in the Quad economies affect about 5 per cent of all exports from developing countries, and 11 per cent of exports from LDCs.[33] It is important to note, however, that a range of preferential arrangements do affect the overall impact on developing countries – a point discussed in more detail below.

The tariff rates applied by OECD countries vary considerably. Those applying to

---

31. For Commissioner Fischler's speech in full see europa.eu.int/rapid/pressReleasesAction.do?reference=SPEECH/03/326&format=HTML&aged=0&language=EN&guiLanguage=en.
32. Hoekman, B. M. and M. M. Koestecki (2001).
33. Hoekman, B. M. and M. M. Koestecki (2001).

agricultural goods, for instance, are generally higher than others; indeed, this has effectively ensured that imports from developing countries are absent over wide ranges of added-value items in the food industry sector, and sometimes even for major agricultural export products in individual developed markets. Developing countries also suffer from the effects of tariffs precisely in those areas where they appear to be most competitive, including sugar, fish, cereals and fruits and vegetables.[34] Export producers in developing countries tend to be SMEs, which find the higher rates particularly difficult to absorb into their operating margins.

OECD tariffs on tropical products are of particular interest to many developing countries. These tariffs are, for the most part, low or non-existent because such goods do not compete with local products, but there are some small significant exceptions. The EU, for instance, maintains several tariff peaks to shield from external competition those of its regions that can produce tropical goods. EU tariff structures are also designed to protect output margins and market access for the developing country members of the ACP countries.[35] Tariffs on bananas are the most egregious that favour the ACP, but exclude others such as Central American exporters. Tobacco and sugar are two other commodities where exporters not benefiting from preferential schemes have been shut out of the market.[36] Tariff peaks are also a significant problem for processed tropical goods (that is, tariff escalation as the level of processing increases). Processed coffee and cocoa, for instance, both attract substantially higher tariffs than their raw and unprocessed equivalents. This effectively shuts developing countries out of the value-added sector and forces them to remain in the volatile, low value-added commodities trade.

The poor performance of developed countries' TRQs is also a cause for concern. In theory, this mechanism allows better market access for a selected group of developing countries. In reality, the average fill rates of TRQs have been low. This reflects discriminatory administrative systems[37] and high 'in-quota' rates that in some cases exceed the Quad's average for agricultural products. The out-of-quota rates are astronomical – including for instance a 130 per cent tariff on above-quota bananas, effectively closing the out-of-quota market for developing countries in this sub-sector. In agricultural and food products, there is little if any developing-country trade exceeding the TRQ levels.[38]

## 7. The gains from developed world liberalization

It is difficult to quantify the impact on developing countries of developed countries' agricultural protection. This is partly because the specific costs of policies depend on

---

34. Hoekman, B. M. *et al* (2001).
35. For more information about this body see the website at www.acpsec.org, which also offers access to the Cotonou Agreement, providing guaranteed preferential market access across a range of sectors (www.acpsec.org/gb/cotonou/accord1.htm).
36. See for instance, Borrell, B. (1999).
37. On the administration of TRQs, see WTO (2001) and OECD (2001C).
38. UNCTAD (2000).

precise information about implementation and flow-on effects. Another problem is that not enough is known about how the distribution of land, capital and labour might affect any welfare gains accruing to developing countries. Nor is enough known about how much rural prices and wages might change as a result of multiplier effects of improvements in agricultural trade. While aggregate data are available on income effects, not enough is known at a disaggregated level, for instance about the multiplier effects of market access changes on domestic agricultural wages and prices. Moreover, much of the modelling work is underpinned by assumptions about supply responses. Though the calculations tend to be sophisticated and are based on available data, we still do not know precisely how producers will react to market access improvements effected via changes in domestic support for agriculture.

Bearing in mind these caveats, the international modelling work on the likely effects of the liberalization of agricultural trade does suggest significant global welfare gains. From a full agricultural liberalization, these may be as high as $20 billion a year for developing countries.[39] Other estimates indicate gains of $15 billion a year to developing countries from a partial liberalization.[40] More recent modelling work, summarized in Table 1, amplifies these results. It shows that reducing direct and indirect agricultural subsidies in the developed world would produce potentially significant gains for agricultural producers in low- and middle-income developing countries and for developed countries' consumers (and taxpayers). These figures should not be accepted uncritically, but they do suggest that substantial overall welfare gains are likely to developing countries.

**Table 1: Enlightened self-interest: gains from agricultural reform for developing countries and gains for the developed world**
(billions of 1997 US dollars)

| Countries/regions | Removal of border protection | Removal of all protection |
|---|---|---|
| Low- and middle-income countries | 22.3 | 26.0 |
| Western Europe | 21.4 | 17.0 |
| United States | 4.3 | 5.0 |

Source: Abbreviated from J. Beghin *et al* (2002).[41]

Declines in developed countries' domestic support (and indeed export subsidies), coupled with reductions in border protection, should affect prices by reducing the global supply of many agricultural products. The price rises are likely to be significant – the price of wheat, for instance, is expected to increase over the 1993 level by 6.2 per cent,

---

39. Binswanger, H. and E. Lutz (2000).
40. K. Anderson *et al* (1999).
41. Caveats to the results cited in the original paper (p.9) apply equally here.

prices of dairy products by 12.2 per cent, and prices of beef and veal by 7.2 per cent[42] —and to have a positive effect on profits and incomes in developing countries.

Against this background, it is possible to compile a short list of the agriculture-related issues that need to be addressed for the Doha Round to deliver on its commitment to be a Development Round. These include:
- Full elimination of export subsidies;
- Sharp reductions in trade-distorting domestic support for each major product line. Most radically perhaps, the base for these cuts should be actual tariff levels, not 'bound' levels;
- A reassessment of some of the Green Box provisions to ensure that those programmes currently in the Box are not distortive; and
- Deep cuts in OECD members' tariffs on agricultural products – with at a minimum a commitment to a two-figure cap on all tariffs (i.e. no 100 per cent tariffs) and significant phase-out commitments.

## 8. Agricultural trade reform by itself is not enough...

While many developing countries will benefit from changes in the international trading regime and are likely to enjoy further positive gains, some may not, at least in the immediate term. Many critics have argued, for instance, that developed countries that are net importers of food may lose as a consequence of the elimination of export subsidies. This argument is overstated. The evidence suggests that the most significant export subsidies are provided when supplies in exporting countries are at their highest and world prices are therefore already low. Much smaller subsidies are provided when prices are high.[43] Thus, export subsidies may benefit low-income food importers the least during their times of greatest need and the most during their times of least need.[44] It is possible to see the same correlation between commodity cycles and food aid (which can serve as another form of export subsidy): often the greatest quantities of food aid are given when world prices are at their lowest.[45]

Many developing countries, not least those in the Caribbean and in the South Pacific, depend heavily on the preferential access provided by the EU and others. They have developed their export-producing sectors to respond to these artificially created incentives. This makes these countries particularly vulnerable to any changes in policies

---

42. N. McCulloch *et al* (2001).
43. Tyers, R. and K. Anderson (1992).
44. It is also erroneous to argue that export subsidies reduce world hunger by cutting world prices. In fact, the use of export subsidies is not calibrated to meet developing countries' food demands. Rather, the mechanism is employed during periods of oversupply, i.e. support is timed to benefit producers in countries using agricultural support and is used less when world prices are high. A better way to assist poor countries would be to replace such support with cash donations at times of need. This would ensure better targeting. As noted in the text, the majority of workers in the developing world are engaged in agriculture, so such an approach would also prevent export subsidies from lowering the incomes of some of the world's poorest people.
45. ABARE (2001).

on preferential agreements, use of the GSP and so on.[46] Preferential arrangements are a vexed issue in the context of the Doha Development Round. They may appear to be valuable to those fortunate enough to benefit from them, but they have served to divide developing countries on the utility of such schemes.

Non-symmetrical market access programmes have several potential difficulties.[47] First, critics have noted that the consequence of preferential arrangements may be to increase the LDCs' or ACP's exports at the expense of other developing countries' exports, though there is some debate as to the magnitude of such a change.[48] Second, there is often uncertainty about whether the preferential access will be maintained, and for how long. This may inhibit or at least distort investment decisions for export industries. Third, a country's growth in incomes as a consequence of improved access may propel it above the threshold of eligibility. This has been a perverse feature, commonly criticized, of the preferential access scheme applied for selected African countries by the US. Fourth, the structure of these mechanisms is such that they may distort LDCs' export profiles towards the improved access, and away from areas of actual comparative advantage.[49] Finally, such arrangements are extremely inefficient transfer mechanisms and can represent a poor form of development aid. One estimate indicates that the cost to the EU and the US of providing US$1 of preferential access exceeds US$5.[50]

Developed-world agricultural liberalization may also affect the poor in developing countries, particularly in the short term, in complex ways, some of them negative. Poor urban workers and farmers, for instance, may stand to benefit from the reduction of the developed world's barriers as a consequence of faster export growth, higher producer prices, increased wages and greater demand for labour. But in the short term, some of the effects of such changes may not be so positive, for two reasons. First, the removal or reduction of developed-world agricultural subsidies (for instance) may raise the prices of internationally traded goods compared with non-traded products. While this may benefit farmers (particularly those that participate in the domestic or export markets) in developing countries, urban poor and/or subsistence farmers in those same countries may experience short-term welfare losses – as noted below. Second, wage levels and employment in developing countries may not move in the expected direction. If, for instance, a developing country protects certain sectors that employ significant numbers of poor people and these are suddenly exposed to more efficient external competition, there is a risk of adverse impacts.[51]

Countries of Sub-Saharan Africa, in particular, appear to have been unable to capitalize on even the modest reductions in developed-world protection of, for instance, agricultural markets. There seem to be two reasons for this. First are the ongoing conflicts

---

46. For this reason, several developed countries (e.g. New Zealand) have eliminated the GSP.
47. Chang, W. and L. A. Winters (2000).
48. Given that preferences do not affect prices in importing countries, consumption in those countries does not increase when preferences are changed.
49. See in particular Anderson, K. *et al* (2001).
50. Beghin, J., and M.A. Aksoy (2003).
51. Winters, A. (2000).

in the region. Second, while agriculture is an important part of many Sub-Saharan African economies, much of it is of the subsistence type, not readily convertible to tradable commodities. Further, the commodities (e.g. coffee and cocoa) that many of these countries have traded internationally have generally suffered reductions in world prices in the past ten years with negative effects on poverty reduction.

More generally, there is a fundamental problem that relates to developing countries' supply responsiveness. Many developing countries' agricultural sectors are unable to respond to changed market conditions swiftly enough to maximize the potential welfare gains. There is in effect a supply response lag to the creation of new demand in developed-world markets. This, combined with the high-cost environment in which their firms must operate (i.e. to meet regulatory and safety requirements to enable exporting), is a significant constraint on their ability to reap the benefits of trade reform.

It is also important to distinguish among the wide range of economies that fall into the developing-country category. In particular, the gains from a decline in developed-country agricultural protection are expected to accrue in the first instance to middle- and upper-income developing countries. These are countries that have reformed their agricultural sectors and therefore stand to benefit most from improvements in global trade access. The likely short-term 'losers' from liberalization are expected to be a small number of LDCs, specifically those whose agricultural reform has lagged and which are net importers of food. Potential improvements in welfare may be negatively affected by distortions in domestic economies.[52]

A further difficulty will be the potential divide between the urban and rural poor in developing countries. Given that the urban poor buy their food, rather than produce it, they are likely to be[53] particularly hard hit by food price rises as a consequence of the elimination of some forms of support. Nevertheless, it is worth remembering that poor households can vary greatly in their composition and structure, so that changes in the international trading regime for agriculture may have important second-round spillovers, many of which can reasonably be assumed to be beneficial.

While there is no doubt that some individual economies would suffer from increases in world prices for agricultural goods, for most of the LDCs any losses are likely to be relatively small. In only a handful of countries, for instance, do the estimated welfare changes represent more than 1 per cent of GDP.

All of the above suggests the need not necessarily for more aid, but better aid. Development assistance should address trade-related policy and public investment priorities to help: expand the ability to respond to new/changed demand; improve the adaptation prospects for countries losing preferences and deal with the potential rise in world food prices (should these emerge as a consequence of agricultural reform). In this regard, the focus could be on building capacity in intellectual property rights management; addressing technical regulations and standards; and encouraging more technology-/know how-related services trade. One practical suggestion might be the use of

---

52. See, for instance, J. S. Wilson (2002).
53. On the gains from multilateral liberalization in agriculture for LDCs, see M. D. Ingco (1997).

fiscal benefits to firms transferring technologies to developing countries (in the same way as many OECD members encourage firms to do this in poorer regions domestically). The developed world's enterprises could, for instance, be encouraged through relaxation of Mode 4 GATS provisions to allow for the temporary employment of science, technology and engineering graduates in OECD countries. Above all, however, any attempt to address these issues needs to be aligned with the domestic priority-setting process.[54]

## 9. Trade and the environment: a not-so-hidden agenda

It appears that any new arrangements to move negotiations forward through the Doha Development Round may include commitments to reduce many subsidies. Unfortunately, however, there is also a very real possibility that this process will be undermined by countries seeking to retain certain subsidies and limit overall reductions. This is not surprising. What is perhaps surprising is the vehemence with which environmental arguments are increasingly used to defend such moves. The European Commission, for instance, recently noted that it subsidizes agriculture 'because ... it contributes to the protection of the environment.'[55] Most recently, Switzerland, France, Norway and Japan have separately emphasized the perceived environmental benefits that some of their subsidy programmes confer, noting in particular the public-good elements of such provision, including limiting erosion, retaining the value of soil and 'preserving' the environmental benefits of, for instance, traditional rice farming in Japan and 'ancient traditions of dairy farming in the Swiss Alps' and so on.[56]

It is important to be clear at the outset what argument is underpinning this approach. Basic principles are a good starting point. There is no doubt that a reduction in subsidies *will* affect the environment in a number of ways – both beneficial and harmful. These impacts occur through *changes* in the:
- structure of production across countries;
- scale of economic activity;
- mix of inputs and outputs; and
- production technologies.

Some of the positive and negative impacts of subsidy reductions may be felt domestically – soil quality, groundwater and surface-water pollution from fertilizer and pesticide run-offs, changes in land use that affect landscape appearance, and so on. Others may have global effects through trans-boundary spillovers (e.g. greenhouse gases), changes in international transport flows and so on.[57] In short, it is important to acknowledge that there may be some truth to the suggestion that a small minority of subsidies

---

54. B. Hoekman, C. Michalopoulos and L.A. Winters (2004).
55. *Le Monde* (Paris: 5 September, 2003).
56. See for instance, the Norwegian Ministry of Agriculture's website (odin.dep.no/ld/html/multifunc/multifunc3.html) and a similar site linked to the Japanese Ministry of Agriculture, Forestry and Fisheries (www.maff.go.jp/e_guide/010.htm).
57. OECD (2001A).

can affect the environment in positive ways.[58] The point is how to ensure that such claims to support the environment through subsidization are legitimately made by governments in response to clearly identifiable demands in a manner that is transparent, contestable and does not distort trade.

That said, such claims should not be used as a reason to freeze or limit subsidy reform. It is not acceptable, for instance, for developed countries to use as an argument for subsidy retention the fact that a loss of subsidy may cause output in a developing country to increase with potential negative consequences for the environment there (or indeed globally). This is a trade-off which developing countries need to consider themselves. After all, no developing country is going to limit its freedom to develop in the same way as developed countries have before them. The developed world's living standards are built on the conversion of natural resources into intellectual and human resources. This substitution of natural capital with human capital is a trade-off that every country regards as its own sovereign choice, and it was reaffirmed by the Rio Declaration.[59]

There are two important and interrelated issues. First, if OECD countries are really so concerned about this, then one response would be a re-focusing of technical and development assistance aimed at alleviating such problems. Take the case of cotton subsidies. OECD member subsidies to cotton farmers lower world prices by some 25 per cent.[60] A reduction in such support would certainly have a positive effect on economic growth through improved market access for a number of developing countries. One of the reasons suggested for retention of such support has been the likely negative effects on the environment as a consequence of raised production in those countries (and the pressure on resources like water and energy).

Uzbekistan has significant cotton interests. Higher world prices would certainly have positive implications for poverty reduction and economic growth in this Central Asian economy. It is also true that increased output may have negative implications for water use and the Aral Sea. The water supply of Uzbek cotton farmers is a dwindling resource. Currently, more than 40 per cent of the water taken from rivers feeding the severely stressed Aral Sea to irrigate the cotton fields of Uzbekistan evaporates before it even reaches those fields (Uzbek systems use open channels, not closed pipes, for irrigation).[61] Further pressure on the Aral Sea water resource would have significant negative spillovers to other parts of the Uzbek economy. What can be done about this?

If those countries using the environment as an argument to avoid subsidy reform

---

58. For more detail on this and other aspects of the environment and the agricultural sector see OECD (2001A).
59. Principle 2 of the Rio Declaration reads: 'States have, in accordance with the Charter of the United Nations and the principles of international law, the sovereign right to exploit their own resources pursuant to their own environmental and developmental policies, and the responsibility to ensure that activities within their jurisdiction or control do not cause damage to the environment of other States or of areas beyond the limits of national jurisdiction. (The Rio Declaration is available at habitat.igc.org/agenda21/rio-dec.htm).
60. See for instance the data available at www.icac.org.
61. TACIS (1999).

are serious about this, then the answer to this problem is not to stall subsidy reform but to focus on how technical and development assistance might plug the gaps. Thus, when market access is improved for Uzbek cotton as a consequence of subsidy reductions, developed countries' policymakers should consider how to fund flanking measures to ameliorate any potential environmental problem (such as technical assistance for improved irrigation techniques).

There is a second important part of the environment-related case for subsidies. This is that there may soon come a point when rents to producers who provide public goods are reduced, with a concomitant decline in the quality of these public goods. The argument runs that maintaining and even increasing subsidies is necessary to prevent the erosion of such public goods.[62] This question needs to be considered in the context of market failure, the valuation of resources and the absence or poor functioning of markets. There are two important distinctions. The first relates to production-related subsidies and the second is decoupled (i.e. non-production-related) support. When the demand for *production-linked* environmental services considered to be public goods is fully satisfied through profitable farming activity at no additional costs and remunerated through market returns, there is no market failure and therefore there is no need for a subsidy.

It is important to acknowledge, however, that there is a potential problem. Take the case of dairy subsidies. Many countries which use these forms of support argue that the subsidy helps in the provision of essential public goods, including, for instance, attractive landscapes (rolling pasture land etc.) that are valued by the wider population. This is sometimes used as a justification for the continuation of production-linked subsidies. Recently, the French Minister of Agriculture sought to make precisely this connection.[63] This argument, which rests on the perceived 'multi-functionality' of agriculture, does not withstand scrutiny. It is true that, where a country reduces subsidies which are associated with particular landscape features, then a market failure may arise. This could occur if, for instance, the subsidy cut causes a reduction of the supply of landscape services that was previously considered adequate.

There is a nuance here. Whether or not a market failure occurs depends on how farmers adjust to lower returns. If the least efficient, highest-cost farmers are driven out of business but their land is acquired by more efficient producers who continue to farm it (albeit less intensively), then the supply of the desired environmental services may not necessarily fall below what is demanded.

If the land goes out of production or is converted to production of non-milk commodities with different (or no) landscape value, there may be an undersupply of

---

62. Public goods are products or services for which consumption and provision cannot be limited to one individual or group of individuals. Two features distinguish these from private traded goods – non-rivalry and non-excludability. Non-rivalry: the benefit from consuming a product or service does not reduce its beneficial consumption by others. Non-excludability: users or potential consumers cannot be prevented from benefiting from the public good once it has been supplied. Also it is impossible to require an individual to pay for the good according to the benefit derived, which would be necessary to avoid free-rider behaviour.
63. *Le Monde* (Paris: 5 May, 2004).

the perceived public good and some intervention may be justified. It is important to note, however, that a simple subsidy payment to the farmer may not be the correct response. Where the demand for such a public good can be identified and quantified, it should be also possible to use market forces through, *inter alia*, enforcing contracts so that the beneficiary pays. For instance, to maintain the agricultural activity associated with the supply of some public goods is, from the farmers' perspective, the provision of services using privately owned resources and the factors of production. Farmers will supply such services if they are adequately remunerated. This is equivalent to the provision of housing facilities and off-farm services provided by farmers to the tourism industry in, for instance, New Zealand and France. In the same way, the remuneration of public goods-related environmental services could be offered by charging all the industries that benefit through, for instance, a tax on their revenues to make the necessary funds available. In this way, the costs of environmental outputs would be internalized in the prices of goods and services provided by the industries that benefit, thus avoiding distortions in the allocation of resources.[64] In short, a win-win solution is possible.

Then there are *non-production-linked* outputs of public goods like the preservation of farm buildings, hedgerows, stone walls and hillside terraces considered as having an aesthetic value. It is worth noting in this regard that the Green Box provision of the AoA allows countries to support these kinds of programme so long as they are not trade-distorting. Many of these programmes may not depend on agricultural production directly and are provided through farmers' own resources. The problem arises when demand for these is not satisfied when the buildings (etc) are not constructed, maintained or preserved or are abandoned. When these features are classified, the important point is the modalities for charging or remunerating their preservation.

In fact, these types of public good concern not only agriculture, but other industries in the region, particularly tourism. Therefore, sustainable financing of solutions for such services should rely on an agreement involving the private sector and public/local entities under clearly defined property rights. Where the cost allocation according to individual benefits received by individuals and groups is not feasible, local or national government programmes may be the only way to provide such public goods, as is the case with other public goods considered to be of historical or cultural value.

There are other non-production linked public goods-related outputs, for instance, the provision of habitat and biodiversity through specific land-management practices including preserving land set-aside from commodity production with specific conservation practices attached to it. Any demand for such services is satisfied only if farmers

---

**64.** To be equitable, effective and minimize competition distortions between sectors and countries, the amount of any subsidy-type payment for providing the public goods in such cases would need to cover the costs incurred to provide it. Therefore, where a link between the provision of the public goods and individual benefits can be established, any sustainable solution for the financing of this should be the result of an agreement involving all beneficiaries (private industries and public local or regional entities, under clearly defined property rights). Legislation sanctioning conservation-easement contracts for conservation, scenic and historical or cultural purposes might also be an appropriate way of harnessing market forces to finance such public goods.

(or other economic agents) are specifically required or remunerated for using their own resources to supply it. The associated resource costs to provide such public goods are directly measurable at market prices and farmers can be remunerated for achieving the desired target levels. The choice of provider/preserver of the public good could be selected by auction.

The point is that it should be possible to distinguish on one hand between payments that do confer a private benefit while securing a significant public benefit (i.e. something that is characterized by non-rival consumption and non-excludability) and on the other hand, payments which largely confer only private benefits. This will be a matter of degree, but surely not one that defies differentiation.

In short, those OECD countries that insist on the need for subsidies, or claim to be concerned about the unintended environmental consequences of their removal, should demonstrate clearly the linkages. Where a case has been made, governments should look more closely at ensuring that public goods like the environment are supported but in a transparent and regularly contestable manner. In particular, such support should not be production-related. In this context, it is worth noting that the EU's CAP reform includes decoupling and cross-compliance requirements ('modulation') – it is not possible to secure the Single Farm Payment, for instance, without demonstrating compliance with a range of environmental and rural development requirements.

## 10. Dealing with 'double whammy' subsidies

Against the above background, we should also acknowledge that many agricultural subsidies are something of a 'double whammy', i.e. the majority of subsidies to agriculture *negatively* affect trade *and* the environment.[65] Unfortunately, there are no reliable estimates of environmentally harmful subsidies (EHS). Typical impressionistic numbers range anywhere from $500 billion to $2,000 billion a year. These take into account non-agricultural subsidies, like support for coal and fishing. Extrapolating data for agricultural subsidies is difficult but not impossible. One reasonably reliable estimate is that for the late 1990s, OECD subsidies to agriculture that were environmentally harmful averaged in excess of $300 billion.[66]

Countries have committed themselves to address subsidies that may harm biodiversity,[67] encourage the consumption of fossil fuels[68] or stimulate over-fishing.[69] The 2002 World Summit on Sustainable Development's Plan of Implementation calls, in several places, for the reform, phasing out or elimination of subsidies that have consid-

---

65. The following draws extensively on the analysis contained in Benitah, M. and R. Steenblik (forthcoming). See also OECD (2005).
66. Van Beers, C., and A. de Moor (2001).
67. Decision VI/15 of the Conference of Parties of the Convention on Biodiversity.
68. Article 2.1.(a) of the Kyoto Protocol.
69. These issues are taken up in a range of ways. The FAO International Plan of Action, for instance, seeks to address over-fishing through a voluntary process. The IPOA is available at www.fao.org. Similarly the FAO Code of Conduct addresses fishing activity in the context of sustainability. This can be accessed at: www.fao.org/fi/agreem/codecond/ficonde.asp.

erable negative effects on the environment and are incompatible with sustainable development. And, in subparagraph 32(i) of the Doha Ministerial Declaration, Trade Ministers instructed the Committee on Trade and Environment 'to give particular attention to: (i) … those situations in which the elimination or reduction of trade restrictions and distortions would benefit trade, the environment and development'.

This is of course not a negotiating mandate. It usefully affirms, however, a connection between subsidies, tariff reform and the environment. In a way, Ministers were stating the obvious. That said, one should also acknowledge that some EHS are *not* trade-distorting. These subsidies would therefore not be covered by current trade-related disciplines. Moreover, even those that are both environmentally harmful and trade-distorting, which may form the bulk of EHS in OECD countries, are subject to disciplines that are generally very weak, though it is hoped that the current Round will strengthen these markedly. Yet it is clear, through the frequent exhortatory statements made by Ministries of the Environment (and others) and NGOs on the need to reduce EHS, that the task of disciplining EHS is one they consider must be taken up by trade negotiators. This has diluted somewhat the emphasis on the environment, since trade negotiators tend to devise rules centred primarily on the trade-distorting effects of subsidies. Thus EHS have come to be treated, effectively, as a 'bycatch' of trade-related subsidy disciplines.

Given that subsidies covered by trade agreements do affect the environment and this imposes both costs and benefits on traders as well as economies, it *is* this chapter's contention that it is appropriate for trade negotiators to reflect on the environmental effects of liberalizing trade agreements. In the aftermath of Cancún, there was a good deal of rhetoric about 'taking stock' and opening up 'new channels of dialogue.' One area in which communication could be improved – *within governments as much as between governments* – is on environmentally harmful subsidies. Trade negotiators who have been preoccupied with the specific Doha negotiating mandates, have not focused on EHS, except those connected with fishing. Interestingly, however, they have not been reticent in noting the benefits for the environment when a subsidy-related dispute is decided in their favour. Meanwhile, officials from Ministries of Environment and NGOs, while keeping the issue alive, do not seem to have pressed their trade counterparts very strongly to be more pro-active on subsidies – again, with the exception of fisheries. This is difficult to understand. While appeals to the environment may appear to be a way of limiting subsidy reductions, the impact on the environment can also justify deeper cuts and stronger disciplines, not least given the huge sums involved in subsidizing environmentally harmful activities.

The AoA's Green Box allows for subsidization of a public good like the environment and imposes disciplines on distortionary measures. Unfortunately, there are several shortcomings. First, the lack of product specificity in the AMS allows members to avoid tariff reductions on sensitive products, and to increase domestic support for favoured products as long as overall reduction commitments are met. Second, subsidies for irrigation and drainage, which are addressed in the Green Box, are considered non-product-specific by definition, even if, because of local climatological and topographic limitations, they support the production of only one or two crops. Third, the way in which foregone resource rent (royalties) is handled remains difficult, particularly when publicly owned natural resources are involved. This has been handled obliquely through the recent dispute over softwood lumber, but is also an issue with regard to fossil fuels, marine-capture fisheries and so on. Numerous state-owned utilities forego charging a market price for access to natural resources used in the generation of, for instance, natural gas and electric power. Many countries also allow access to publicly owned land for grazing, charging well below its market value. Charging users for water they pump out of groundwater aquifers – even when those aquifers are being overdrawn – is similarly rare.

Fish subsidies are a powerful example of the application of environmental concerns to assist in ensuring reductions to these simultaneously trade-distorting measures. Subsidies for the building of fishing vessels have led to woeful consequences for fish stocks under national jurisdictions which have then been visited on high-seas fish stocks as underutilized vessels look for employment further afield. The sharp rise in high-seas fishing over the past two decades, both legal and illegal, has been linked to past subsidization programmes, including those for fish production and processing, which has placed considerable pressure on global fish stocks. Over 27 per cent are described by the FAO as either overexploited or depleted and, more worryingly, only 1 per cent of the global fishery resource is on the road to recovery.[70]

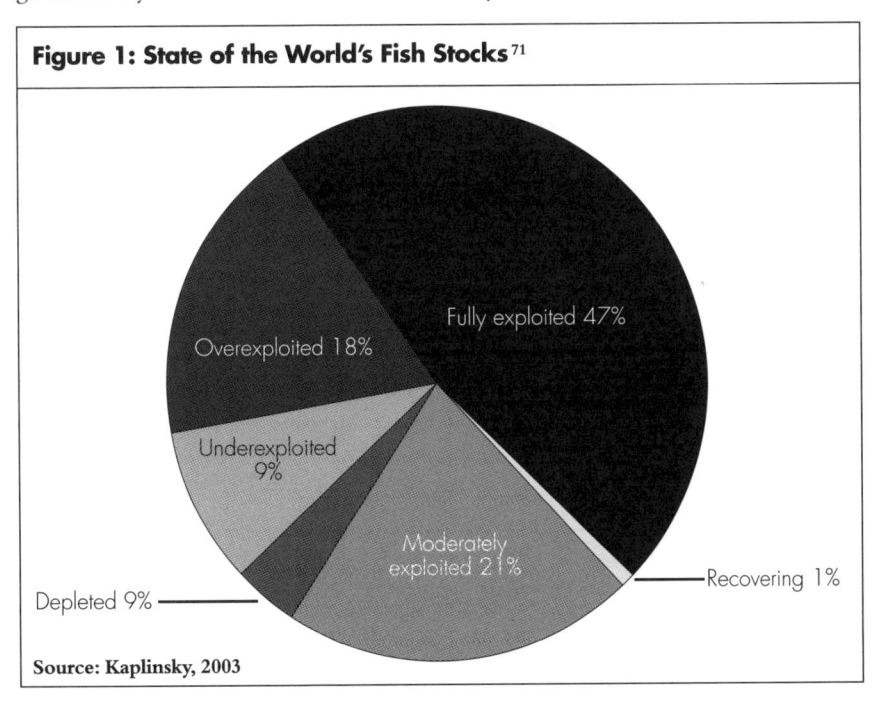

**Figure 1: State of the World's Fish Stocks**[71]

- Fully exploited 47%
- Overexploited 18%
- Underexploited 9%
- Moderately exploited 21%
- Recovering 1%
- Depleted 9%

Source: Kaplinsky, 2003

---

70. Food and Agriculture Organization (2002).
71. Food and Agriculture Organization (2002).

Figure 1 illustrates the extent of the problem.[72] These estimates are, however, only as good as the fishing data supplied by countries. Recent evidence suggests that statistical misreporting by some countries, including ones which have retained their fishing industry through subsidies, may mask even more serious declines in global fish stocks.[73] Moreover, a recent study by scientists in Canada reveals that the commercial exploitation triggered by subsidies can cause a catastrophic and irreversible decline in stocks. According to their research, fish stocks collapse by about 80 per cent within the first 10 to 15 years of commercial exploitation and then stabilize at around 8 to 10 per cent of the original numbers. This research indicates that conservation of stocks based on recent data alone is flawed, as it seriously underestimates this problem.[74]

Addressing fish subsidies is important, but should not be the end of the discussion. The role that international trade rules applied through the WTO might play in constraining other subsidies and protection-related support should be pursued as a priority. At the very least, WTO members should accelerate work on identifying where those links between environmental damage and trade distortions are the strongest, and adapt their positions in the Subsidies and Countervailing Measures Agreement, AoA and GATS negotiating groups accordingly. While it may be too late in the current trade round to do much more than focus on fisheries subsidies, it will be important to manage this process correctly so that it can be a suitable model for future attempts to make those linkages.

The WTO negotiations may help shift the burden of proof for establishing whether a particular subsidy is trade-distorting. The conclusion of the Round may also herald new disciplines for economic activities currently not covered, or only weakly covered, by trade rules – e.g. subsidies affecting trade in services. There are a number of other interesting questions related to the pursuit of environmentally harmful subsidies through the WTO. Some NGOs have proposed that the WTO should tackle EHS head on. On the face of it this appears an attractive possibility. The WTO has instruments that are enforceable and effective in a meaningful (i.e. economic) way. That said, there are potential difficulties associated with a pursuit of EHS through the WTO. Adding 'environmental damage' (however defined) as a criterion for WTO rules may raise a number of thorny questions, particularly in cases where remedies require a demonstration of adverse environmental effects. How, for instance, might a Disputes Panel consider the environmental harm inflicted, or the adequacy of the management system being applied by the subsidizing country? Could measures be designed (even contemplated) only on environmental externalities that are trans-boundary in nature (such as greenhouse gases) or also ones that are confined within the borders (decline in water use or biodiversity) of the subsidizing economy? Should developing countries be given more latitude to damage the environment, as a consequence of SDT?

---

72. Fishing Atlas CD ROM appended to Food and Agriculture Organization (2002).
73. See, for instance, R. Watson and D. Pauly (2001).
74. R. Myers and B. Worm (2003).

## 11. Conclusion

This chapter has argued that a meaningful attempt to tackle export subsidies, domestic support and tariff policies is vital. The implications of this are significant for both developed and developing countries. As the primary suppliers of agricultural subsidies, OECD members have a responsibility to consider the impact their agricultural policies have on other countries, particularly when those policies have a negative effect on the poor. This responsibility coincides with self-interest, since subsidization and protecting domestic markets impose costs on importers, exporters and on consumers and taxpayers. Reductions in agricultural support have win-win effects for both developed and developing countries. Notwithstanding this, while global reform of agricultural policies is a good start, it is not in and of itself a sufficient condition for poverty alleviation. Reform needs to be supplemented by better strategies for development assistance.

Above all, fundamental reform of agriculture must be pursued with the vigour, and indeed the rigour, it requires. It should not be derailed by spurious environmental considerations. Rather, while trade negotiators should bear such issues in mind when negotiating liberalization, there should be sufficient flexibility to address genuine and well supported public good-type initiatives that relate to the environment. Where support is provided, this needs to be contestably and transparently dealt with. Specifically, the focus on non-production-related support for agreed public goods needs to be matched with a rapid diminution of product-related support for public goods like the environment. The potential to reap considerable further win-win-win gains is therefore significant.

This paper has suggested that the WTO is the right place to tackle subsidies that have 'double whammy' effects. The way it handles fish subsidies will be a test case, but there are some important points to bear in mind. These include an assurance that the disciplines applied to constrain and eliminate EHS are consistent with WTO agreements and that the recourse to dispute settlement procedures is both clear and explicit. That said, nothing can conceal the fact that the complicated relationships between EHS and trade, and the use of WTO disciplines to address them, throws into sharp relief a number of intriguing questions that go to the heart of the future of the WTO. These are urgent issues and, in the interests of sustainable development, negotiators should not shy away from them.

## 12. Annex

| Estimated welfare effects of liberalization: summary of recent studies | |
|---|---|
| Dessus et al. (1999)<br>Billion 1995 US$ in 2010 | Total<br>Total with productivity growth |
| Anderson et al. (2001)<br>Billion 1995 US$ in 2005 | Agriculture<br>Manufacturing<br>Total |
| Dee and Hanslow (2000)<br>Billion 1995 US$ in 1995 | Primary and secondary<br>Tertiary<br>Total |
| World Bank (2002)<br>Dynamic<br>Billion 1997 US$ in 2015 | Agriculture<br>Manufacturing<br>Total |
| DFAT (1999)<br>Billion 1995 US$ | Total |
| World Bank (2002)<br>Dynamic with productivity growth<br>Billion 1997 US$ in 2015 | Agriculture<br>Manufacturing<br>Total |
| World Bank (2002)[a]<br>Static<br>Billion 1997 US$ in 2015 | Merchandise trade<br>Services<br>Total |
| Brown et al. (2001)<br>33 per cent reductions<br>Billion US$ | Agriculture<br>Manufacturing<br>Services<br>Total |
| DFAT (1999)<br>50 per cent reductions<br>Billion 1995 US$ | Total |
| Dessus et al. (1999)<br>Full OECD liberalization and 50 per cent developing country reduction<br>Billion 1995 US$ in 2010 | Total<br>Total, with productivity gains |

a. This scenario relates to developing-country liberalization only.
*Other notes*:
Definitions of developing countries vary across the models.
Dessus et al. use a dynamic linkage model and trade elasticities for a relatively short period of three to five years. The dynamic estimation allows trade openness to influence total factor productivity. The liberalization is from the situation in 1995.
Anderson *et al.* use a steady-state Global Trade Analysis Project (GTAP) model, with longer-term trade elasticities. Liberalization is following the implementation of Uruguay Round agreements in 2005. They assume no additional agricultural liberalization between 1995 and 2005.
Dee and Hanslow use a static modified GTAP model with foreign direct investment. The model

|  | Developing countries | Industrial countries | Total |
|---|---|---|---|
| | Complete liberalization | | |
| | 64 | 18 | 82 |
| | 757 | 455 | 1,212 |
| | 43 | 122 | 165 |
| | 63 | 24 | 87 |
| | 108 | 146 | 254 |
| | 69 | 65 | 134 |
| | 134 | -1 | 133 |
| | 203 | 65 | 267 |
| | 142 | 106 | 248 |
| | 42 | 65 | 107 |
| | 184 | 171 | 355 |
| | | | 750 |
| | 390 | 196 | 587 |
| | 149 | 97 | 245 |
| | 539 | 293 | 832 |
| | 1,073 | | |
| | Partial liberalization | | |
| | 8 | 3 | 11 |
| | 43 | 168 | 211 |
| | 50 | 340 | 390 |
| | 101 | 511 | 613 |
| | | | 380 |
| | 43 | 30 | 73 |
| | 292 | 620 | 912 |

incorporates monopolistic competition and imperfect capital mobility. Liberalization is following the implementation of Uruguay Round agreements in 2005.
The World Bank uses a model related to GTAP and a later version of the GTAP database than the other studies. The dynamic estimation allows productivity growth to be a constant function of the export-output ratio. Liberalization is from the situation in 1997.
DFAT uses both static GTAP and dynamic APC-cubed models.
Brown *et al.* use the static Michigan model of World Production and Trade, with monopolistic competition.
More information about the GTAP may be found at www.gtap.agecon.purdue.edu/default.asp.
**Source: OECD (2002).**

Chapter 4 | **Agricultural Commodities, Trade and Sustainable Development**

## References

ABARE, *Export Subsidies in the Current WTO Agriculture Negotiations* (Canberra: 2001).

Anderson, K. *et al*, 'The cost of rich (and poor) country protection to developing countries', *Journal of African Economics* (2001).

Anderson, K., E. R. Widodo and M. D. Ingco (1999), 'Integrating Agriculture into the WTO: The Next Phase,' Paper for the WTO/World Bank Conference on Developing Countries in a Millennium Round, (Geneva: 1999). Available at www.worldbank.org/research/trade/archive.html/).

Baldwin, R. E., 'Trade and Growth: Still Disagreement about the Relationships,' OECD Economics Department Working Paper No. 264 (Paris: 2002).

Beghin, J., and M.A. Aksoy, 'Agricultural Trade and the Doha Round, Preliminary Lessons from Commodity Studies' (Washington: World Bank, mimeo, 2003).

Beghin, J., D. Roland-Holst, and D. van der Mensbrugge, 'Global Agricultural Trade and the Doha Round, What are the Implications for North and South?' Paper presented to OECD/World Bank Global Forum on Agriculture (Paris: OECD, 2002).

Benitah, M. and R. Steenblik, 'Environmentally Harmful Subsidies and International Instruments,' OECD Working Paper (Paris: OECD, forthcoming).

Binswanger, H. and E. Lutz, 'Agricultural Trade Barriers, Trade Negotiations and the Interests of Developing Countries,' Paper for the UNCTAD X High Level Round Table on Trade and Development Directions for the 21st Century (Bangkok: 2000).

Borrell, B., *Bananas: Straightening our Bent Ideas on Trade as Aid*, Centre for International Economics (Canberra/Sydney: 1999).

Chang, W. and L. A. Winters, 'How Regional Blocs Affect Excluded Countries: The price effects of Mercosur' (Washington: World Bank, 2000). See: www.worldbank.org/html/dec/Publications/Workpapers/wps2000series/wps2157/wps2157.pdf.

Dee, P. and K. Hanslow, 'Multilateral Liberalization of Services Trade,' Australian Productivity Commission Research Paper, (Canberra: 2000).

Dessus, S. K., K. Fukasaku and R. Safadi, 'Multilateral Tariff Liberalization and Developing Countries,' OECD Development Centre, Policy Brief No 18 (Paris: 1999).

DFID, *Trade Liberalization and Poverty* (London: 2002).

Dollar, D. and A. Kray, 'Trade, Growth and Poverty,' World Bank Working Paper no. 2615 (Washington: 2001).

Food and Agriculture Organization, *The State of World Fisheries and Aquaculture* (Rome: 2002).

Frenkel, J. A. and D. Romer, 'Does Trade Cause Growth?' *American Economic Review*, vol. 89 (1999).

Hanmer, L., J. Healey and F. Naschold, 'Will Growth Halve Poverty by 2015?' ODI *Poverty Briefing* (London and Oxford: Overseas Development Institute and Oxfam, 2000).

Hoekman, B. M. and M. M. Koestecki, *The Political Economy of the World Trading System: The WTO and beyond* (Oxford: Oxford University Press, 2001).

Hoekman, B. M., C. Michalopoulos and L. A. Winters, 'Special and Differential Treatment of Developing Countries in the WTO: Moving Forward after Cancún,' *The World Economy*, Vol. 27, pp. 481-506 (2004).

Hoekman, B. M., F. Ng and M. Olarreaga, 'Eliminating Excessive Tariffs on Exports of Least Developed Countries,' Policy Research Working Paper 2604 (Washington: World Bank, 2001).

IMF, *World Economic Outlook Trade and Finance* (Washington: September 2002).

Ingco, M.D., *Has Agricultural Trade Liberalization Improved Welfare in the Least Developed Countries? Yes*, International Economics Department, International Trade Division, World Bank (Washington: 1997).

Khan, M. H., 'Rural Poverty in Developing Countries', *Finance and Development* (Washington: IMF, December 2000).

McCulloch, N., L. A. Winters and X. Cirera, *Trade Liberalization and Poverty: A handbook*, (London: DFID and Centre for Economic Policy Research, 2001).

Myers, R., and B. Worm, 'Rapid Worldwide Depletion of Predatory Fish Communities,' *Nature*,

Vol. 423, pp. 280-283 (2003).

Nordstrom, H., D. Ben-David, and L. A. Winters, *Trade, Income Disparity and Poverty* (Geneva: WTO, 2001).

OECD, *Agriculture Policies at a Glance* (Paris: 2004).

OECD, *Agricultural Policies in OECD Countries: Monitoring and evaluation* (Paris: 2000).

OECD, *Agricultural Trade and Poverty: Making policy count* (Paris: 2003).

OECD, *Environmentally Harmful Subsidies: Challenges for Reform* (Paris: 2005).

OECD, *Improving the Environmental Performance of Agriculture: Policy options and market approaches* (Paris: 2001A).

OECD, *Open Markets Matter: The benefits of trade and investment liberalization* (Paris: 1998).

OECD, *Sustainable Development: A Framework for Peer Reviews and Related Indicators,* Document no. SG/SD (2002) 3 (Paris: 2002).

OECD, *The DAC Journal: Development Co-operation 2000 Report* (Paris: 2001B).

OECD, *The Uruguay Round Agreement on Agriculture: An evaluation of its implementation in OECD countries* (Paris: 2001C).

Oxfam, *Rigged Rules and Double Standards: Trade, globalization and the fight against poverty* (Oxford: 2002). Also available at www.maketradefair.com/stylesheet.asp?file=26032002105549&cat=2&subcat=6&select=13.

Prassad, E. S. and J. R. Gable, 'International Evidence on the Determinants of Trade Dynamics,' IMF Working Paper, Number 97/172 (Washington: 1997).

Rodriguez, F. and D. Rodrik, 'Trade Policy and Economic Growth: A Skeptic's Guide to the Cross-Country Evidence,' Centre for Economic Policy Research, Discussion Paper Series, No 2143 (1999).

Spicer, M., 'Europe's Agriculture Debacle,' *Wall Street Journal* (New York: 30 October 1997).

TACIS, *Report on the Uzbek Agriculture System: The Case of Water and Cotton* (Tashkent: unpublished report) European Commission Delegation, 1999).

Tyers, R. and K. Anderson, *Disarray in World Food Markets: A Quantitative Assessment* (Cambridge: Cambridge University Press, 1992).

UNCTAD, 'The Post-Uruguay Round Tariff Environment for Developing Country Exports: Tariff Peaks and Tariff Escalation,' document no. TD/B/COM.1/14/Rev. 1 (Geneva, 2000).

Van Beers, C., and A. de Moor, 'Public Subsidies and Policy Failures: How Subsidies Distort the Natural Environment, Equity and Trade, and how to Reform them', PowerPoint presentation to the World Summit on Sustainable Development (2001). www.earth-summit.net/presentations /gabs_de_moor.ppt.

Watson, R., and D. Pauly, 'Systematic Distortions in World Fisheries Catch Trends,' *Nature*, Vol. 414, pp. 534 – 536 (2001).

Wilson, J. S., 'Liberalizing Trade in Agriculture: Developing Countries in Asia and the Post–Doha Agenda,' Policy Research Working Paper (Washington: World Bank, 2002),.

Winters, A., 'Trade and Poverty: Is there a Connection?', *Trade, Income Disparity and Poverty* (Geneva: World Trade Organization, 2000).

World Bank, *Global Economic Prospects* (Washington: 2001).

World Bank, *Global Economic Prospects* (Washington: 2002).

World Trade Organization, Doha Declaration (2001).

World Trade Organization, *Market Access: Unfinished business* (Geneva: WTO, 2001).

# Chapter 4 | Agricultural Commodities, Trade and Sustainable Development

# Chapter 5

# Conspiracy of Silence: Old and New Directions on Commodities

Duncan Green[1]

## 1. Introduction

*'There is, on this subject of commodities, a sort of conspiracy of silence. There are no simple solutions. Many of the remedies introduced in the past – especially the major commodity agreements – have failed and we do not want to repeat these experiences. Yet there is no justification for the current indifference.'* President Jacques Chirac, Paris, February 2003.

This chapter summarizes the main aspects of the crisis affecting agricultural commodities, both those that compete with Northern agriculture (e.g. sugar, maize) and the non-competing commodities such as coffee and tea, also known as tropical commodities. It

---
1. This chapter is an edited version of a paper presented at the Barcelona dialogue in 2005. It draws on an earlier paper for DFID, co-written by the author with Ian Gillson, Steve Wiggins and Nilah Pandian (Gillson, Green *et al*, 2004).

examines and compares the main approaches taken both within the mainstream policy community and among a wider range of thinkers and advocates. A final section compares the impact and feasibility of these approaches and discusses the degree of complementarity between them. The chapter identifies six main currents of thought:

1. **'Mainstream macro'**: WTO agriculture negotiations; compensation and aid schemes
2. **'Mainstream micro'**: Diversification; market-based price risk management
3. **'Sustainable commodities'**: improved environmental management; fair trade; organics; corporate social responsibility
4. **'National coordination'**: state marketing boards; producer organizations; increased attention to quality and product differentiation
5. **'International coordination'**: supply management; harmonization of standards
6. **'Corporate concentration'**: competition law; monitoring and transparency.

## 2. The problem

The 'commodity problem' is often described as a combination of declining terms of trade (commodity prices rising less rapidly than those of manufactures) and price volatility. Producers therefore face the dual problem of low returns and high risks.[2] More recently, a third element has been widely discussed, namely corporate concentration in commodity supply chains, which are held both to drive down prices and further reduce the share of export price going to farmers.[3]

### 2.1 Long-term decline in prices

The hypothesis that in the long run the price of primary commodities declines relative to manufactures[4] has been repeatedly tested and found valid.[5] Over the past four decades, real prices for agricultural commodities declined by about 2 per cent per year. If prices for the ten most valuable agricultural export commodities of developing countries had risen in line with inflation since 1980, these exporters would have received around $112 billion more in 2002 than they actually did. This is more than twice the total amount of aid distributed worldwide.[6]

Theoretical analysis suggests that agricultural commodity prices fall relative to others because of relatively inelastic demand and the lack of differentiation among producers. Moreover, the decline is likely to continue. On the supply side, technological improvements, increased competition, reduced protection of markets and devaluation of some national currencies (e.g. CFA franc) have all contributed to increases in production. On the demand side, the development of synthetic substitutes and slower population growth will act to depress demand growth.

---

2. Page & Hewitt (2001).
3. Gibbon (2004b).
4. E.g. Prebisch (1950); Singer (1950).
5. E.g. Spraos (1983); Bloch & Sapsford (2000).
6. FAO (2004).

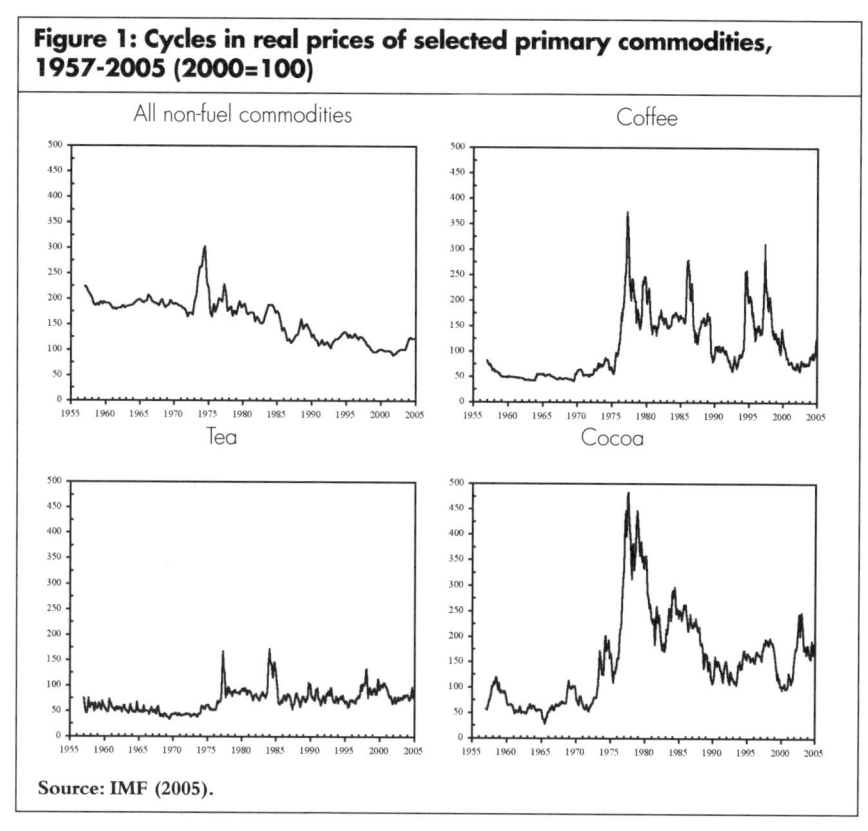

**Figure 1: Cycles in real prices of selected primary commodities, 1957-2005 (2000=100)**

[Charts showing price cycles for: All non-fuel commodities, Coffee, Tea, Cocoa, from 1955 to 2005]

Source: IMF (2005).

Price trends vary between commodities. The UN notes 'the two groups for which the developing countries account for the largest shares in world exports, namely tropical beverages and vegetable oilseeds and oils, show the highest rates of decline in prices.'[7] However, whereas the growth of demand for traditional agricultural commodities (such as coffee) has weakened, that for some products has been on the increase. These new dynamic products include fruit, vegetables, fish and dairy products. The differences reflect, in part, changing consumer habits.[8]

However, there appears to have been a breakpoint in the long-term trends in the mid-1980s. Prior to then, prices fluctuated widely while the overall trend declined steeply. Since then, however, both the fluctuations and the trend have flattened out. This is explained in part by a slowdown in the growth of prices for manufactured goods.[9] For some authors, this strengthens the case for looking for progress within commodities, rather than in an exit into manufacturing or services.[10] Moreover, many prices have recovered since 2001, driven partly by demand in China. Opinions differ over whether

---

7. UN (2000).
8. UN (2002).
9. FAO (2004).
10. Kaplinsky (2003).

this is just another price spike or part of an extended 'supercycle' – a period of high prices that defies the rules of boom and bust.[11] The recovery has been much stronger in some commodities than others. Compared to 2000 prices, for example, cereals showed a 20 to 30 per cent increase by 2004, whereas tropical commodities varied from a 70 per cent increase for palm oil and cocoa to a price fall in sugar, coffee and tea. (See the Appendix to this chapter).

## 2.2 Price volatility

In addition to their long-term decline, the prices of many agricultural commodities show a high degree of volatility, caused by time lags between production decisions and delivery to the market; delayed and inappropriate responses by producers to price signals; inelastic supply; and natural shocks. The characteristic shape of commodity price cycles is one of 'flat bottoms punctuated by occasional sharp peaks,'[12] i.e. periods of low prices endure for longer than price spikes. This trend is illustrated in Figure 1.

## 2.3 The economic impact of price decline and volatility on developing countries

These problems face all countries that produce commodities but are more serious for 'agricultural commodity-dependent developing countries.' ACDDCs are defined as being those countries that are more dependent on agricultural commodity exports and specialize in producing one or a few commodities.[13] Many of them are LDCs or among the EU's associated countries in Africa, the Caribbean and the Pacific. Almost all the countries in Sub-Saharan Africa rely on primary commodities (including non-agricultural) for over half of their exports (see Appendix). Over time, more successful developing countries have diversified either into more dynamic sectors within commodities, or out of agriculture altogether. Non-LDC developing countries reduced the share of tropical beverages and raw materials in their agricultural exports from more than 55 per cent in the early 1960s to around 30 per cent in 1999–2001. But in the LDCs, these products increased from 59 per cent to 72 per cent of agricultural exports during the same period.[14]

## 2.4 Social and environmental impact of agricultural commodities

In many ACDDCs the producers and workers directly affected by agricultural commodity exports are among the poorest of the population. Cocoa, for example, provides livelihoods for 14 million rural workers on big plantations and a further 2.5 million small producers. Coffee provides income for 25 million producers. In banana, palm oil and tea

---
11. Financial Times (2005).
12. Gilbert (1999),
13. Dehn (2000).
14. FAO (2004).

plantations, NGOs claim that the downward pressure on prices has triggered a 'race to the bottom' in wages and working conditions, including casualization of labour, the use of child labour, increased workloads and reduced benefits such as health provision, schooling and housing. However, according to Gibbon, 'Large-estate commodity production has fared much better than smallholder production since the advent of structural adjustment… Countries with smallholder-based systems, because they are poorer and less economically diversified, have been much more exposed to the commodity crisis.'[15]

Structural adjustment programmes have thus had the reverse effect to that intended, which was to increase producer incomes by raising the share of export prices going to farmers. Instead many countries have witnessed a downgrading of quality, and progressive marginalization of producers within supply chains increasingly dominated by large, usually transnational, corporations.

A number of authors raise concerns about environmental impacts. Intensification in commodity production can lead to soil erosion and exhaustion, reduced biodiversity, increased pollution (e.g. through pesticides) and can divert scarce water supplies. At a global level, there are concerns over the use of fossil fuels (e.g. in fertilizers) and the impact on climate change of intensive soil use.[16]

## 3. Mainstream approaches

This section reviews what can be categorized as 'mainstream' views on problems and solutions to commodity dependence. These currently hold sway in influential institutions such as the World Bank, bilateral donor agencies such as DFID and more broadly among politicians, civil servants, consultants and academics. Categorizing any set of views as 'mainstream' is necessarily both a simplification and a caricature: views within these circles are not monolithic; differences and debates are vigorous and the boundary between 'mainstream' and 'alternative' is both porous and blurred. Within the mainstream paradigm, the solution to commodity dependence generally lies in diversification, either horizontally into other products, preferably non-agricultural, or vertically into higher value-added links in the supply chain.

The first part of this section deals with macro solutions, including the role of international trade rules, Northern subsidy regimes and aid flows. The second section goes more 'micro', exploring mainstream thinking at sectoral and firm level within developing countries.

### Macro approaches

The nature of the debate varies greatly between so-called 'competing commodities,' produced in both developed and developing countries (e.g. cotton, sugar, rice) and non-

---
15. Gibbon (2004b).
16. Clay (2004).

competing or tropical commodities such as coffee and cocoa. For competing commodities, the crucible of discussion is the Doha Round of WTO negotiations and to a lesser extent in regional trade negotiations. Here, issues such as Northern subsidies and market access for commodities in both North and South are seen as central to improving the lot of ACDDCs. Within competing, and to a lesser extent, non-competing commodities, the issue of preference regimes and their erosion by multilateral liberalization is becoming important. The mainstream debate on tropicals largely revolves around financing diversification and improvements in productivity.

## Competing Commodities

The generally accepted view is that through a combination of subsidies and restrictions on market access, government intervention in the North has disrupted the natural order of economic development. In the early 1960s, developing countries had an overall agricultural trade surplus of almost $7 billion per year. By the end of the 1980s, however, this surplus had disappeared. During most of the 1990s and early 2000s, developing countries were net importers of agricultural products. The change has been even more pronounced for the LDCs.[17]

### 3.1 Northern subsidies

The most trenchant view of the reasons for this apparent anomaly comes from Kevin Watkins. In Chapter 3 of this book, he argues that the distribution of opportunity in agricultural trade is shaped not by comparative advantage, but by comparative access to subsidies – an area in which rich countries have an unrivalled advantage. The WTO's Agreement on Agriculture was designed to accommodate, rather than constrain, EU and US subsidies.

The anti-subsidy argument points out that the AoA treats developed and developing countries in a discriminatory manner. Developed countries tend to use subsidies to support their agricultural sector, while cash-strapped developing countries use tariffs. Thanks to a deal between the EU and US during the Uruguay Round, the AoA places no upper limit on subsidies but does constrain the use of tariffs. This deal introduced a crucial distinction between 'trade-distorting' and 'non-trade-distorting' subsidies. Trade-distorting subsidies, such as payments per head or per bushel, were to be reduced, but non-trade-distorting subsidies, such as payments that were decoupled from production, were not. While payments per bushel are clearly likely to affect production decisions more than subsidies for songbirds or hedgerows, arguments remain over the impact of payments that fall between these two extremes.

Watkins concludes that the distinction over trade distortion is 'unworkable and unwarranted.' The World Bank largely agrees, pointing out that from 1986-88 to 2000-02 domestic subsidies in the OECD rose by 60 per cent, even as they shifted to less

---

17. FAO (2004).

distorting forms. Quantity thus undermined the change in quality. According to the Bank, the effects of decoupling on production 'have been modest. In many cases over-production has continued.'[18]

Subsidies also come under attack for their environmental impact. Clay argues that globally, subsidy regimes result in more environmental impacts than any other single set of policies. Producers who are not subsidized often cut corners to remain competitive.[19] However, others (both mainstream and beyond) believe subsidies do not merit their prime suspect status. Unsurprisingly, the EU and US claim that their decoupled payments are indeed non- or minimally trade-distorting. On the progressive end of the spectrum, some authors argue that subsidies are a symptom of over-production, not a cause. The real culprit, they believe, is the abandonment of supply management in the North. The answer is thus a return to supply management, not an attack on subsidies.[20]

The AoA draws a distinction between domestic subsidies and what it terms 'export competition' measures, including direct export subsidies. The case against export subsidies is broadly accepted. The EU is responsible for 90 per cent of them, and after years of resistance agreed in the WTO's July framework in 2004 to negotiate an end date for such subsidies. In any case, export subsidies are in decline, falling globally from $7.5 billion in 1995 to $3 billion in 2001.[21]

### 3.2 Market access and preferences

Within the mainstream, there is general agreement that trade liberalization leads to growth, which leads to poverty reduction, and that both developed and developing countries would benefit from lowering their tariffs. Indeed, due to higher average tariffs in developing countries, the World Bank's models predict that global liberalization would actually benefit them more.

There is broad agreement on the developmental benefits of Northern market access, e.g. reduction in tariff peaks on particular developing-country exports, and in *tariff escalation on processed goods*, which deters higher value-added production in poor countries. But there is disagreement on the appropriate tariff regimes in developing countries. Orthodox economists tend to stress the benefits of liberalization and the growing importance of South-South agricultural trade, while others raise concerns that liberalization paves the way for expansion of agribusiness in developing countries. Some NGOs criticize liberalization on infant-industry grounds, arguing that at early stages of development tariff protection is often necessary.[22]

Meanwhile, the thorny issue of preferential access to developed countries' markets for certain categories of developing countries is becoming increasingly prominent. The

---

18. World Bank (2005).
19. In Chapter 6 of this book.
20. Ray *et al* (2003).
21. FAO (2005). For excellent summaries of the evidence on export competition and other aspects of the WTO negotiations on agriculture, see also FAO Trade Policy Technical Notes, www.fao.org/trade/policy_en.asp.
22. Oxfam (2005). See also Chapter 2 in this book.

subject applies both to competing and non-competing commodities. Commodity protocols attached to the Cotonou Agreement extend quota access to the highly protected European markets for bananas, beef and veal, rum and sugar to countries of the ACP group. For many ACP states, these generate foreign exchange and employment. In some cases wide-ranging preferences have also encouraged export diversification. Examples include Mauritius (from sugar to clothing and services) and Zimbabwe (from tobacco to textiles, clothing and horticulture). In general, however, preferences are criticized for having stifled diversification, by making commodity-dependence profitable.

The structure of preferences is under assault both from reforms such as the EU's drive for Economic Partnership Agreements and from the issue of preference erosion. As developed countries' tariff barriers come down, the benefits afforded by preferential access also fall. Within the WTO, Northern negotiators are concerned that preference erosion is turning a group of ACP countries into blockers who stand to gain more from defending their preference margins than from benefits such as increased market access.

### 3.3 South-South trade

UNCTAD points out that South-South trade has increased faster than South-North trade in almost all commodity groups and all regions in recent years.[23] It believes that increased demand for commodities in developing countries, particularly Asia, could considerably boost world demand both for raw materials and food products. A 'window of opportunity' could thus open up over the next few years, allowing developing countries to substantially improve export earnings from commodities. Clay agrees that South-South trade is a boom area, but is pessimistic about its poverty-reducing potential.[24] In South-South trade, there is far more concern about price than any other factor. What may be developing globally is a trade system where volume and value are important in developing countries, and quality and uniqueness in developed countries. Small-scale farmers will be torn between trying to improve standards to access better prices in Northern markets, or stay with rock-bottom prices but expanding volumes in the South.

### Tropical Commodities

Compared to the WTO debates on competing commodities, the mainstream policy discussion on tropical commodities is remarkably threadbare, mainly consisting of condemnations of past remedies such as supply management, exhortations to diversify, largely unsuccessful attempts to harness market-based mechanisms in order to smooth price volatility, and increased financial flows to compensate for falling prices and pay for diversification efforts.

---

23. UNCTAD (2005).
24. See Chapter 6 of this book.

## 3.4 Compensation schemes and commodity funds

Both the IMF and the EU have operated schemes that made financial transfers to national governments in compensation for falls in export earnings. The EU-ACP STABEX arrangement was established in 1975 under the first Lomé Convention and continued until the recent Cotonou Agreement. In the form in which it operated in the 1990s, the instrument had serious drawbacks. First, transfers had to be used by the recipient government to support the commodity sector that had suffered the price falls, even if this aggravated commodity dependence. Second, the EU placed ever greater restrictions on the use of transfers. Third, time delays meant that support often arrived just as prices were rebounding, exacerbating the impact of price instability.

With the entry into force of the EU-ACP Cotonou Agreement, a new instrument was established to compensate countries for sudden falls in export earnings: the FLEX. FLEX allows ACP governments to use the finance for a wider range of purposes, e.g. to safeguard macro-economic and sectoral reforms. Initial experience has shown that several countries that experienced significant losses in export earnings were not eligible for compensation, due to stringent eligibility criteria.[25] It has therefore been proposed to lower some eligibility thresholds. Had the proposed criteria been applied from 2000–02, ACP countries would have received €255 million through the FLEX system, six times more than was actually disbursed.

A number of proposals have also been made for introducing voluntary commodity levies to fund demand-, efficiency- and livelihoods-enhancing measures, often for the coffee sector. UNCTAD and Oxfam have both proposed an 'international diversification fund'.[26] Walter Zwald proposed (to the ICO) for importers to pay a voluntary levy of $20/tonne into a coffee fund that would raise an estimated $84 million per year. The fund would be used for promotional activities aimed at expanding demand and for a range of production-related activities.[27] There are a number of problems with these proposals as they currently stand. In particular, there is no guarantee that participating enterprises will not pass the cost of the levy on to consumers in the form of higher sale prices or back to producers in the form of lower purchase prices.

The attention paid to aid and compensation schemes is intended to wean ACDDCs off preferences and commodity dependence and in the process, reduce obstacles to multilateral trade liberalization. Rarely is the question asked, 'is lack of money really the problem?' Small and vulnerable economies may simply have no competitive advantage in anything, without undergoing a drastic fall in wages and/or a massive devaluation.

## 3.5 Price and volume risk, debt relief and poverty strategies

Commodity price risks have not been sufficiently considered in debt relief schemes

---

25. European Commission (2004).
26. UNCTAD (2004b); Oxfam (2004).
27. Zwald (2001). The ICO revised the proposal to spend a minimum of 80 per cent on assistance to coffee workers with primary health care and education for their children (ICO, 2001).

such as the HIPC initiative. A substantial drop in prices of key export commodities can threaten the ability to exit from unsustainable debt. Out of 42 HIPCs, 37 rely on primary commodities for more than half of their merchandise exports.[28] The net present value of debt-to-export ratios deteriorated after decision points in 2001 in 15 HIPCs, of which 13 were in Africa.[29] Uganda found itself in an unsustainable debt situation at completion point due to steep declines in the price of coffee,[30] and completion-point debt relief for Burkina Faso had to be topped up by $129 million because of the decline in price of its main export, cotton.[31]

In addition, there remains concern about the low priority accorded to the agricultural sector in PRSPs, and the consequent impact on levels of investment, e.g. in rural infrastructure.

### 3.6 Is there a place for tropical commodities in the WTO?

Part 4 of GATT 1994 provides a comprehensive legal basis for dealing with tropical commodities in the WTO. This is described in sub-section 6.3 below. Article 8 obliges members to develop a joint action plan to achieve the objectives of Part 4, but to date, this has not happened. Oxfam has in the past called for a Trade and Commodities working group at the WTO, which would address these issues. Currently, however, there is little prospect of such a group appearing. The most determined drive for a comprehensive approach has come from Kenya, Uganda and Tanzania, in two submissions to the Committee on Trade and Development in 2003 and 2004.[32] These touch on supply management, the impact of structural adjustment and market concentration.

The commodity crisis was recognized in the draft text for the Cancún ministerial, which instructed the Committee on Trade and Development to work on 'the dependence of many developing countries on a few commodities and the problems created by long-term and sharp fluctuations in prices of these commodities.' That agreement fell with the collapse of the ministerial (although this paragraph was never disputed). The subsequent July Framework Agreement merely included commodities in a list of 'other development issues' to be 'taken into consideration, as appropriate, in the course of the agriculture and NAMA[33] negotiations.'

#### Micro approaches

In recent decades, mainstream thinking has become disenchanted with issues such as raising productivity through investment in infrastructure, R&D and technical assistance.

---

28. FAO (2004).
29. IMF and World Bank (2002a).
30. IMF and World Bank (2002b).
31. UNCTAD (2003a).
32. WTO (2003); WTO (2004).
33. Non-Agricultural Market Access, covering tariffs on industrial goods, forestry products and fisheries.

Overproduction and falling prices have raised doubts about increasing productivity even faster – average yields for the major agricultural export commodities increased by almost one-third over the past two decades.[34] Instead, most donors have moved towards encouraging exit from commodity dependence, either through diversifying within agriculture or (increasingly) moving out of agriculture and exploring options in manufacturing and services. The global aid budget devoted to agriculture fell from $6.2 billion to $2.3 billion between 1980 and 2002.[35]

### 3.7 Reducing dependence on agricultural commodities

There are three diversification routes available to ACDDCs: horizontal diversification into alternative crops; vertical diversification into agricultural products and processes that capture a higher proportion of the value chain; and diversification into non-agricultural activities such as manufactures and services. Of these, the last is generally seen as the only solution in the long run.

#### Horizontal diversification

Diversification into other internationally traded agricultural commodities has a disadvantage: with few exceptions, the prices of all agricultural commodities appear to be in long-term decline, so the problem of declining terms of trade will remain. In order to limit risk, countries need to diversify into several different commodities. For a small country, this may imply quantities that are too small for efficient production, transport or marketing.[36] Moreover, for smallholders in developing countries, existing patterns of diversification for food crops may be so entrenched that they constitute a barrier to further diversification into new cash crops.[37] The significant investment associated with tree crops (e.g. cocoa and coffee) also makes producers reluctant to destroy these in order to move into other crops. A further problem is that of 'adding-up'. An agricultural commodity's price can become further depressed if all countries diversify into the same product simultaneously – prawns and pineapple became notorious examples in the 1980s.[38]

A further possibility is to diversify into crops for the domestic market. A number of countries have achieved take-off by producing domestic cereals, rather than by export-led growth.[39] For some LDCs import substitution at either a national or regional level may be the way forward.

#### Vertical diversification

Higher value-added agricultural exports offer good prospects for long-term growth due

---
34. FAO (2004).
35. DFID (2004).
36. Page & Hewitt (2001).
37. Gibbon (2004a).
38. Page (1990).
39. See Chapter 2.

to their relatively high income elasticities.⁴⁰ However, there are a number of difficulties with this approach, including the high costs associated with storing and processing.⁴¹ Other obstacles are poor infrastructure, lack of investment, high marketing costs and rising product standards. In many of the poorest countries the recent trend has been *away* from vertical diversification, not towards it: among LDCs, processed primary commodities fell from 24.5 per cent of commodity-sector exports in 1981-83 to 11.1 per cent in 1997-99.⁴²

### Diversification into new activities

The main benefits of diversification away from primary commodities are reduced risk and more stable export revenues. A number of developing countries have succeeded in diversifying into areas such as manufacturing and services. For manufactures, this has mainly been the case in Asia (e.g. Malaysia, Indonesia) and Latin America (e.g. Brazil). For services, the Caribbean has shown some success in tourism and financial services. This has often involved an enhanced role for the state, for example in industrial policy. High investment and savings were significant in developing supply capacity, while public investment in infrastructure and education, as well as foreign direct investment, played key roles.⁴³

Nevertheless, diversification into manufactured products and services presents its own challenges. Established competition is fierce. Banking systems and capital markets in many ACDDCs, particularly in Sub-Saharan Africa, are underdeveloped, making it difficult for new producers to raise the capital to move into new sectors. Kaplinsky questions whether diversification into manufacturing remains the best option.⁴⁴ He believes instead that a new quality- and product-enhancing approach towards commodity sectors holds the possibility of rising terms of trade for at least some producers, with a more stable price regime.

### 3.8 Market-based price risk management

As donors have given up on supply management for agricultural commodities, they have switched their attention to market-based risk-management instruments such as futures, options and swaps. These are intended to enable producers to limit the risks arising from price volatility. In 1999, the World Bank, with the assistance of UNCTAD, convened an International Task Force to assist developing countries in piloting these approaches.

Although the use of derivative instruments is not widespread in ACDDCs, some African countries have sold forward their cocoa and cotton exports.⁴⁵ Several reasons

---
40. Gibbon (2004a).
41. Delgado and Siamwalla (1997).
42. Lines (2004), citing data from UNCTAD.
43. Page & Hewitt (2001).
44. Kaplinsky (2003).
45. UNCTAD (2003a).

have been put forward for the narrow use of these instruments in developing countries: limited know-how and awareness, regulatory and institutional barriers, and creditworthiness problems. Unlike coffee, many commodities are traded without futures markets but only by private contracts between buyers and producers, greatly complicating the use of derivatives. Finally, derivatives are unsuitable for addressing long-term instability and they cannot maintain higher prices for sellers.

Six years on, the ITF has yet to produce significant breakthroughs. According to delegates at the Annual Meeting of the ITF in Rome in May 2004, pilots and research continued to show bottlenecks and constraints: for example, the minimum size of commercially viable transactions (put at $50,000 in premiums per client by one finance house) was proving extremely hard to generate. Micro-insurance, along the lines of microcredit, also seemed to offer little hope, given its much higher demands in terms of data, proof of loss and danger of moral hazard.

### 3.9 Conclusion

Mainstream discussions on competing commodities appear far more vigorous and hopeful than those on non-competing tropical commodities, where the debate resembles little more than a dispirited counsel of despair. Resigned to falling prices and marginalization, policymakers and opinion formers can only advocate aid, managed decline (e.g. by smoothing prices) and exit for a residual group of poor countries that have failed to find the way out of commodity dependence. One author likened such 'let them diversify' exhortations to Marie Antoinette's 'let them eat cake' advice to the starving French people.

## 4. Sustainable commodities

Those trying to influence the social and environmental impact of commodity production have largely focused on progressive versions of process and production methods. These have provided a means of channelling a premium to poor producers and good environmental practices from socially conscious consumers, through a variety of labelling schemes. In recent years, a number of corporate-driven schemes have followed suit, which both hold out the possibility of influencing much greater volumes of production, and the threat of significantly watering down the standards involved. Moreover, concerns have been raised about the potential for both niche and mainstream labelling schemes for small-scale producers.

### 4.1 Environmental impact

Table 1 summarizes the main environmental impacts of a range of commodities. These are in addition to the wider impact of industrial agriculture in areas such as climate change (use of fossil fuel-based inputs and release of carbon from soil depletion) and loss of biodiversity.

## Chapter 5 | Agricultural Commodities, Trade and Sustainable Development

### Table 1: Environmental impact of commodity production

| Commodity | Forests cleared for planting | Excessive use of pesticides | Water | Other |
|---|---|---|---|---|
| Cocoa | Yes | Yes | - | Clearings open way for illegal timber and wildlife exploitation |
| Coffee | Sometimes (e.g. Côte d'Ivoire) | - | Processing pollutes local supplies | - |
| Cotton | - | Uses 25% of global insecticides and 10% of pesticides | 73% of cotton is produced on irrigated land – cf. disappearance of Aral Sea | Loss of soil fertility |
| Oil Palm | Yes | - | - | Air pollution from clearance fires; soil loss; soil fertility |
| Soya | Yes, especially in Brazil and Argentina | - | - | Rapid spread of GM soya increases farmers' dependence on chemical herbicide and Monsanto; soil erosion |
| Sugar | No | No | The third thirstiest of commodities – needs 1,500-3,000 litres per kg of sugar cane | Water pollution from processing run-off |
| Tea | - | Yes | Yes | Soil fertility |

Source: Based on IIED *et al*, 2004

The standard environmentalist solution to such issues is better management practices. BMPs involve maintaining and building soils, maintaining natural ecosystem functions on farms, reducing total input use and using inputs more efficiently, and reducing waste or marketing by-products from materials that were previously considered waste.[46] Clay sees some conflict between social and environmental objectives. He points out that few BMPs are appropriate for small-scale farmers attempting to produce on more marginal lands and at scales that are often not competitive, while evidence suggests that the most environmental impacts per hectare of production of commodities come from small-scale producers. However, he sees crop selection as offering some room for progress, with perennial crops the most promising.[47]

---
46. Clay (2004).
47. See Chapter 6.

## 4.2 GMOs: problem or solution?

Clay also considers the controversial issue of genetically modified organisms. Following the introduction of GMOs, pesticide application per hectare has fallen, but overall more herbicide is used as more marginal lands are brought into production. Moreover, there are initial signs of growing pesticide resistance. This raises the spectre of farmers having to hike pesticide use to kill increasingly resistant bugs. Research in China on Bt cotton suggested that the best path to minimize pesticide use and maximize producer income lay in a combination of GM and integrated pest management.[48] GMOs can facilitate soil conservation via the use of no-till cultivation practices.

## 4.3 Niche markets: fair trade and organic agricultural commodities

Fair trade organizations have created a parallel marketing chain that allows consumers to pay a premium that directly supports agricultural producers. This constitutes a different approach to marketing, in that buyers are concerned about the nature of production, not only the characteristics of the product.[49] Proponents of fair trade argue that paying producers a 'living' price, above the cost of production, is the only sustainable long-term strategy. They also point to the positive impact of the community projects funded by such schemes.

Fair trade commodities represent a small share of world trade in commodities. Westlake[50] estimates that fair trade coffee (the most important fairly traded commodity) only accounts for 1.0 to 1.5 per cent of global trade in coffee. However, year-on-year growth far exceeds that of trade as a whole, with UK fair trade produce sales rising 46 per cent in the year 2002-03. Moreover, a number of large supermarkets have launched their own fair trade marked own brand coffee. They were joined in 2005 by Nestlé, which launched a 'Fairtrade Partners Blend.' According to calculations for coffee by Daviron & Ponte,[51] fair trade purchasing returns between 12 and 21 per cent of the retail price to the producer co-operatives. Yet even the higher end of this spectrum is only what farmers achieved in the mainstream market in the 1970s and 1980s under the ICA.

The emergence of organic commodities has allowed some other areas of production to be marketed at a price premium. Organic coffees, in particular, are frequently cited as a reason for US coffee consumption not falling, despite health concerns.[52] In principle, an increase in organic production should assist poor producers, since the poorest farmers are the least able to acquire chemical fertilizers and sprays. However, in practice the processing and marketing of these commodities is more complex than for

---

48. Clay (2004).
49. Page (2003).
50. Westlake (2002).
51. Daviron & Ponte (2005).
52. In the US the market for organic and speciality coffees has been growing annually at around 30 per cent since 1999 and today accounts for 17 per cent of coffee imports by value and for 40 per cent of coffee retail sales (Ponte, 2002).

those traditionally produced. The system requires that the commodity be traceable from its source through the value chain. This requires comprehensive inspection and certification, which is much easier for large farms in developed countries than for scattered smallholders in developing countries.[53] The price premiums obtainable from organic commodities may not cover the additional marketing, certification and inspection costs and would yield lower returns than investing similar resources in efficiency- or quality-enhancing measures at the national level. Moreover, as organics have increased their market share, the large supermarkets have moved in, squeezing down profit margins and squeezing out small producers. Vorley concludes that 'organic and high-welfare production is not a refuge for smaller scale producers in modern agrifood systems.'[54]

Clay[55] is also sceptical on the environmental impact of organics. Organic production can produce as much soil erosion as conventional agriculture and more than no-till agriculture. Organic agriculture uses water less efficiently than well managed conventional farms. Finally, the natural chemicals used in organic agriculture (e.g. copper, sulphur, nicotine and rotenone) can be far more toxic than many synthetic chemicals used in conventional agriculture.

### 4.4 Corporate social responsibility

The growth of the fair trade market and public concern over the social and environmental impacts of commodity production have prompted responses from mainstream traders, processors and retailers. In coffee, roasters, roaster/retailers and roaster/coffeehouse chains have devised alternative sustainability standards, aimed more or less explicitly at deflecting more radical initiatives. Amongst the best known are Starbuck's proprietary 'Coffee and Farmer Equity Programme' and the Common Code for the Coffee Community.

Gibbon and others are sceptical, arguing that these second-generation initiatives water down standards on fair trade, confuse consumers by blurring the boundaries between fair trade and non-fair trade products, load the costs of compliance on to producers while giving little back in the shape of price premiums, are skewed heavily towards estate production, with little attention to smallholders, and more generally add to standards proliferation.[56] Daviron & Ponte suggest that the best way to deal with this proliferation of standards is to set up 'multiple certifications' which group together 'high-bar' standards such as fair trade and organic, in contrast to 'low-bar' industry-driven standards such as the CCCC.[57] However, introducing such an intermediate tier of labelling is likely to confuse consumers even more!

---

53. Wheeler (2001).
54. Vorley (2004).
55. In chapter 6 of this book.
56. See Chapter 7.
57. Daviron & Ponte (2005).

## 4.5 Conclusion

Environmentally sustainable, fair trade and organic commodities face a number of challenges in the years ahead. Firstly, they must reconcile the tensions between social and environmental goals through some degree of standards harmonization; secondly they have to deal with the problems of success, whether through corporates launching watered down versions of fair trade marks that confuse consumers, or scaling up organic production, which drives down margins and squeezes out small producers. Thirdly they will have to deal with the underlying issue that new standards tend to place extra burdens on small producers and favour large-scale agriculture.

## 5. National coordination: the state and producer organizations

The SAPs of the 1980s and 1990s dismembered many state-led coordination and support structures, through the abolition of marketing boards, cutbacks in sources of finance and sharp reductions in technical assistance. Small-scale farmers were left atomized and weakened, easy prey for more powerful sections of the value chain such as traders and retailers, who moved into the vacuum left by the retreat of the state. Much of the current debate revolves around a revived role for the state. A parallel discussion considers other ways to revive producer coordination, such as the promotion of independent producer organizations and contract-farming.

### 5.1 State marketing boards

Often producing a narrow range of agricultural commodities on which they depend for foreign exchange and government revenues, and enjoying only limited shipping outlets, ACDDCs have traditionally relied on national stockpiles to regulate export supplies. These were until recently run by state-owned marketing boards, or *caisses de stabilisation*, which also collected output from small and large producers. The national stockpile was therefore part of a much larger exercise.[58] For marketing boards, the government would normally set an annual price at which it would purchase the commodity through intermediaries, who were given a fixed margin. *Caisse de stabilisation* systems controlled export contracts but did not handle, export or acquire physical ownership of the commodity. Marketing boards and *caisses de stabilisation* had the advantage that farmers knew the price they would receive at harvest. By aggregating the output of a large number of small producers, they also made it easier to demand better prices from buyers.

The records of marketing boards have been mixed. In the late 1970s and early 1980s, they struggled to determine the right level of support prices. In several instances, the value of administered prices was not sufficiently adjusted to reflect inflation,

---

58. UNCTAD (2003a).

exchange-rate movements or world price trends. If administered prices were too low, farmers were cheated, while excessive prices created financial difficulties for the marketing board. In addition, they provided little incentive for quality improvements and suffered from inefficiency and rent-seeking behaviour, including corruption. Nevertheless, some argue that they played a vital role in the development of agricultural exports and the policy of dismantling them as part of SAPs has been widely criticized.[59] Apart from stabilizing prices, the boards provided ancillary services such as extension, inputs, product distribution and credit.[60] They played a role in building quality standards, which helped to establish national reputations and attract premiums for quality.[61]

FAO summarizes the positive and negative impacts of the retreat of the state, pointing out that while it did indeed lead to the predicted increase in the proportion of sale price reaching the farmers, there was a sharp fall in the overall price, which largely wiped out this benefit. Moreover, poor market infrastructure and information channels left the farmers vulnerable to price volatility and exploitation by trading companies. In many countries, both yields and quality of commodities have fallen.[62]

## 5.2 Producer organizations

A closer examination of the role of producer organizations in improving the outcomes for small farmers and poor farm labourers could also produce new policy ideas. At least five types of producer organization can be identified: large estates, small estates, large modern co-operatives, small co-operatives and contract-farming and outgrower schemes.[63] Scale and organizational model affect the benefits that accrue to farmers. For example the FNC, the Colombian national coffee growers' federation, claims 500,000 members with an average of 2 ha of coffee each. FNC operates an extension service with over 800 staff, as well as its own agricultural colleges and an R&D centre. It runs a price-stabilization scheme and has diversified downstream into freeze-drying and own-label sales. Co-operatives in Africa, on the other hand, have often failed to grapple successfully with the market and high demands on quality and reliability.

In cotton, post-liberalization structures fall into three groups: geographical monopolies (Ghana, Mozambique), systems with numerous players (Tanzania, Uganda) and oligopolies (Zimbabwe, Zambia). Gibbon concludes that the last category produces the best outcomes, by combining the positive benefits of competition with a scale that can deliver price stabilization and other benefits. 'Rebuilding local-level economies of scale is becoming a strategic issue in the wake of increasing buyer-drivenness on a global plane on the one hand, and the fragmentation that has frequently followed market liberalization on the other,' he argues.[64]

---

59. See, for example, UNCTAD (1998a); WTO (2003).
60. UNCTAD (1998b).
61. Gibbon (2004a). See also Chapter 7 of this book.
62. FAO (2004).
63. Gibbon (2004).
64. Gibbon (2004).

### 5.3 State or producer? Putting Humpty together again

Whether a return to state marketing boards is either desirable or feasible is a moot point. Responding to the needs of small or least developed ACDDCs may require an enhanced role for the state. The challenge is to ensure that the state equips poor producers to engage with the market on more beneficial terms. Successful Latin American initiatives in the 1980s/90s focused on providing services such as information for new entrants and new buyers. General state support to enhance and diversify assets, and to increase productivity and value added, is likely to form a growing part of mainstream approaches. Measures include access to finance, rural credit facilities to non-farm activities, extension services and training. Improving social and physical infrastructure, health and education will also enhance productivity.

In conjunction with international schemes, national supply management approaches have also been encouraged. UNCTAD cites Malaysia's levy on palm oil production, imposed when prices are high and then used in times of low prices to subsidize the use of palm oil in a non-traditional way, namely, for electricity generation.[65] In West Africa studies by the French government have concluded that the remaining *caisses de stabilisation* are more effective at protecting small cotton growers from price volatility than market-based risk management.[66] The researchers propose the creation of national 'stabilization fund mechanisms,' which could be either privately or publicly run. In either case they would require a single nationwide purchasing organization, taking a share of any surplus in good years and redistributing it to farmers and ginners in bad years.

If donors are to revisit the issue of state marketing boards, they need to consider the pressures on state trading enterprises within the WTO – largely targeted at developed countries' enterprises, such as the Canadian Wheat Board. Any rules that inadvertently prevent a new generation of more effective state interventions in ACDDCs would have negative consequences for the poor.

Gibbon agrees that new ways of balancing market power must be found, but concludes that the place to look is in interventions that scale-up the competitiveness and bargaining power of smallholders. These need accompanying measures to rebalance power in global supply chains (discussed in the next section).[67] Murphy foresees strong opposition from national and international traders,[68] while Lines argues for a pragmatic combination of state and producer-led approaches:

*'Efforts should be supported to find effective replacements for some of the functions of former marketing boards. This means fostering organisations that assist farmers with market intelligence, the development of cooperatives, extension advice, access to credit and physical inputs, and schemes to make the most of premium market niches. They should be farmer-based where possible, government-run where not.'*[69]

---

65. UNCTAD (2003b).
66. Gergely (2004).
67. See Chapter 7.
68. Murphy (2002).
69. Lines (2004).

## 5.4 From coffee to wine: quality-based commodity production

In several sectors, the demise of state regulation has had a severe impact on quality control. Private buyers often pay the same price irrespective of quality, while specialty retailers and traders are overcoming the problem by establishing vertical links to estates, bypassing small producers.[70] Several agencies and authors have looked at the issue of quality, particularly in the case of coffee. In 2002, the ICO agreed a Coffee Quality Improvement Programme. This required members to withdraw low-quality coffee from the market and implement quality-improvement programmes. However, the means of enforcing compliance was never clear, and the programme was made voluntary as a condition for the US rejoining the ICO in 2004.[71]

Optimists are undaunted and advocate a 'wine makeover' for coffee, with coffee houses educating the palate of coffee drinkers. This should be done within mainstream markets, not as a new niche exercise.[72] Kaplinsky holds up Jamaican Blue Mountain Coffee as an example of such 'winification,' as well as the Specialty Coffee Association of Costa Rica, formed in 1999 to pursue product and process upgrading and selling directly to roasters and retailers.[73] Daviron & Ponte suggest that developing countries need to use geographical indications to promote their own coffee to consumers, thereby increasing their bargaining power in the value chain.[74]

This may all be bad news for smallholders, if international traders turn to tighter forms of vertical integration. In the case of specialty coffees this typically means buying from estates. In the case of cotton, where large producers are often absent, it typically takes the form of outgrower schemes. Gibbon points to the twin needs to keep smallholders in commodities like cotton 'in the system' and to enable those in crops like coffee to *get back into* the system.[75]

## 5.5 Conclusion

Where state coordination has avoided dismemberment, as in West Africa, there are strong arguments for retaining it. Elsewhere, efforts may be better spent finding other solutions. It is hard to argue against a focus on producer organization, supported by the state in an enabling role. The hard question is, can it work? How can producer organizations become a significant counterweight in an ever more unbalanced supply chain? How can they counter the many pressures that are steadily squeezing small-scale producers out? An emphasis on producer empowerment could also conflict with international supply management, which relies on national supply-management schemes as a building block. The next section discusses such issues.

---

70. Daviron & Ponte (2005).
71. Daviron & Ponte (2005).
72. Daviron & Ponte (2005).
73. Kaplinsky (2003).
74. Daviron & Ponte (2005).
75. See Chapter 7, sub-section 6.4.

# 6. International coordination and supply management

## 6.1 Boosting demand

FAO advocates generic promotion campaigns in consumer countries, pointing to the long-running UK campaign promoting bananas as a source of energy, which contributed to a threefold increase in consumption, making them the most popular fresh fruit in the country.[76]

## 6.2 Standards

The World Bank has drawn attention to the proliferation of international quality and health standards, and their potential to exclude small-scale farmers.[77] New standards are being introduced by governments (e.g. in animal health) and the private sector (e.g. supermarkets in horticulture). Approaches to this include harmonization of the standards demanded for the same product by different importing countries and establishing, where appropriate, equivalence between developing- and developed-country standards.[78] Donors have set up a trust fund to support developing countries' participation in the Codex Alimentarius Commission, which sets health and trading standards for food. At a national level, training in standards compliance is frequently offered by the World Bank and other donors.

## 6.3 Supply management

Ever since the demise of the ICAs, one of the most polarized debates around the commodities issue has been that of supply management at an international level. For some, it is, if not a magic bullet, an essential first step in any attempt to address the commodity crisis. For others, it is both a political impossibility and a distraction from more important issues.

John Maynard Keynes included a commodity control organization in his grand design for the Bretton Woods institutions.[79] However, the US opposed any restriction of free trade.[80] The GATT has allowed commodity agreements in some circumstances, specifying in article 38 that contracting parties shall:

*'where appropriate, take action, including action through international arrangements, to provide improved and acceptable conditions of access to world markets for primary products of particular inter-*

---
76. FAO (2004).
77. World Bank (2005).
78. See for example the now legendary case of Mauritanian camel cheese, where EU health rules required would-be Mauritanian exporters to use automatic milking equipment – which does not exist in camel-size models, www.geocities.com/madhukar_shukla/mauritaniancheese.html.
79. Keynes (1943).
80. Henningson (1981).

*est to less-developed contracting parties and to devise measures designed to stabilize and improve conditions of world markets in these products including measures designed to attain stable, equitable and remunerative prices for exports of such products.'*[81]

Measures taken in compliance with a commodity agreement are allowed as exceptions to normal MFN treatment under Article 20, subject to agreement by all contracting parties.

The 1970s saw a brief period of 'commodity power' (1973–79), which put control of supply in the hands of developing-country exporters. Collective action was taken first for phosphates and then, in 1973–74, for crude petroleum. In the case of these (non-agricultural) commodities, the strategy worked. They were supplied by developing countries and enjoyed strong international demand, mostly in developed countries. Stocking costs were modest while the commodities were not easy to substitute. This seemed to show that concerted producer supply control could raise prices.

International momentum built up in the 1970s for an Integrated Programme for Commodities. UNCTAD took the lead in promoting the IPC, which had as an objective to raise the price of commodities. The Common Fund for Commodities was envisaged as an instrument to fund buffer stocks of core commodities that were to form the key element of the IPC.[82] The Agreement establishing the CFC was signed in 1980 but only became operational in 1989. By then, the world had changed and the mood among policymakers had swung decisively against intervention in the market. International efforts for primary commodities collapsed, often as consuming countries withdrew. Many of the ICAs have reduced their activities to those of study groups. The CFC was left with a much smaller budget than first proposed, to undertake technical assistance in developing countries (focusing on individual commodities) and multi-country projects examining market chain strategies.[83]

A number of reasons have been advanced as to why the ICAs failed. Some believe that the breakdown reflects the difficulties of supply management in an environment of productivity increases.[84] Others propose that it is difficult, if not impossible, to agree on price ranges[85] or to determine accurately the long-term price trend. Lack of enforcement mechanisms and the 'free-rider' problem[86] have also been suggested. The ICAs' failure to actually curb supply has been cited, while in the case of competing commodities, such as sugar, the impact of developed countries' farm policies played a role in undermining the agreement.[87] On the other hand, it has been argued that many of these challenges could have been surmounted had there been sufficient political will and finance.[88]

---

81. GATT (1986). The wording dates back to the Kennedy Round of GATT negotiations, concluded in 1965.
82. The proposed core commodities were: cocoa, coffee, sugar, rubber, wheat/coarse grains, jute, tropical timber, copper, cotton, lead/zinc, nickel, olive oil and tin.
83. UNCTAD (2003b).
84. Reinhart & Wickham (1994).
85. Gilbert (1996).
86. Cashin et al. (1999).
87. Koning (2004).
88. Rangarajan (1993); Robbins (2003).

**Figure 2: Monthly New York coffee futures**[89]

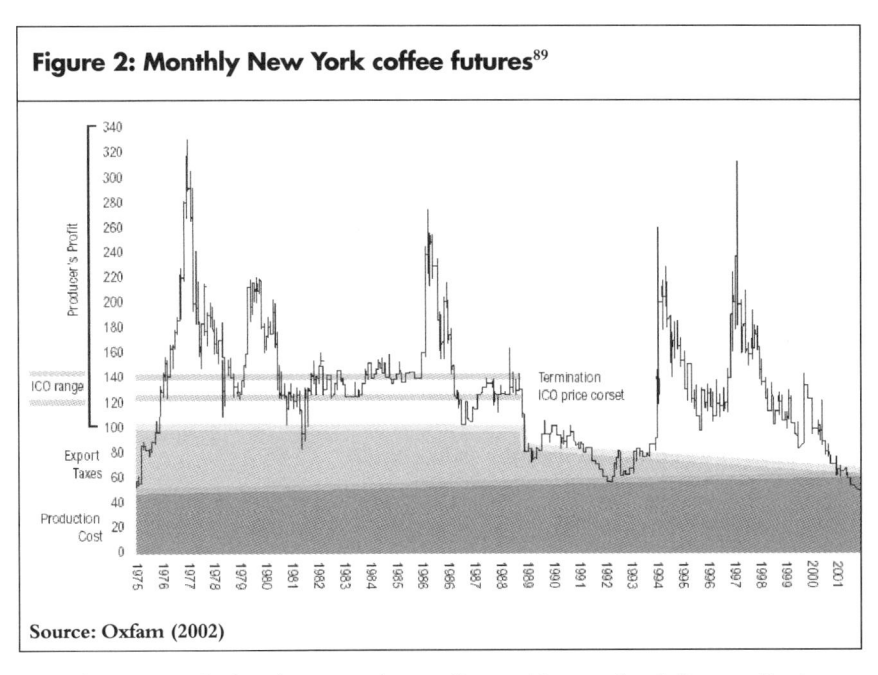

Source: Oxfam (2002)

After OPEC, the best known and most discussed International Commodity Agreement is that for coffee. Oxfam views the International Coffee Agreement from 1964-89, when it had 'economic clauses' imposing export quotas, as a 'golden era of good and stable prices.'[90] Until 1989, governments in both producing and consuming countries sought to agree to predetermined supply levels by setting export quotas for producing countries. The aim was to keep the price of coffee relatively high and stable, within a band from $1.20 – $1.40 per pound. The agreement succeeded in stabilizing prices and persistently raised them by 24 to 30 per cent over what would otherwise have been market-clearing levels.[91] As Figure 2 illustrates, from 1975 to 1989, though prices fluctuated significantly, they remained relatively high and rarely fell below the price floor. In the six years following the collapse of export quotas for coffee, the international price fell 60 per cent.[92]

In recent years, an increasing number of commentators have returned to the issue of international supply management. Lines and Robbins both advocate moving away from buffer stocks and export controls towards controlling production.[93] Murphy believes a key weakness of the first generation of ICAs is that they were commodity-specific, and so precluded any chance of trade-offs between commodities. She argues for restoring UNCTAD's role as 'an obvious forum to house such a multi-commodity approach coupled with one or more funding mechanisms.'[94]

---

89. Monthly, nominal spot prices. Real prices (taking inflation into account) show an even sharper long-term decline.
90. Oxfam (2002).
91. Palm & Vogelvang (1991); Hermann *et al.* (1993).
92. Gibbon & Ponte )2005).
93. Lines (2004); Robbins (2003).
94. Murphy (2004).

But other authors see the return of ICAs as doomed to fail. Firstly, consumer countries would be highly unlikely to sign them. Secondly, at a national level, SAPs have destroyed the market coordination mechanisms required to enforce ICAs. Only if these mechanisms were restored, would any international initiatives be able to function. Both problems are clearly visible in relation to the recent attempts in the coffee sector to re-launch looser or more indirect forms of international agreement. The Association of Coffee Producing Countries, formed in 1990, introduced a voluntary quota-based programme that foundered in the face of Brazilian overproduction, while the Coffee Quality Programme was effectively shelved in return for the US rejoining the ICO, as discussed above.

## 7. Corporate concentration

### 7.1 Market concentration and the value chain

Agricultural products are linked to final consumers through global value chains. A value chain describes the full range of activities that are required to bring a product from the growth of a primary commodity, through the intermediary phases of processing to delivery to final consumers and final disposal after use.[95] ACDDCs are capturing less and less of the value of their markets. This is not just a developing-country phenomenon. In the US in 1900, a farmer received about 70 per cent of every dollar spent on food. Today it is about 3 to 4 per cent.[96]

Two closely related changes have occurred in the market structure for most agricultural commodities. First, farming is highly fragmented, and the destruction of marketing boards removed an intermediary that could improve farmers' bargaining power.[97] Second, the international markets have become much more concentrated. Large trading companies dealing in many commodities have replaced smaller, specialized companies, while the total share of all trading companies has fallen relative to direct purchases by processors or final sellers. In cocoa, the number of trading houses in London shrank from 30 in 1980 to around ten in 1999. Similarly, the six largest chocolate manufacturers account for 50 per cent of world sales. Grain trading, storage, processing and milling is also dominated by a few big companies. Three or four companies control 60 per cent of the terminal grain-handling facilities, 61 per cent of the flour milling, 81 per cent of the maize exports and 49 per cent of the ethanol production in the US.[98]

The growing role of integrated companies also leads to more direct control of what is produced. These interacting trends mean that some of the services formerly provided by governments, e.g. finance and stockholding, are now provided by foreign companies, decreasing the share of commodity income remaining in the producing country. For coffee, Figure 3 shows how relative income within the value chain has changed over the years. Producer countries achieved their peak share under the ICA in the late

---

95. Kaplinsky (2000).
96. Clay (2004).
97. UN (2000).
98. FAO (2004).

**Figure 3: The inter-country distribution of income: percentage share of final retail price**

- consumer countries
- transport and weight loss
- post farm producing countries
- growers share

Source: Kaplinsky, 2003

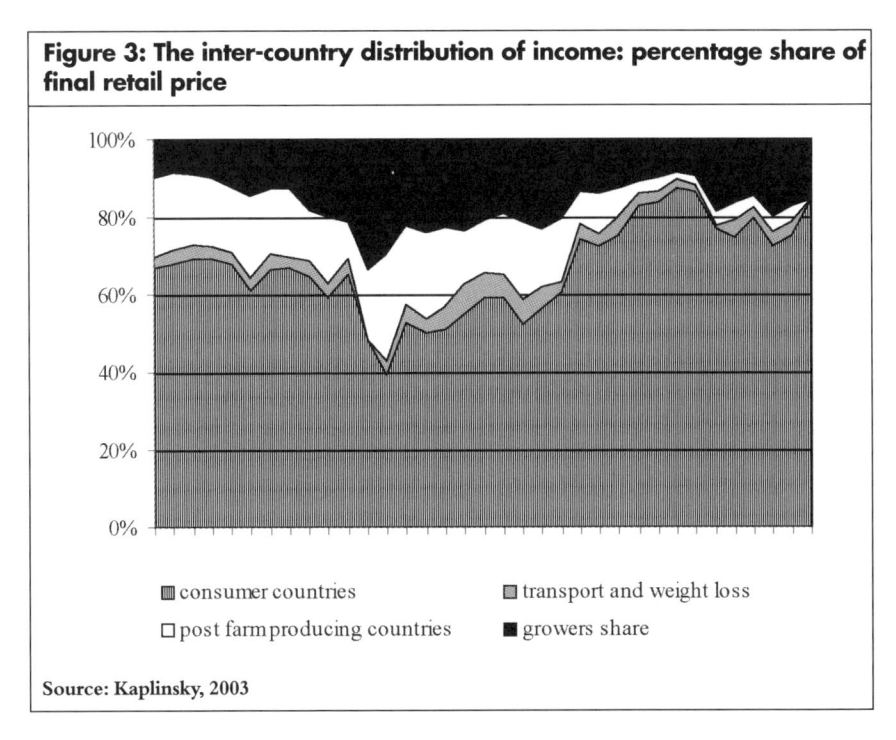

1970s, but since then have steadily lost ground. In the early 1990s export earnings by coffee-producing countries were some $10 to 12 billion and the value of retail sales about $30 billion. Now the value of retail sales exceeds $70 billion but coffee-producing countries only receive $5.5 billion.[99] The asymmetry of power in the coffee chain helps explain the growing inequality of incomes. Importers, roasters and retailers compete with each other for a share of the rents but combine to ensure that few of these accrue to producer countries.[100] Real profits in agricultural commodity chains are made by those who control critical points along the chain, own established brands or have access to shelf space in supermarkets.[101]

## 7.2 Distributional implications

Not only has corporate concentration diminished the slice of value accruing to developing-country producers, it has shifted the balance of power against small-scale farmers. Vertical coordination and concentration create 'insiders' and 'outsiders.' The suppliers who have deep enough pockets, low enough costs and the right kind of technology can benefit as 'insiders'. Vorley cites the example of dairy in Brazil,[102] where before the 1990s most of the main processing firms were central co-operatives. Deregulation of

---
99. Osorio (2002). Nestor Osorio is the Executive Director of the ICO.
100. Fitter & Kaplinsky (2001).
101. UN (2002).
102. Vorley (2004).

the dairy market between 1989 and 1993 saw almost all of these co-operatives sold to multinationals. The top three dairy processing companies in Brazil – Nestlé, Parmalat and Brazilian-owned Vigor – had 53 per cent of the market in 1996. Dairy companies have consolidated their supply bases to reduce transaction costs. The number of farmers delivering milk to the top 12 companies, for example, decreased by 35 per cent between 1997 and 2000, and the average size of those farm suppliers increased by 55 per cent.

Concentration does not only apply to consumer-country traders and retailers. Supermarkets have spread rapidly in developing countries. In Latin America, for example, supermarkets increased their share of food retailing from less than 20 per cent in 1990 to 60 per cent in 2000. Worldwide, the top 30 supermarket chains now control almost one-third of grocery sales.[103] Consequently, small farmers producing for the domestic market increasingly face the same barriers to entry as those trying to export. The majority of smaller and family-scale enterprises (the 'outsiders') are thus left as residual suppliers to bulk commodity or wholesale markets, where corporate concentration is steadily driving down farmgate prices.

### 7.3 Proposals to reduce the adverse impact of market concentration

A number of measures have been proposed that would contribute to reducing market concentration in these segments of the marketing chain. National and international competition law is one way. Tanzania, Uganda and Kenya have also requested that the WTO examine steps to deal with anti-competitive behaviour of large foreign firms and to improve the bargaining position of small producers *vis-à-vis* these firms.[104] Unfortunately, this proposal fell victim to the broader argument on 'new issues' in the WTO, and competition was dropped in the July 2004 Framework agreement on the Doha Round. Some authors and NGOs believe a pro-development competition agreement is more likely to be achieved outside the WTO, elsewhere in the UN system.

Vorley points out that national competition law could address some of these issues, but only if it shifts from its current focus on consumers and retail prices (i.e. monopoly/oligopoly) to one on producers and farmgate prices (monopsony/oligopsony).[105] Gibbon[106] dismisses this as a practical solution because of the difficulties in determining what constitutes oligopsonistic behaviour. For example, the EU bases its competition law on the actions of firms, whereas in commodity markets, firms behave in a less obvious way, benefiting from their market power rather than plotting behind closed doors. Other problems arise over remedies – how could developing countries enforce competition law, since they cannot easily impose fines or ban mergers.

Improving monitoring and transparency is less ambitious, but may be more achievable. Vorley calls for the restoration of the defunct UN Centre on Transnational Corpo-

---

103. FAO (2004).
104. WTO (2003).
105. Vorley (2004).
106. Chapter 7 of this book.

rations in a monitoring role.[107] Current WTO rules require governments to complete questionnaires about any state trading enterprises operating in their country. That approach could be expanded to include any company, public or private, with more than a given percentage of the import or export market. In June 2004, delegates from 70 countries attending a World Farmers' Congress organized by the International Federation of Agricultural Producers adopted resolutions to collect and publicize concentration information and demand that government anti-trust agencies provide economic impact statements of proposed mergers and joint ventures. IFAP supports introducing a pre-established level of concentration that triggers a presumption of a violation of anti-trust law.[108] Vorley also points to the potential for consumer transparency via double pricing, which was piloted in 1999 in France. For fruits, tomatoes and cucumbers, as well as imported produce, every retailer was temporarily obliged to display the price the grower received in addition to the retail price.

**7.4 Conclusion**

Since the demise of supply management, corporate concentration has been the most significant change in the global commodity trade and it is only likely to grow in importance and extent, despite efforts to promote developing countries' processing and trading capacity. This raises two questions for policymakers. To what extent does corporate concentration change the debate on the commodity crisis, making some remedies more difficult and others more practical? Second, what combination of carrots and sticks, and hard and soft law, is required to control concentration and ameliorate its negative impacts on producers? While maximalist positions such as a binding international competition agreement are likely to prove elusive, the issue may be amenable to 'soft law' approaches such as transparency and reporting requirements. Here the last decade of corporate campaigning has armed NGOs and unions with useful experience.

## 8. General conclusion: comparing the approaches

The failure to tackle the link between commodity dependence and extreme poverty has been called a 'conspiracy of silence' by President Chirac of France, and described as the 'major sin of omission' in current international efforts to reduce poverty.[109] New thinking and a vastly increased level of ambition is required to end the conspiracy, and this chapter has surveyed what is currently on offer. The approaches described vary in ambition, social and environmental impact, and in their political and technical feasibility. Table 2 summarizes these qualities. Moreover, the approaches are not entirely de-linked. Some reinforce and complement each other, while others may even undermine each other. The synergies between the approaches are shown in Table 3.

---

107. Vorley (2004).
108. IFAP (2004).
109. UNCTAD (2004a)

## Chapter 5 | Agricultural Commodities, Trade and Sustainable Development

### Table 2: Summary of interventions for sustainable commodities

| PARADIGM | Proposed Solution | Poverty Impact | Environmental Impact |
|---|---|---|---|
| MAINSTREAM MACRO | WTO: cut subsidies, open markets | Limited. Large farms main beneficiaries | Good in North. Could be negative in South (spread of industrial agriculture) |
| | Compensation and aid schemes | Depends on DC governments | Depends on DC governments |
| MAINSTREAM MICRO | Diversification: horizontal, vertical or out of agriculture | High in long term, but in short term depends on labour intensity of new activities | Depends on nature of new production, e.g. more chemical-intensive agriculture |
| | Market-based price risk management | Low, since the mechanisms are largely inaccessible to Southern agriculture; could lead to increased overall production | Neutral |
| SUSTAINABLE COMMODITIES | Environmental Better Management Practices | Could be negative, if excludes Southern agriculture, or positive, by reducing input costs | Positive |
| | Fair Trade | Positive | Could be negative, since Southern agriculture less amenable to BMPs |
| | Organics | Could be negative, if excludes Southern agriculture, or positive, by reducing input costs | Could be negative, depending on what replaces chemical inputs |
| | Corporate Social Responsibility | Depends if broader reach is undermined by weaker standards, plus exclusion issue | Depends whether broader reach is undermined by weaker standards |

| | Who needs to agree/accept? | Political Feasibility | Technical Feasibility | Comments |
|---|---|---|---|---|
| | OECD governments (trade and agriculture ministries), DC governments for Southern liberalization | High in North, since win-win, but agribusiness lobby strong | High | More important for competing commodities than tropicals. Supply response may mean benefits are short-lived |
| | OECD governments (finance ministries) | High | High | What exit routes for remaining ACDDCs exist - is shortage of $ really the problem? |
| | DC governments, producers, supply chains | Easy to say | very hard to do! | Remaining ACDDCs are a residual category of those countries that have so far failed to diversify; so bound to be hard. |
| | Financial providers; farmers | High | Low | Six years into the World Bank's programme, there is very little to show for it. Triumph of ideology over pragmatism. |
| | Producers; supply chains; consumers | Market-driven, so feasible if incentives are there | High | Role of GMOs likely to surface in debate |
| | Consumers (rest will follow, if price premium sufficient) | Market-driven, so feasible if incentives are there | High | Market share + threat of dilution from CSR initiatives are main challenges |
| | Consumers (rest will follow, if price premium sufficient) | Market-driven, so feasible if incentives are there | High | Not clear who benefits from organics apart from health conscious consumers and retailers |
| | Can be corporate-driven e.g. reputation risk management, or consumers | Market-driven, so feasible if incentives are there | High | Doubts over whether CSR is driven by desire for real impact, or reputation management |

# Chapter 5 | Agricultural Commodities, Trade and Sustainable Development

**Table 2 continued**

| PARADIGM | Proposed Solution | Poverty Impact | Environmental Impact | |
|---|---|---|---|---|
| NATIONAL COORDINATION | Defend/revive state marketing boards | High, *if* previous problems such as low farmer prices, corruption etc can be overcome | High, since provides channel for disseminating BMPs | |
| | Producer organization | High | Neutral, unless POs used as channel for disseminating BMPs | |
| | Quality and differentiation based on Geographical Indicators | High, if does not exclude Southern farmers | Neutral | |
| INTERNATIONAL COORDINATION | Supply Management/ ICAs | High | Neutral | |
| | Standards: harmonization, equivalence, DC voice in setting | Could reduce exclusionary impact of standards | Neutral | |
| CORPORATE CONCENT-RATION | International competition law | High, if leads to higher producer prices | Neutral | |
| | National competition law | High, if leads to higher producer prices | Neutral | |
| | Increased corporate monitoring, transparency | Unclear | Neutral | |

| Who needs to agree/accept? | Political Feasibility | Technical Feasibility | Comments |
|---|---|---|---|
| DC governments and (preferably) donors | Low. High level of donor hostility and scepticism on practicality | Low. Hard to restore state coordination once privatization has taken place and value chains consolidated. | Best option may be to defend remaining marketing boards, but look for other options elsewhere. |
| Producers; DC governments; buyers | High, at least for limited degree of coordination around extensions services, credit | High, at least for limited degree of coordination around extensions services, credit | Spans huge range from basic technical assistance to real shift in producer power within GVCs |
| Consumers; Producer; DC governments | High | Depends on commodity – coffee and tea most promising | Only relevant to a few commodities like coffee that can be 'winified' |
| Producer and consumer countries, if want GATT legality | Low. Consumer countries unlikely to support | Low. Intractable problems with free riders, new entrants, substitution | Magic bullet or massive distraction? Depends who you ask… |
| Consumer and producer governments | Limited, if seen as watering down health standards | Possible, given political will | Sensible step, given inexorable proliferation |
| Consumer and producer governments | Low. US unilateralism + corporate resistance | Low. Hard to prove, plus hard to impose penalties on international firms. | Unlikely in short or medium term |
| Producer governments, Northern companies | Medium. Corporates may abandon marginal countries, but would stay with profitable ones | Low. Would DC governments be strong enough to ban mergers, impose penalties on TNCs etc? | Coordinated approach between DCs eg via UNCTAD would reduce danger of corporate backlash |
| Northern companies, possibly pushed by Northern governments via reporting requirements | Medium. Corporate resistance, but transparency = motherhood and apple pie. | High | Relatively easy win, but how much impact would it have? |

### Table 3 Summary of interactions and complementarities between approaches to the commodity problem

| Paradigm | Mainstream micro | Sustainable Commodities | National Coordination | International Coordination | Corporate Concentration |
|---|---|---|---|---|---|
| Mainstream macro | Complementary | WTO may be barrier to Social/Environmental PPMs; compensation schemes cd be linked to BMPs | WTO could restrict operation of state marketing boards but strengthen protection of Geographical Indicators; compensation schemes could fund technical assistance, credit etc for producer organizations | WTO legitimizes but restricts ICAs by insisting they include consumer countries. WTO could play a role in harmonizing standards. Compensation schemes could fund work on standards compliance | WTO could require transparency on corporate concentration |
| Mainstream micro | | Sustainable commodities could be part of diversification strategies; PRM largely irrelevant to small producers | Differentiation via GIs could be part of differentiation strategy; producer organizations and marketing boards could have scale to use PRM | No links | No links |
| Sustainable Commodities | | | Complementary: marketing boards and producer organizations provide channel for spread of BMPs, technical assistance. Fair trade encourages producer organization. | Sustainability standards may need to be harmonized to reduce burden on Southern agriculture; international supply management rules could require BMPs | No links |
| National Coordination | | | | Restoration of national supply management an essential condition for any international agreements – an exclusive emphasis on producer empowerment could undermine that | Strongly complementary. Producer organizations would be able to take advantage of curbs on corporate power in supply chains |
| International Coordination | | | | | No links |

## References

Aksoy, M.A., & J.C. Beghin (eds), *Global Agricultural Trade and Developing Countries* (Washington: World Bank, 2005).

Bloch, H. & D. Sapsford (2000), 'Whither the terms of trade? An elaboration of the Prebisch-Singer hypothesis', *Cambridge Journal of Economics* 24: 461–81.

Cashin, P., C. McDermott & A. Scott (1999), 'The myth of commoving commodity prices', IMF Working Paper. Washington, DC: IMF.

Clay, J., 'World Agriculture and the Environment' (WWF, 2004).

Daviron, B., & Ponte, S., *The Coffee Paradox: Commodity trade and the elusive promise of development* (London: Zed Press, 2005).

Delgado, C. & Siamwalla, A. (1997), 'Rural economy and farm income diversification in developing countries', IFPRI Markets and Structural Studies Division, Discussion Paper 20.

Dehn, J. (2000a), 'Commodity price uncertainty and shocks: Implications for economic growth', World Bank.

Dehn, J. (2000b), 'Private investment in developing countries: The effects of commodity shocks and uncertainty', World Bank.

DFID, 'Official Development Assistance to Agriculture,' Working Paper 9 (London: 2004).

DTI, 'Strategy Paper on Commodities,' www.dti.giv.uk/ewt/commo.pdf (London: 2004).

FAO (2004), 'The State of Agricultural Commodity Markets'.

FAO (2005), 'Export competition: selected issues and the empirical evidence', Trade Policy Technical Note No. 4.

*Financial Times* (11 April 2005), 'On the climb: a natural resources boom is unearthing both profits and perils.'

Fitter, R. and R. Kaplinsky (2001), 'Who gains from product rents as the coffee market becomes more differentiated? A value chain analysis', IDS Bulletin 32 (3): 69–82.

GATT, *The Text of the General Agreement on Tariffs and Trade* (Geneva: 1986), available at www.wto.org/english/docs_e/legal_e/gatt47_01_e.htm.

Gergely, N. (2004), 'Etude sur les mécanismes possibles d'atténuation des effets de la volatilité des cours du coton en Afrique'.

Gibbon P., 'Commodities, donors, value-chain analysis and upgrading', background paper presented at the IIED/ICTSD Windsor Dialogue (2004a).

Gibbon P., 'The commodity question: new thinking on old problems', paper for FAO symposium (Rome: 2004b).

Gilbert (1996), 'International commodity agreements: An obituary notice', World Development 24 (1): 1–19.

Gilbert, C. (1999), 'Commodity risk management for developing countries', Paper prepared for the Third Meeting of the International Task Force (ITF) Meeting held in Geneva, 23–24 June.

Gillson, I., Green, D., Pandian, N. and Wiggins, S. (2004), 'Rethinking Tropical Agricultural Commodities', Working Paper for DFID.

Green, D. and J. Morrison (2004), 'Fostering pro-sustainable development agriculture trade reform: strategic options facing developing countries', ICTSD.

Henningson, B.E. (1981). 'United States agricultural trade and development policy during world war II: the role of the Office of Foreign Agricultural Relations', Ph.D. diss., University of Arkansas.

Hermann, R., K. Burger and H. Smit (1993), 'International commodity policy: a quantitative analysis', London: Routledge.

IFAP (2004), 'World farmers' congress adopts agriculture concentration remedies', Press Release, 26th World Farmers' Congress, International Federation of Agricultural Producers, 4 June, http://www.ifap.org/wfc04/pressconcenhtml.html.

IIED, Rabobank and ProForest, 'Better Management Practices and Agribusiness Commodities' (2004).

IMF and World Bank (2002a), Initiative for Heavily Indebted Poor Countries – Status of Implementation, Washington, DC.

## Chapter 5 | Agricultural Commodities, Trade and Sustainable Development

IMF, International Financial Statistics (Washington: 2005).

IMF and World Bank (2002b), The Enhanced HIPC Initiative and the achievement of long-term external debt sustainability, Washington, DC.

Kaplinsky, R. (2000), 'Spreading the gains from globalisation: what can be learned from value chain analysis', IDS Working Paper.

Kaplinsky, R. (2003), 'How Can Agricultural Commodity Producers Appropriate A Greater Share Of Value Chain Incomes?', paper for FAO Symposium.

Keynes, J.M. (1943). 'The international regulation of primary products', reprinted in D. Moggridge (ed.), Collected writings of John Maynard Keynes, London: MacMillan & Cambridge University Press.

Koning, N., M. Calo and R. Jongeneel, (2004), 'Fair trade in tropical crops is possible: International commodity agreements revisited', North-South Discussion Paper no. 3, North-South Centre, Wageningen.

Lines, T. (2004), 'Commodities Trade, Poverty Alleviation and Sustainable Development', paper sponsored by the Common Fund for Commodities for UNCTAD XI.

Murphy, S. (2004), 'UNCTAD XI: Challenging the Commodity Crisis', IATP.

Osorio, N., 'Technological Developments in Coffee: Constraints encountered by producing countries' (London: International Coffee Organization, 2002).

Oxfam (2002), 'Mugged: Poverty in your coffee cup', Oxfam International.

Oxfam, (2004), 'The commodities challenge: towards an EU action plan', Oxfam International.

Oxfam (2005), 'Kicking Down the Door: How upcoming WTO talks threaten farmers in poor countries', Oxfam International.

Page, S. (1990), 'Trade, finance and developing countries: Strategies and constraints in the 1990's', USA: Barnes & Noble Books.

Page, S. (2003), 'Towards a global programme on market access: opportunities and options', Report for IFAD, Overseas Development Institute.

Page, S. and A. Hewitt (2001), 'World commodity prices: still a problem for developing countries?', Overseas Development Institute.

Palm, F.C. and B. Vogelvang (1991), 'The effectiveness of the world coffee agreement: a simulation study using a quarterly model of the world coffee market' in O., Guvenen, W.C Labys and J-B. Lesourd, (eds.) International Commodity Market Models, London, Chapman and Hall.

Prebisch, P. (1950), 'The economic development of Latin America and its principal problem', Santiago: UNECLA.

Rangarajan, L. (1983), 'Commodity conflict revisited: From Nairobi to Belgrade', Third World Quarterly 5(1).

Ray, D., de la Torre Ugarte, D., Tiller, K. (2003), 'Rethinking US Agricultural Policy: Changing Course to Secure Farmer Livelihoods Worldwide'.

Reinhart, C. and P. Wickham (1994), 'Commodity prices: cyclical weaknesses or secular decline?', IMF Staff Papers 41 (2).

Robbins, P., Stolen Fruit: The tropical commodities disaster (London: Zed Books, 2003).

Singer, H. (1950), 'The distribution of gains between investing and borrowing countries', American Economic Review, Papers and Proceedings, 40: 473–85.

Spraos, J. (1983), 'Inequalising trade? A study of traditional North/South specialization in the context of terms of trade concepts', Oxford: Clarendon Press.

UN (2000), 'World commodity trends and prospects', Note by the Secretary-General, New York: UN.

UN (2002), 'World commodity trends and prospects', United Nations General Assembly. A/57/381. New York.

UNCTAD (1998a), 'Trade and Development Report', E.98.II.D.6, United Nations: New York and Geneva.

UNCTAD (1998b), 'The least developed countries report', 1998, E.98.II.D.11, United Nations: Geneva.

UNCTAD (1999), 'The impact of changing supply and demand market structures on commodity prices and exports of major interests to developing countries', TD/B/COM.1/EM.10/2.

UNCTAD (2003a), 'Economic development in Africa: Trade performance and commodity dependence', United Nations: New York and Geneva.

UNCTAD (2003b), 'Report of the Meeting of Eminent Persons on Commodity Issues', TD/B/50/11, United Nations Conference on Trade and Development.

UNCTAD (2004a), 'The Least Developed Countries Report', Geneva.

UNCTAD (2004b), 'Economic Development in Africa: Trade Performance and Commodity Dependence', Geneva.

UNCTAD (2005), 'International Trade Negotiations, Regional Integration And South-South Trade, Especially In Commodities'.

Vorley, B. (2004), 'Food, Inc. Corporate concentration from farm to consumer', UK Food Group

Watkins, K. (2004), 'WTO Negotiations on Agriculture: Problems and Ways Ahead' ICTSD.

Westlake, M. (2002), 'The world coffee economy and coffee in Africa, Africa Beverages Report for DFID.

WTO, 'Paper on the need for urgent action in the WTO to deal with the crisis situation created by the long-term trend towards decline in prices of commodities to the trade and development of developing countries which are heavily dependent on their exports', Communication from Kenya, Uganda and Tanzania, Document No. WT/COMTD/W/113 (Geneva: 19 May, 2003).

WTO, 'Declining Terms of Trade for Primary Commodities,' Submission by Kenya, Uganda and Tanzania, Document No. WT/COMTD/W/130 (Geneva: 6 May, 2004).

# Chapter 5 | Agricultural Commodities, Trade and Sustainable Development

# Chapter 6

# Commodity Production and Trade: Public Policy Issues

Jason W. Clay

## 1. Introduction

The world is producing more food than ever before. However, after decades of declining numbers of hungry in the world, the number of people who go hungry is increasing. Between 1997 and 2001, the number of hungry people globally increased by 18 million to a total of 798 million, most of them landless. The World Food Programme provides food to about 90 million people every year, but the remainder are beyond the reach of the international community. In part, infrastructure is the problem, as many of the hungry live in remote places where they neither have access to sufficient food nor the possibility to grow subsistence crops. In many cases, it is not clear that availability would result in more people being able to acquire food. The issue is income rather than access.

To put this in context, in India, despite overflowing granaries, about 20 per cent of the country's population are still hungry. This situation is more and more common – as food production goes up and price comes down, a significant proportion of the world's population cannot afford food, at least at current prices. Some people spend upwards of 75 per cent of their income on food but still go hungry. Producing more food is not the answer, and even producing food that is less expensive is not likely to address the issue either. Similarly, handing out food to increasing numbers who need it is nothing more than a sticking plaster, even though it can prevent thousands of deaths a day.

The final point is clear: food production strategies and poverty alleviation strategies, while not unrelated, need to be de-linked. Producing more food will not necessarily feed more people. The focus now needs to be on creating more jobs, income and equity. Some have referred to the problem as one of a 'famine of jobs and livelihoods' rather than a lack of food. Over the past 35 years, the production of food has increased faster than population growth. Today, everyone on the planet could have a daily diet of 2,800 calories and there would still be food reserves.

The majority of those who cannot afford the food that they and their families need live in rural areas. However, for the most part they do not own or rent land, so rural development programmes intended to boost the livelihoods of small farmers must trickle down if they are to reach them.

This, then, is the context in which commodities and sustainable development need to be analyzed.

## 2. Global agricultural commodities – production and markets

To have a useful discussion about commodities, it is important to start with some essential background information. There are a number of myths about agricultural commodity production. Five appear to be key to this discussion, as they will influence not only the policy tools being discussed but also the strategies and goals.

### 2.1 Myth 1 – most agricultural commodities are traded internationally.

In 2000, a number of crops were produced primarily for export (e.g. coffee with 76 per cent traded internationally; tea with 50 per cent; cocoa virtually 100 per cent; soya beans 57 per cent; palm oil 47 per cent; cashews 62 per cent, rubber 84 per cent; tobacco 83 per cent; shrimp from aquaculture 91 per cent; salmon from aquaculture 95 per cent). However, this is not the case for food staples: many are produced primarily for domestic consumption. These include orange juice (with 13 per cent sold internationally), sugar from cane (16 per cent), bananas (21 per cent), cotton (26 per cent), wood pulp from plantations (12 per cent), wheat (22 per cent), rice (4 per cent), corn/maize (14 per cent), sorghum (13 per cent), cassava (9 per cent) and beef (23 per cent). In fact, when horticulture and fruit are taken into account, some 90 per cent of all food is consumed in the country of production.[1]

## 2.2 Myth 2 – most commodities are produced in developing countries and consumed in developed ones.

While this holds for crops that can be produced primarily in the tropics, it does not hold for crops that can also be produced in temperate zones or for total food production. The US is the largest producer and exporter of soya beans, corn/maize and sorghum, and is the largest exporter of wheat. The US, EU or Australia are the main producers and exporters of beef and salmon, and the US, EU or other developed countries are major producers and exporters of orange juice, sugar, cotton, wood pulp from plantations, tobacco and rice. In fact, in order to meet their current food needs, a number of developing countries are significant importers of agricultural commodities. Oxfam estimates that some 20 per cent of global grain exports are used for famine victims and refugees. In general, developing countries are net importers of all cereals and developed countries are net exporters. Similarly, with the exception of Latin America, developing countries are net importers of meat, and developed countries are net exporters.[2]

## 2.3 Myth 3 – most people eat a wide range of foods.

In fact, rice, wheat, corn and cassava account for 73 per cent of global food caloric demand. By adding four more cultivars – potatoes, sorghum, bananas and sweet potatoes – the total percentage of food calories is about 90 per cent. This is not to say that vegetables and fruits are not essential to diet and health, but rather that only a handful of commodities are key when addressing hunger (a shortage of calories in the diet).

## 2.4 Myth 4 – the price of food is increasing.

This is perhaps the most complicated myth. While the price of food to the ultimate consumer may be rising in specific instances, the price paid to producers, when adjusted for inflation, for nearly every staple foodstuff, is lower than a generation ago. According to the *Economist*, the price of most foods is at the lowest level it has been at for any time for which there are records. Furthermore, the percentage of total household budget that people in developed countries pay for food has declined to an all-time low (e.g. about 14 per cent in the US). By contrast, the poor in developing countries can pay as much as 75 per cent of their income for food and still be hungry.

Another complicating factor is that not only has the percentage of income spent on food tended to decline, but the percentage of the money kept by farmers has declined as well. In the US in 1900, for example, a farmer tended to receive about 70 per cent of every dollar spent on food. Today it is about 3-4 per cent on average, less on commodities and more on fresh fruits and vegetables. Farmers receive 1-2 per cent of the price consumers pay for a loaf of bread or a box of breakfast cereal. Farmers in devel-

---

1. Clay 2004
2. Clay 2004

oping countries do a little better. And, globally, farmers receive about a third of the total food value, but given today's trends, estimates suggest that they will receive about 10 per cent in 25 years.

### 2.5 Myth 5 – Agriculture represents a declining share of commerce in most countries.

One of the things that is happening is that more value is being added to agriculture than ever before. For example, farmers represent 0.9 per cent of US GDP, but the entire food market chain is about 14 times that big. In most other countries, both of these figures are larger, making agriculture a very significant, if not the most significant, driver of total commerce.

## 3. Agricultural commodities and price volatility

Considerable attention has been paid to the decline in commodity prices. Even more important than price declines, however, is the volatility of commodity prices. A study commissioned by the World Bank[3] to stimulate discussion at a recent board meeting had a number of interesting findings. The most significant, perhaps, is illustrated in Figure 1.

With Figure 1 as a backdrop, the authors of the report offered a number of observations:
- Commodity prices are more volatile and more subject to shocks than are the prices of tradable industrial goods.
- Some commodities experience shocks more frequently than others.
- Commodity price shocks tend to persist.
- The maximum impact of a price shock is typically achieved after about four years.
- Long-term impacts can persist for much longer – some situations will take as much as 20 years to return to the starting point if nothing else happens in the interim.
- Since the 1973 energy crisis, global commodity prices have become much more volatile.
- Shocks and economic growth are closely related, and large negative shocks cannot be offset by later positive developments through economic growth.
- Poverty tends to increase from negative shocks due to declines in growth and incomes.
- Positive price shocks tend to be "buffered" from producers (i.e. not passed on as quickly as negative shocks): commodity booms are not as good for producers as commodity busts are bad.

However, another issue that was not raised in the above-mentioned paper may be significant for our discussion. Namely, what is the impact of a sharp price spike on longer-term agricultural commodity prices? Put another way, could abrupt changes in agricultural subsidies in developed countries, or in developing ones as well, trigger

---
3. ARD, PREM and FRM 2004

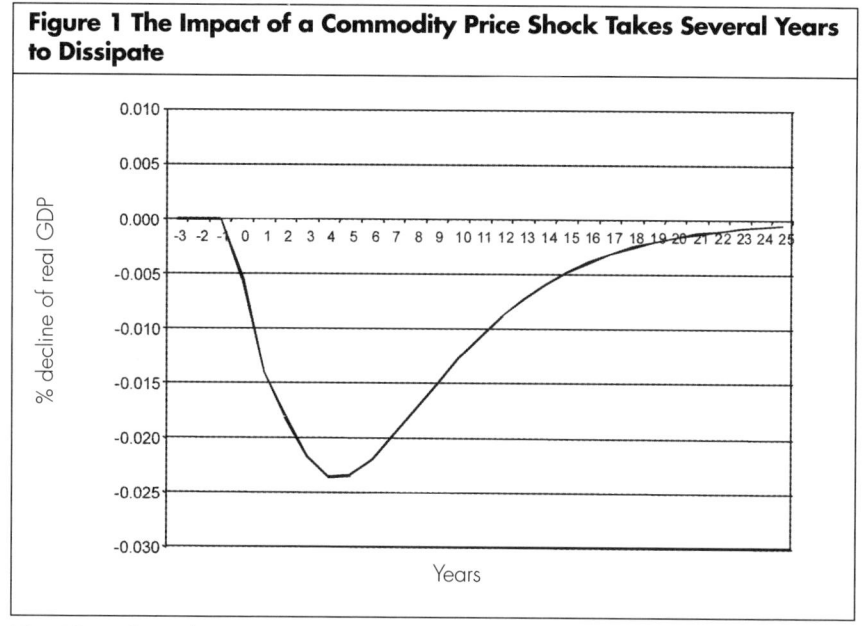

## Commodity Production and Trade: Public Policy Issues | Chapter 6

**Figure 1 The Impact of a Commodity Price Shock Takes Several Years to Dissipate**

Note. Figure shows the impact of a two- standard- deviation change of the country-specific commodity price index (Deaton Miller index) on real output (GDP) in a typical low-income country The impact is the percentage change in GDP for low- income countries, on average.
**Source: World Bank staff calculations**

shocks throughout the world for the affected commodities? Given the price elasticities of many agricultural commodities, a sharp or even a small rise in price of a given commodity is likely to trigger a large producer response that could result in precisely the type of picture (and the associated consequences laid out above) depicted in Figure 1. The factors that might affect the extent and duration of the impact would be whether it was an annual, semi-annual or perennial crop. The longer the productive life of the crop, the longer the impact on the market.

## 4. Competitiveness in commodity production

There are at least five trends of note regarding competitiveness in agricultural commodities.

### 4.1 Trend 1 – Competitiveness through technology (e.g. genetics, management, inputs)

The first trend is that significant genetic and technical gains have allowed production of many commodities to increase far more rapidly than the area under production. Since 1900, the area under cultivation globally has increased by about a third, but total production has increased some six-fold. This trend pushes producers (large and small) to become much more competitive to stay in business. This contributes to competitiveness through reductions in the costs of production.

### 4.2 Trend 2 – Competitiveness through globalization

In 1900, most European and North American countries were self-sufficient in agricultural products, at least those that could be grown in temperate areas. Colonies gave colonial powers access to tropical agricultural products as well (e.g. rubber, coffee, sisal, jute, cocoa, bananas and cotton). With the growth of populations in the North as well as the fact that many Northern countries did not have their own colonies, international trade in agricultural commodities began in earnest. This trend contributed to competitiveness via access to technology, infrastructure, markets and capital.

The competitiveness gained this way was not just about agricultural production but also about trade, manufacturing of food products based on those commodities, and the distribution of those manufactured products. In short, globalization of trade through colonial structures created competitive advantages for certain groups throughout the market chain, not just at the producer end.

### 4.3 Trend 3 – Competitiveness through policies

The public-sector policy dimensions that shape competitiveness take two forms – preferential access of foreign producers to domestic markets, and domestic agricultural subsidies. Regarding the first, after the world wars in the past century, the number of colonies decreased. Former colonial powers usually gave former colonies some form of preferential access to their domestic markets. At the same time, after World War II, food security and domestic food production were important political issues, particularly in Europe. Over time, the use of trade policy instruments such as tariffs and subsidies escalated and spread throughout the world, at least to countries which could afford them.

Over the past 10-15 years, the International Monetary Fund (IMF) has restructured many developing country economies. A cornerstone of this restructuring has been the removal of agricultural subsidies and protective tariffs, as well as the privatization of commodity marketing. However, until the subsidy regimes are similarly dismantled in developed countries, producers and food manufacturers in developing countries will not be competitive within most international markets.

In this context, the EU began to reduce the preferential access of former colonies to EU markets over the past decade. This was done not by eliminating preference but by extending it to a larger class of countries based on their level of development. The EU has still not reduced commodity-specific subsidies for its domestic producers and this has led, in the case of sugar, to the protection of sugar beet producers and the subsidized export of their product while at the same time allowing some cane sugar producers access to the EU market. This is a fairly expensive and inefficient policy.

As the WTO begins to rule on subsidies (e.g. bananas, cotton and sugar) it is clear that the ability of former colonial powers to give preferential market access to former colonies will be reduced, if not eliminated. This will also happen with the protection of domestic producers. This issue is not limited to developed countries. Many Asian countries protect domestic rice production through subsidies and trade barriers. China protects its soya producers through tariffs on raw and processed soya from abroad. India and Pakistan protect both sugar and cotton through a host of different policies.

These three trends have helped shape commodity competitiveness throughout the past century. Competitiveness, in this context, has been increasingly determined by cost of production and increasing efficiency either of production, transport or processing and manufacturing. As subsidy regimes are dismantled either voluntarily or as a result of WTO or IMF pressure, governments are losing the ability to prop up less efficient producers. While the main focus of subsidy discussions has been on the US and EU, subsidies have had significant impacts in many developing countries too.

## 4.4 Trend 4 – Competitiveness through comparative advantage

Many countries have a 'natural' comparative advantage for producing crops that is related to their environments and climate. The US is well suited to produce maize, soya, wheat, meat, fruit and vegetables. Likewise, many developing countries have a comparative advantage in tropical crops such as coffee, cocoa, rubber, cashews, palm oil or even wood pulp from plantations, when compared to developed countries, which lie mostly in temperate zones.

However, it is important to look at the world in terms of evolving trends, not past performance. As technology allows for the genetic manipulation of crops like soya beans, the US is losing its comparative advantage to countries such as Brazil, where the longer growing season allows more harvests. Similarly, wild harvested timber for pulp wood made the US and Canada strong pulp producers in the past, due to the uniformity of the trees and the relatively small number of species. New technology, however, makes single-species plantations in the tropics where trees grow all year round much more competitive than in the past. It appears this will be the trend in the future.

Similarly, fish protein (from capture fisheries and increasingly from aquaculture) is an important income generator for developing countries. In spite of high fishing subsidies in developed countries, by 2001 developing countries accounted for about half of the $56 billion export value of fisheries products.[4] In 2002, the $28 billion in gross exports generated by fisheries from developing countries resulted in some $18 billion in net revenues. That was nearly twice their net export revenue from coffee, bananas, natural rubber, tea, rice and all other meats combined.

This may call for fundamental shifts in our approaches to commodities. Valdimarsson of the FAO[5] predicts that between 1997 and 2020, the developing countries'

---
4. Valdimarsson 2004
5. Valdimarsson 2004

percentage of all fisheries product exports will increase from 72 per cent to 79 per cent. In the same period, Valdimarsson expects the percentage of fisheries production from aquaculture in developing countries to increase from 31 per cent to 41 per cent (since 1970, global aquaculture production has grown by 9.2 per cent per year). Moreover, during the same period, food fish consumption in developed countries is predicted to remain static, while in China it will increase more than 36 per cent and in all other developing countries by about 61 per cent. In short, production, consumption and exports will all be in and among developing countries, representing a trend that needs to be taken into account in building an agricultural commodities strategy. For example, increases in soya consumption are static in the EU and US but are growing dramatically in China and throughout Asia.

Moreover, many producers in the US, Europe and Japan are affected by high land values, high labour costs, regulations, and other factors that are far less significant in many other countries. This means that even though the climate and quality of the land may be good, such countries will lose their advantage to others. In this climate, the most efficient producers in Southern countries are likely to come to dominate much of global production and international trade. Given that consumption in developed countries is rather flat, and that food manufacturing may also come to be more efficient near the sources of production, food manufacturing is likely to shift to developing countries, and trade among developing countries will likely increase.

### 4.5 Trend 5 – Competitiveness on domestic markets

Many developing country producers could not compete on price within their own domestic markets with producers from other developing or even developed countries. For example, Brazil has a competitive advantage to produce sugar. If allowed, Brazilian sugar could be produced and exported to most other sugar-producing countries at costs below those of domestic production. In fact, analysts looking at changes in EU sugar policies predict that Brazil would fill at least half of the newly opened market and perhaps much more. Similarly, US maize and Australian wheat can be grown and shipped to most parts of the world at lower prices than the production costs of domestic producers. This is because American and Australian producers are extremely efficient at producing these crops, and many of their costs are amortized over large volumes due to their scale.

The issue that this raises is rather simple: there may be 30–50 countries in the world that do not have any ability to produce even the most basic food needs in their countries compared with other efficient producers. However, since the population of many of these countries is primarily agricultural, allowing cheaper imports will not only force many out of farming as a market activity, it will reduce all the employment associated with it in the local economy. This issue will be extremely important for many developing countries.

## 5. Other commodity production issues

### 5.1 Multi- vs. single-commodity producers

Most commodities around the world (with the exception of small-farmer crops such as coffee) are produced by individual farmers who focus most if not all of their attention on a single crop or on a small number of crops grown in rotation (e.g. soya/maize or soya/maize/cotton rotations in the US and Brazil respectively). Very few producers of any scale or commercial market integration produce more than two to three commodity crops at any single time. Even most small farmers produce only one to two commodity crops, often grown in association with other subsistence foods, to generate most of their income. In general, the global trend is to produce greater volume of fewer crops to reduce the cost per unit of production and remain competitive. Globalization accelerates this process, but the trend has been present for a century.

### 5.2 High-tech vs. low-tech production

The production of most food, agricultural commodities and fibres, and the vast majority of what is traded internationally, comes from high-input, intensive production systems. Even the production of most foods that are consumed fresh (e.g. vegetables and fruit) comes increasingly from high-input agriculture. In fact, the inputs used for market-oriented horticultural production even in developing countries are far more high-input than most agricultural commodities. Similarly, the production of most non-food industrial crops also comes from high-input, intensive production. These crops include cotton, wood pulp, rubber, tobacco, sisal, hemp, flax and jute, but these crops combined represent only a tiny fraction of the land that is devoted to food crops.

The current answer to feeding the world is in large-scale, high-input, monoculture agricultural production systems that have existed for only 50-100 years. The environmental problems caused by such production systems perpetuate and intensify earlier agricultural impacts that degraded parts of the Andes, Meso-America, North Africa and the Middle East, as well as parts of Europe, South and South-east Asia and the Great Plains of the United States. Nevertheless, low-input cultivation systems, as they were practised in the past, cannot meet the food and industrial needs that people around the world have come to expect. Somewhere between these two extremes are systems of production that are more sustainable and productive and that make better use of fewer resources than either the less input-intensive or the more input-intensive systems that currently dominate.

### 5.3 Subsistence or export-led agriculture

Around the world, agriculture is practised by a range of producers whose practices differ in intensity, scale and focus. Whether they sell 100 per cent of their product to markets or are primarily subsistence-oriented and only sell surplus into markets, agricultural producers are increasingly in competition. Globalization will only accentuate this process.

What does this mean for farmers globally? For the past few years, the total number of farmers in the world has declined in absolute terms and the number of farms has declined even more. The productivity of farms, by contrast, has increased considerably. Simultaneously, the number of hungry people in the world (excluding China) increased by an average of 11 per cent from 1970 to 1990. In Africa, between 1980 and 2000 the number of hungry people actually increased in absolute terms. Over the past 35 years, per capita food production has grown 16 per cent faster than population. Still, people are hungry. In Africa, agriculture employs about two-thirds of the labour force, accounts for 37 per cent of GNP and is responsible for half of exports. Still, the sector is doing little to generate wealth among the poor. In South Asia, agriculture generates 27 per cent of the GNP but also has little impact on reducing inequality.

Hunger and malnutrition are more about distribution and income than they are about agricultural production. But, in all likelihood, this will not always be the case. Production will not keep pace with population and consumption increases in the future as it has in the past. In fact, cereal yield growth rates have declined for nearly 16 years. Furthermore, per capita land and water quality, and availability of these inputs for agriculture, are declining.

### 5.4 Value-added production and development

Farmers and those who work with them have long wanted to find viable ways to add value to the commodities that they produce, rather than sell raw materials while others make most of the money beyond the farm gate. Farmers in the US traditionally added value to their maize and soya production by feeding livestock to produce milk, meat, and eggs. However, small producers cannot achieve the efficiency of very large operations.

## 6. International market trends that affect commodities

There are a number of market trends that influence commodity production and trade. Many of these trends have not been created by government regulations (or lack thereof) but by the private sector and consumer perception. The challenge is to examine these trends closely to understand where the leverage points are for change, either within public or private sector policies.

### 6.1 Trend 1 – Consolidation and integration within the food market chain

Perhaps the single most important issue that has arisen in the past 10-20 years with regard to food and agricultural commodities globally is integration and consolidation.

Less than half as many large, multinational companies exist today as did 20 years ago. The consolidation has occurred both horizontally and vertically. Globally for any single commodity, only some 300–400 buyers make key purchasing decisions, not millions of consumers.

Nowhere is this clearer than with the spread of supermarkets. In China, supermarket sales went from 0.4 per cent of retail sales in 1995 to 6.5 per cent by 2000. In the last decade in 10 Latin American countries, supermarkets increased their share of food sales from 10-15 per cent to almost 60 per cent. In South Africa, supermarkets have increased their share of total food sales by 55 per cent. These trends occur because supermarket chains can achieve efficiencies of scale, product standardization and quality, and satisfy increasingly global food tastes and preferences.

Similar efficiencies are being driven on the production side, where higher quality, larger volume and lower costs are the order of the day. Market prices are greatly influenced by the largest, most efficient producers. These producers don't set prices, but they tend to influence them – especially to lower prices. The efficiency of market dominators must be matched by government interventions (e.g. protection, subsidies or tariffs), subsidies from nature (e.g. environmental impacts), or lower profit margins and standards of living for less efficient producers, including small-scale producers.

## 6.2 Trend 2 – Increased consumer concerns about the quality of food

Globally, consumers are sending clearer signals than ever before about what they want (or more often, don't want) in their food – higher quality as well as healthier, safer and tastier products. This has been fanned, especially in Europe, by a succession of mad cow disease, foot and mouth, E coli, salmonella, PCBs, dioxins, contaminated fishmeal in feeds, etc. However, the concerns are not limited to Europe. Organic food consumption and production in the US (40 per cent of global) is another indication of consumers' food residue and health concerns. In China, the market for green food products has exploded, and similar moves are under way elsewhere in Asia and Latin America.

Residues in food, food bioterrorism and food traceability are putting pressure on production systems to trace a product from 'field to fork' or from 'pond to plate.' Furthermore, such systems are not limited to the actual commodities themselves, but also to all inputs. For plants, this includes fertilizers and pesticides. For animals, it includes eggs, seed and feed. Whether plant or animal, product residues are also being monitored, and it doesn't matter whether the residue comes from the environment or was introduced specifically by the producer. Residues are increasingly not tolerated.

NGOs and consumers have driven the GMO debate and have forced the private sector to separate and label GM products, at least in the EU and Japan. While many large-scale traders resisted this move, commodities have long been differentiated based on size, quality and other attributes that people are willing to pay for. The largest unintended consequence of the GMO issue is that it is 'de-commodifying' some agricultural food commodities (e.g. maize, soya, and rape/canola). This is happening not only with regard to segregating the unprocessed commodity, but also differentiating animals, for example, that have not been fed with any GM ingredients. This has tremendous implications for what can be done within commodity systems (both production and trade).

Whether the concerns are always well founded or not, they are real. As a consequence, most food companies are exploring ways to ensure that they have more control over the production processes for agricultural commodities as well as overall product quality. Certification is one way to do this, as is ownership of an increasing portion of the market chain. In some instances, companies are developing their own producer guidelines, which producers who want to sell products to them are required to follow. Because this is voluntary, it does not fall under the WTO programme.

There are a few other trends in the global market that should be noted.
- There is an increasing use of producer contracts to guarantee production for buyers and to reduce risks (e.g. residues, product safety, traceability).
- There is a significant increase in product testing throughout the market chain arising both from bioterrorism concerns (in the US) and food safety and GMO issues (in the EU and Japan). Such testing provides financial incentives for products to be segregated once tested.
- Retailers are acting as watchdogs and even developing first- and second-party certification programmes and standards.
- As a consequence, Eurepgap (1,700 companies representing 70 per cent of food sales) has developed unified industry standards for such products as fruits, vegetables, meat and coffee and has certified more than 20,000 producers in 60 countries. Other standards are being added. This has implications for segregation and differentiation of mainstream commodities.
- In the face of all these trends, the main consumption increases globally are likely to be in developing countries and as of this time, there is far more concern about price than any other factor. What may be developing is a trade system where volume and value are important in developing countries, and quality and uniqueness in developed countries.

## 7. The subsidy regime and commodity production

There are a few key, underrepresented themes in the subsidy debate around commodities.

### 7.1 Subsidy regimes in developing countries

Much of the subsidies and tariff protection in developing countries has been dismantled as part of restructuring programmes with the IMF and others. However, while the subsidies that remain are not as large in value or focused on as many commodities as those in developed countries, they are nonetheless extremely important for producers. Subsidies and protection in developing countries, while only a fraction of the value of those in the EU, US, and Japan, are still quite significant in some countries and for certain crops. Elimination of such subsidies due to WTO rulings could have significant impacts. It will be important to phase out such programmes gradually so as not to produce the kinds of 'exogenous shocks' described previously in this paper.

## 7.2 Subsidies and the global environment

Considerable attention has been focused on the impact of developed-country subsidy regimes on poverty. While this issue is clearly important, there are other equally important impacts of subsidy regimes. Globally, subsidy regimes result in more environmental impacts than any other single set of policies. Producers whose production or exports are subsidized or whose markets are protected have an unfair advantage over those who do not receive similar support. To compete, producers who are not subsidized often cut corners to reduce their costs of production and remain competitive.

## 7.3 Subsidies and Better Management Practices

Subsidies can also be the greatest impediment to the adoption of BMPs (better management practices). When producers make profits because of subsidies, they have little incentive to change. As prices decline, however, efficiency becomes more and more important. Given that decline, it is likely that some of the most innovative BMPs for commodity production are being developed at this time. It would be important to document and disseminate those practices throughout the world, not least because research shows that most BMPs pay for themselves within two to three years and make more money than less efficient practices. It is important to monitor what happens to producers who benefited from past subsidies: their strategies may be a key place to look for innovation.

## 7.4 Production without subsidies

The vast majority of agricultural production is not subsidized. For example, there are few direct subsidies or market supports for horticultural crops – the higher-priced fresh fruits and vegetables that many eat every day. Subsidy regimes tend to be focused on durable commodities, which can be produced and substituted for each other all around the world, encouraging international trade.

Globally, subsidies affect only a handful of commodities: e.g. sugar, cotton, dairy, fisheries and rice. Some subsidies, while not globally significant in terms of overall trade, can have severe regional consequences (e.g. the EU olive oil subsidies on the greater Mediterranean production area). The EU's subsidy regimes for sugar and dairy products (including subsidized exports so that the EU is the second largest exporter of sugar after Brazil and the largest exporter of dairy) and the US subsidy regime for cotton are perhaps the most important subsidy regimes globally. The US subsidizes rice production, but only 4 per cent of rice produced each year is traded internationally.[6]

---

6. FAOSTAT 2002

## 8. Changes in production and marketing – the impacts on poverty and the environment

More food is being produced per capita than ever before, yet there is increasing poverty and hunger. Food security has not been addressed because people cannot afford to buy the food that is often available. Moreover, trends in food production efficiency tend to marginalize not only many small-scale producers but, in some cases, virtually any producers of some commodities in certain countries. Increased food production in places such as India and China have been somewhat de-linked from poverty alleviation, malnutrition and rural development. Those who fight this trend have often succeeded in creating little more than poverty maintenance programmes that might maintain a current lifestyle for another generation, but they do not fundamentally increase benefits to the poorest of the poor. It is important to take a step back and see if it makes sense to de-link poverty, income, asset-building and malnutrition programmes from agricultural production programmes.

Globally, food production is becoming more intensive as well as more vertically and horizontally integrated. For the past 30 years, concerns about food availability and food security have spurred drives to increase production as well as productive efficiency. There has been a simultaneous increase in the vertical integration of food production systems that have increased overall efficiency by reducing the number of players. Such shifts are not neutral. For example, supermarkets increasingly send clear signals about what they do and do not want (see the previous comments about Eurepgap). With consolidation comes standardization and trends toward monopolization.

It seems clear that it is possible to increase food production through traditional agricultural production programmes, but that these programmes may not be the only or even the best ways to reduce poverty or malnutrition. Furthermore, it is not clear that agricultural production programmes can continue to result in higher yields and production if the environmental impacts of agriculture are not brought more in line with sustainability. Here are just a few trends in this regard:

- More than half of all habitable land on the planet is used for agriculture or livestock. Some 90 per cent is farmed unsustainably (e.g. there is a net loss of soil nutrients and soil carbon each year), so new land (0.25 to 0.5 per cent per year) must be brought into production.
- Some 70 per cent of all water used by humans is used for agriculture. More than 60 per cent of irrigation water is wasted, but solutions are expensive and are not available to most small farmers.
- Many of today's production packages have reached technological ceilings. For example, rice yields are seen to be as high as they can go commercially with today's technology. Another technological breakthrough will be needed to achieve higher levels of production.
- Most biodiversity is in the soil and in areas of agricultural use, yet current production systems are mining the soil for short-term gains and market advantage.

- Inputs such as fertilizers to offset some of these issues do not appear to be long-term solutions. For example, the amount of nitrogen required to produce a unit of maize in the US doubled from 1970 to 1990. Quick, technological fixes may not provide continuous improvements in productivity and food availability in the future.

In short, the environmental impacts of agricultural production over the past 30 years, while often improved from the practices of a century ago, are still unacceptable. Fortunately, some production strategies are being developed that will help. For example, in many parts of the world it is more profitable to rehabilitate degraded land than to clear natural habitat and incorporate it in agricultural production. Similarly, abandoning the more marginal areas (say from 5-15 per cent) on most farms actually increases total production, reduces costs and impacts (up to 50 per cent of environmental impacts) and increases profits. However, few of these solutions are appropriate for small-scale farmers attempting to produce on more marginal lands and at scales that are often not competitive. To put it another way, addressing the environmental impacts of production on small farms is much more difficult than it is for medium- to large-scale farms. This has implications for policy.

## 9. Winners and losers from commodity trade liberalization

There will be winners and losers throughout the market chain from commodity trade liberalization. In order to understand the impacts, it is important to have a clear understanding of the following:
- which commodities will be affected by liberalization,
- which commodities can be substituted for them by producers, manufacturers or consumers,
- which producers will be affected,
- what impacts will be felt by whom throughout the market chain, and
- what interest, if any, consumers have in the issue.

However, trade liberalization is only one factor, albeit an important one, that will affect trade. It is equally important to identify where increased demand for commodities is likely to arise as well as where the low-cost traders and food manufacturers are likely to be in the new commodity world. Most studies suggest that overall consumption in developed countries will increase only slightly if at all for many commodities. This is already true for soya in Europe and bananas, coffee, rubber and fish protein, among others, in Europe and North America. With the exception of paper pulp, the consumption of most agricultural commodities is actually stable or declining in developed countries.

Increases in consumption are likely to result from growth in the South. Sustained 8 per cent or more growth in China has not just increased the demand for raw materials. It has also driven demand for more calories and higher-protein diets. In fact, the entire expansion of soya in South America is linked to the increased consumption of animal protein in China. People are 'eating up the food chain.' Since China's population has not increased during this period, the entire increase is due to increased consumption. China is not only importing resources to satisfy this consumption, in 2003 it became the largest agricultural producer globally, surpassing the US.

China demonstrates another likely trend in food commodity chains. Historically, most commodity trade was not only dominated financially but managed physically by developed countries. Goods were often shipped to developed countries, held or transformed there and then reshipped. This is changing. Overheads in developed countries (from labour and management costs to warehousing and compliance with regulations) are becoming more burdensome. In the recent past, China bought its soya from the US; now it buys from Brazil. China is already investing in Brazil's port and transport infrastructure to improve that country's efficiency. This is likely just the start of a trend.

It is more efficient to deal directly with the main producers. For this reason, many of the developed-country traders and processors will likely be cut out of the South-South trade that will dominate the next 20-50 years of agricultural production unless they shift their operations to the new centres of production. This is what ADM, Cargill and others are doing for soya in Brazil and Nutreco and Stolt are doing with salmon in Chile.

However, a number of countries (perhaps 30-50 and most in sub-Saharan Africa) have little that they can produce competitively for sale on world markets. Trade liberalization may actually accentuate such countries' plights. Currently they protect their agriculture through trade barriers. In the future that may not be possible. Yet efficient commodity producers could likely produce and ship half way around the world products that would be cheaper and often of higher quality than those produced locally. Unfortunately, while such imports would put local producers out of business, it is not clear whether, without agriculture, many locally would have money to buy the imported food at any price, since food production is the largest sector in most of those economies.

Even gaining access to EU and US markets is not likely to help most producer countries. Sugar illustrates the problem. Recent research suggests that, conservatively, half of any increased imports of sugar in the EU that might result from reforms in the sugar regime would come from Brazil. In fact it could be higher. Every tonne of sugar Brazil produces will tend to lower its production costs.

## 10. Looking ahead – The changing role of the public sector for achieving a pro-poor and pro-environment commodity agenda

There are two major trends in the role of the public sector in any pro-poor or pro-environment policy agenda. The first is the reduction of the role of government and the resources available to government in almost every country. The second is the increasing focus on security and terrorism. While eradicating poverty is considered somewhat important as a strategy for reducing the number of potential terrorists, little money is being spent on it. Environment is nowhere to be found in the new counter-terrorism strategies of developed countries.

What, then, are the trends of government with regard to commodity food production? Simply put, less of everything. Here are a few examples of the implications:
- Fewer regulations for agriculture and less funding for the monitoring and/or enforcement of existing environmental laws and performance standards.
- Less funding for agricultural research and extension.
- Less funding for residue and product testing and a shifting of responsibility (and cost) to the producer or producer country. This is also being privatized (and becoming a cost of doing business) through HACCP or Eurepgap. Producer countries are required to show traceability.
- Decentralization of power to lower units of government where local élites often have interests in agriculture and natural-resource exploitation. This often produces neither pro-poor or pro-environment results.

## 10.1 Licence to operate

Agricultural production does not take place in a vacuum. This is especially true for commodity production. Scale and capital investment are important. Governments, neighbours, society at large, NGOs and even food manufacturers and retailers have an interest in the impacts of farming. The pressures that these groups can bring on farming have been referred to as the 'licence to operate.' This licence to operate is changing. Here are a few recent changes:
- In the past, producers were required to obey the law (though it was not always enforced). This has shifted to obeying the law in the consumer country. This is a result of private-sector initiatives, testing, and countries' ability to require of other producers what they require of their own.
- In the past, the goal was to do no harm or to produce with no net loss. This was driven by NGOs, local government and buyers. Today this is shifting to doing good and performing 'beyond compliance.' Even the International Finance Corporation (IFC) of the World Bank requires its borrowers to go beyond just obeying the law.
- In developing countries, cheap food for cities may well be the most important issue in food companies' licence to operate. While this may lead to a flood of imports and displace local farmers, governments may see it as preferable to food riots or the strengthening of urban-based political opposition. WTO decisions may encourage this trend by reducing protection.
- There is also a shift in emphasis from scale *or* equity to scale *and* equity. In the past, it was accepted that it was impossible to achieve both. Today, it is increasingly required to achieve equity as well as produce at a scale that makes one competitive on global markets. Some experiments suggest that both can be achieved through worker equity programmes (employee stock option plans - ESOPs); joint ventures between investors, producers, food manufacturers and retailers; and worker incentive programmes. Brazil has more of these experiments under way in agriculture than any other country. They can be found in sugar, fruit concentrate, palm oil, forestry, mixed rotation farms (maize,

Chapter 6 | **Commodities, Trade and Sustainable Development**

soya, cotton) and coffee. In each of these cases, workers not only earn wages, they also receive bonuses or equity.

## 11. The increasing role of the private sector and its implications

The last 20 years have been marked by a number of interesting trends. These include reductions in the budgets of most governments for agriculture, the reduced role of government in product inspection and testing, and now the increasing pull-out of subsidy programmes, first in developing and now finally in developed countries. The private sector is filling this void in a number of ways. There are, first of all, the Eurepgap-type programmes described above, where the private sector is certifying production processes and product origins, to ensure compliance with laws. There are also programmes where companies are attempting to reduce the social and environmental impacts of the production of specific commodities. This is being done out of financial opportunity, corporate responsibility, market position, consumer demand, or a combination of the above. Finally, there are eco-label and certification programmes that are voluntary in nature yet where the private sector is attempting to exert pressure over the entire production chain.

### 11.1 Better Management Practices (BMPs) and commodity production

Perhaps no private-sector initiative is more at the heart of sustainable commodity production than the adoption of BMPs. Many companies are involved in the identification, analysis, adaptation and adoption of BMPs to reduce the impacts of commodity production. In most cases, the companies are looking for win-win situations where producers and others can all benefit from BMPs through increased efficiency and profitability. BMP-based investor, buyer and government screens are being created for key commodities to send mutually reinforcing signals to producers. While few BMPs are scale-neutral, there are BMPs for every type of producer. Here are a few of the issues raised. BMPs:
- are different for different crops. There is no one-size-fits-all approach that will work. There is still much to be learned across commodities.
- improve product quality, reduce risks and residues, and increase overall efficiency.
- reduce environmental and social impacts (e.g. soil degradation, input use and waste, while increasing productivity, worker income and profits).
- pay for themselves within two to three years, some more quickly. The BMPs that do not pay for themselves can be sequenced so as not to put financial pressure on producers.
- are not always immediately bankable, so short-term financial lending may be required during an initial transition until banks see that they are profitable.
- social BMPs are probably the least understood but have the greatest potential (e.g. education, worker incentives, ESOPs, equity, and working with neighbours and local communities).

Producers create most BMPs to solve problems. One way to encourage the development of BMPs is to set rigorous yet achievable standards and let producers find their own ways to achieve them. Instead, many programmes tell producers how to farm. They tell them what to think, not how to think. This undermines innovation.

## 11.2 The limitations of eco-labels to commodity production

Most eco-labels and fair trade certification programmes have tried to create parallel marketing chains which pay a premium that supports the environment and producers. Eco-labels are intended primarily to create markets for differentiated products rather than be applicable to commercial commodity production on a large scale. In short, they create niche markets. From a commodity point of view, most eco-labels are sticking plasters. The most important way to change commodity production would be to develop certification programmes that are measurable and within the grasp of a far larger share of producers. The private sector needs to drive these for them to have widespread uptake, unless the programmes actually increase net profits to producers. To be credible, programmes must measure and demonstrate results against baseline performance. Finally, to be financially sustainable, certification systems need to be limited to monitoring and measuring the most significant impacts, rather than laundry lists of them.

Side-by-side comparisons of eco-label/certification programmes for the same commodity (e.g. shrimp, coffee or bananas) show most eco-labels to be subjective. The approach tends to be prescriptive – do this or don't do that. They do not measure performance or results, and they do not have baseline data against which to show improvement. As a consequence, few eco-labels can back up the marketing claims they make.

Organic is a good example. It is process-oriented and does not measure results. Natural chemicals are used instead of synthetic ones. Integrated pest management, tillage and mulching are used instead of pesticides. But what are the results? Organic production can produce as much soil erosion as conventional agriculture and more than no-tillage agriculture. Organic agriculture uses water less efficiently than well-managed conventional farms. Finally, the natural chemicals used in organic agriculture (e.g. copper, sulphur, nicotine and rotenone) can be far more toxic to the environment and biodiversity than many synthetic chemicals used in conventional agriculture.

Why are these issues important? Because we need to compare different production standards on the same grounds. In a recent WWF project to reduce toxicity of potato production in Wisconsin, most organic growers could not be certified because they were too toxic. And, while only 5 per cent of producers in the state were certified, in only three years total toxicity was reduced by 50 per cent in the state and the number of producers using class 1 or 2 chemicals was reduced from 35 per cent to less than 2 per cent.

Organic agriculture as it is currently promoted cannot move conventional producers step by step to more sustainable practices. Moreover, organic certification tells producers what to do or not to do rather than identify standards and let producers find ways to achieve them. A recent study on PCB and dioxin contamination in farmed salmon in Canada showed that the organic farmed salmon had far higher levels of contaminants than other farmed or wild salmon. This is related to organic standards that accept trimmings and waste from wild fish as sources of feed. While using waste is laudable, it is not acceptable in global trading systems where such waste is known to store the bio-accumulated toxins from pollution in the natural environment.

Fair trade does not address environmental impacts directly, though certification is often linked to organic or other environmental standards. In addition, fair trade is not fair for everyone, only for small-scale producers. While this may or may not be a laudable goal, it is not going to change most commodity production systems and the myriad of people who depend on them. It may be possible to better address poverty through equity-based programmes rather than small-farmer programmes.

## 12. Problem areas with commodity production and sustainable development

A number of problematic areas have been identified in this paper with regard to commodity production and sustainable development. A few important issues, however, do not fit in the outline of this paper. They are addressed here.

### 12.1 The focus on commodities has not been particularly balanced or thoughtful

To date, the social and poverty-alleviation focus has been more on structural and macro issues, while the environmental focus has been on micro, farm-level issues. Either approach, by itself, misses key problems and opportunities.

On the environmental side, much of the focus has been on reducing impacts of individual producers. Those problems can be fixed without addressing the larger cumulative impact or carrying-capacity issues. It is now clear that the production of commodities can have aggregate impacts on biodiversity and eco-system functions. For example, the expansion of coffee (Vietnam, Sulawesi, Central Africa and most recently in Myanmar), cocoa (West and Central Africa, Sulawesi and most recently Vietnam), soya (Brazil, Paraguay and Bolivia) and palm oil (Malaysia, Indonesia, New Guinea and parts of Central and South America) can reduce biodiversity and eco-system functions.

Does paying a fair-trade price for coffee change market structures or simply act as a price guarantee? Does paying a fair-trade price address a fundamental issue such as overproduction? In fact, does a fair trade price actually encourage more planting of coffee by fair-trade producers?

Globalization is likely to increase production in a number of commodities (e.g. sugar, cotton, soya, corn/maize, dairy) and more than likely cause international prices to decline even more sharply. This could have negative implications for poverty and hunger.

A business case analysis suggests that many of the more marginal lands (e.g. steep slopes, riparian areas and watersheds) are not profitable to farm even in the short term.

The most effective regulations might be those that are based on a good business case where there is self-interest to do it right. However, many of the more marginal areas are farmed by resource-poor farmers who have little choice. Evidence around the world suggests that the greatest impacts per hectare of production of commodities come from small-scale producers who cannot afford better land or better practices.

## 12.2 Value of strategic alliances and partnerships

No single stakeholder group or set of government or private-sector policies will make the international commodity system significantly better. Commodity markets involve many players, and if the goal is to use the market to make commodity production more sustainable then many different actors in the marketing chain will need to be involved. Several groups are attempting to bring different players together for coffee (e.g. producers, traders, NGOs, food manufacturers and retailers). There are similar groups working on cotton (e.g. groups led by the Organic Cotton Exchange, Oxfam and WWF). The IFC and WWF-US are bringing together producers, buyers, manufacturers and retailers to explore using BMP-based screens to reduce impacts of producing such commodities as soya, sugar and cotton. WWF, NACA, FAO and the WB created the Shrimp Aquaculture and the Environment Programme to work with shrimp aquaculture producers to reduce the impacts of shrimp production. A similar programme is now being started by NGOs, producers, and researchers for salmon and bivalve aquaculture.

## 12.3 Most agricultural poverty-alleviation programmes are actually poverty-maintenance programmes

There is no entitlement to farm and there will be fewer farmers each year. The poorest of the poor in rural and urban areas do not own land. There is a need to shift our emphasis from small-farmer and poverty-alleviation programmes to viable scale and equity programmes. There are a number of new ways to address equity issues that are also scaled up to work in most commodity markets. They need to be better understood. These include ESOPs (employee stock option plans or worker-owned businesses) and joint ventures for production, value-added manufacturing, processing and marketing. We need to identify, adapt and extend to new areas the different ways that are being used to address equity issues around the world. We need to be learning rather than reinventing.

## 12.4 Producing food in the future will be about managing change and how to think, not what to think

No matter what the competition or the price trends are today, they will worsen in the future as a result of globalization. Given the reduction of price supports, trade barriers etc., the tendency will be for producers to cut corners. Most of the corners cut will be those that are least regulated. Those producers who learn faster will survive. Production efficiency strategies, BMPs, new crops etc. take some time to disseminate globally. Even under the best of conditions it can take eight years or more to disseminate BMPs unless they are patented information and a company is disseminating the technology to make money, e.g. Roundup Ready soya.

## 13. The way forward

Here are a few thoughts on moving the commodity and sustainable development agenda forward.

***Be strategic. Not all crops or impacts are equal.***

One needs to choose the crop carefully depending on the geographical focus, whether the goal is to reduce poverty, hunger or environmental or social impacts, or some combination of these. Some crops lend themselves to poverty strategies (e.g. perennial crops in the tropics that are labour-intensive and don't lend themselves to mechanization, such as coffee, cocoa, fruit crops, palm oil and rubber; annual, horticultural crops that are labour-intensive, e.g. fruit and vegetables; and organic or other crops where labour is substituted for other inputs). In general, perennial crops tend to have fewer environmental impacts, tend to be less easily mechanized, and tend to longer investment periods that discourage larger, more capital-sensitive investors. For all those reasons they tend to be ideal for long-term poverty reduction strategies.

***Focus on how to think, not what to think.***

Don't be prescriptive and give producers solutions. Instead, help them understand how to solve problems and innovate. Work with producers to help them understand better management practices and continuous improvement. After all, today's BMP will be tomorrow's norm, and the day after that the obsolete practice we are trying to get rid of. Finally, each producer has access to different resources and the optimal combination will be different for each of them as well as for each crop.

***Work with farmers to reduce impacts and increase profits.***

The overall goal is to make sure that farmers can still be financially viable in 25–50 years because they are adopting and using sustainable production practices. To do this, they will need to use inputs more efficiently. They will need to find ways to sell waste or use it to reduce input costs. Everything about survival in more open, competitive commodity markets in the future will be about efficiency.

***Use the power of the market system to change it.***

Focus on producers, key market-chain players and governments. The goal should be to develop longer-term partnerships that reduce risks and costs throughout the chain, using both carrot and stick incentives. In all likelihood, profits will have to be found within the current price structure rather than by obtaining price premiums.

*Focus on one commodity at a time.*

Agriculture does not have impacts: specific commodities do. Agriculture is not traded on local or international markets, specific commodities are. We need to target key commodities, and then identify those stakeholders who have the largest interest in sustainable production of them to ensure that production can continue indefinitely. This includes producers, society, government, buyers, manufacturers, retailers and investors.

*Farming isn't an entitlement.*

Many if not most small-farm development strategies are more about poverty maintenance than poverty alleviation. Globally the trend is for fewer, more productive, larger farms. Bucking this trend will be difficult if not impossible. That being said, however, it is not impossible to find both scale and equity solutions. The largest sugar plantation in Brazil is owned by the workers, who have contracted with competent managers and turned a profit for eight years running. The largest passionfruit processing plant in the world is jointly owned by two producer cooperatives and a workers' union. The loans to buy the plant and provide working capital to it were provided by the Brazilian government, but a European bank was also prepared to provide the funding, working with the largest juice company in Europe and the third largest food retailer in the world.

*Focus on objective results, not subjective or prescriptive processes.*

Only a few key impacts are truly significant (e.g. environmental, social or price). Identify key impacts, establish baseline performance data, then identify acceptable performance levels for the future. Work with producers, key market-chain players and government regulators to encourage performance that exceeds compliance.

*Sustainable agriculture requires entrepreneurs.*

Agriculture is the largest inherited profession on the planet. It is also the profession that has the smallest percentage of new entrants. As a consequence, there is considerable room to bring new ideas, innovations and approaches to the sector. At present, EARTH University in Costa Rica is the only agricultural university in the world that requires each undergraduate to identify a business, write a business plan, borrow money at local interest levels, run the business, pay themselves a salary, and sell it out in order to graduate. Agriculture needs more job makers and fewer job takers.

## References

ARD, PREM and FRM (the World Bank), 2004, 'Exogenous Shocks in Low Income Countries: Policy Issues and the Role of the World Bank,' document prepared for a Technical Briefing to the Board, March 9.

Clay, J., 2004, *World Agriculture and the Environment,* Washington DC: Island Press.

Gillson, I., D. Green and S. Wiggins, 2004, 'Rethinking Commodities,' Working Paper for the Renewable Natural Resources and Agriculture Team, DFID Policy Division, June.

Thurow, R and J. Soloman, 2004, 'As Hunger Rises in Line with Food Production, India Shifts Its Strategy', *The Asian Wall Street Journal,* June 25-27, 2004.

Valdimarsson, G., 2004, 'A Future for Socially Responsible Aquaculture: A View from the FAO,' Talk given to AquaVision 2004, Stavanger, Norway.

# Chapter 7

# Commodity Policy in an Era of Liberalized Global Markets

Peter Gibbon[1]

## 1. Introduction

Classically, the 'commodity question' has been conceptualized as having two elements. The first was commodity price volatility. The second was decline in relative prices, an issue first raised by Prebisch and Singer in 1950, who both argued that volatility and relative price decline were linked, via reference to the notion of inelasticity in demand for commodities. The Prebisch-Singer analysis still forms the basis for most common under-

---

1. This chapter is a combined, edited and updated version of a paper from the Windsor dialogue in 2004, 'Commodities, Donors, Value-Chain Analysis and Upgrading,' and a paper from Barcelona in 2005, 'Market Power, Monopsony, and the Commodity Question.' The former was prepared for UNCTAD in 2003. The latter was a shortened version of a paper commissioned by UNDP, 'The Commodity Question: New thinking on old problems,' October 2004, and we thank Kevin Watkins and UNDP for permission to reproduce it. Thanks also go to Stefano Ponte and Frantzeska Papadopoulou-Zavalis for comments on an earlier draft. The usual caveats apply.

standings of the 'commodity question' today.[2] However, the last decade has seen a widespread acceptance that the question also includes a third element, namely oligopolistic market structures on the demand side. Concentration amongst Northern-based international traders, processors and retailers is today mentioned as a critical dimension of the commodity question not merely by producing countries' governments and concerned NGOs, but also by the World Bank[3] and the European Commission.[4]

This chapter reviews more and less mainstream policy options in relation to the commodity question in the light of both its classical definition and the emerging concern about oligopoly. It begins by updating the evidence concerning commodity price decline and volatility, and examining the implications for macro-economic performance and livelihoods in producing countries. It then turns to the issue of oligopoly, where it considers evidence on market concentration and monopsonistic behaviour. This is followed by a discussion of the main policy options in the area, which have received attention from international donors since the beginning of the 21st century. The chapter then turns to what might be called an 'alternative' policy agenda on commodities.

Throughout, the main focus is on a specific agro-commodity, namely coffee. This is because this product has been the subject of more recent documentation, analysis and policy proposals than any other. However not all agro-commodities resemble coffee, either in respect of historical forms of international market regulation or current market structure or relevant policy options. For this reason, a secondary focus on cotton is provided.

## 2. Declining prices and the management of international commodity trade

Agro-commodity prices were declining throughout the 20th century, but for most commodities this decline has accelerated in the wake of the collapse of International Commodity Agreements (ICAs). These years have also seen a gradual disengagement of donors from commodities. This development reflects changing geopolitical as well as economic conditions (see Section 6.1 below).

Under the agreements, recommended prices were established and defended, either on the basis of producing-country export quotas or centrally held buffer stocks. Price levels above the recommended price were achieved for most of the lives of the coffee and rubber agreements, and for around half the life of the cocoa and sugar ones. According to Hermann *et al.*,[5] at least one of the agreements (that for coffee) persistently raised

---

2. Prebisch (1950) and Singer (1950) argued that the decline in relative prices of commodities was structural, since demand for commodities was inelastic while demand for manufactures was elastic. Instability around a declining price curve was induced via the interaction of inelastic demand with a supply position that could be highly variable due to accidents of nature, as well as the tendency for price increases to generate over investment in producing countries.
3. Cf. Lewin *et al.* (2004).
4. European Commission (2004).
5. Hermann *et al.* (1993).

prices by 24 to 30 per cent over what otherwise would have been market-clearing levels. In any event, over the six years following the collapse of the ICAs for coffee and cocoa, international prices for these products fell between 60 and 65 per cent.[6]

**Table 1: Export prices of coffee and cocoa in the wake of the collapse of ICA and ICCA (1990 prices = 100)**

|  | Average price, final six years of agreement | Average price, first six years after collapse | Average price, second six years after collapse |
|---|---|---|---|
| Coffee (economic provisions ended 1988) | 182.3 | 109.8 | 145.3 |
| Cocoa (economic provisions ended 1989) | 151.7 | 98.6 | 103.7 |

Source: GATT/WTO, various

But the apparent success of the ICAs in pushing commodity prices higher became a source of tension between the two sets of parties to the Agreements. Consuming countries never wholly accepted that they should be used to defend long-term floor prices, let alone push prices higher, and as the 1980s unfolded the political reasons for their silence on this question disappeared. In addition there were problems in securing the agreement, or even participation, of all major supplying countries. Critical issues here were new players that had entered the market in order to exploit the price improvements attained as a result of the Agreements, and side-selling outside them by producer member countries.[7] According to Maizels[8] total volumes of world commodity exports increased by 40 per cent during the 1980s, despite a series of functioning export quota and buffer stock schemes. None of the agreements in question, except that for natural rubber, survived the end of the 1980s.

International prices for both coffee and cotton declined by over 50 per cent in real terms between 1982 and 2002, and in both cases have been recently at 30-year lows. Cotton, and particularly coffee, prices are also subject to high levels of volatility. Since the collapse of the International Coffee Agreement in 1988-89, coffee supply has increased substantially, mainly on the basis of new production in Brazil and Vietnam, while aggregate demand has changed little. In the case of cotton, which was never governed by an ICA, supply has been fairly stable but demand has contracted, as synthetic fibres have replaced natural ones in textile production.

The phenomenon of stable or increasing supply in the face of declining prices is

---

6. Gibbon & Ponte (2005).
7. Mshomba (2000), Gilbert (1996), Bates (1997).
8. Maizels (2000).

partly related to low costs of production in certain countries. In the case of coffee, Vietnam's production costs appear to be low enough to provide incentives to increase robusta output even at current prices. Meanwhile Brazilian coffee producers can now cultivate natural arabicas at lower cost than has been the case historically, through the adoption of new farming systems. In the case of cotton, producers in Brazil have again been able to cultivate profitably under current prices. Both coffee and cotton production in Brazil, and coffee in the important state farm sub-sector in Vietnam, are organized on the basis of large estates. Here, previously unattainable economies of scale in input use, irrigation, use of farm machinery and transport/marketing can all be now realized.

Although in this period intellectual recognition of the validity of the Prebisch-Singer thesis extended to the Bretton Woods institutions for the first time,[9] the 1980s also witnessed new analyses of commodities, focusing on possible negative effects of commodity price rises. One of these was the 'Dutch disease' thesis,[10] which argued that booms in a single large tradable sector impose heavy adjustment costs on other tradable sectors. This happens because resources are withdrawn from other tradable sectors, not only to feed the sector, which is booming, but also to support an induced growth of demand for non-tradables. Earnings brought in by the booming sector also induce a rise in real exchange rates, which in turn worsens the competitiveness of other tradable sectors. A second narrative questioned the capacity of developing countries' governments to correctly manage commodity price increases, with the dissipation of revenues in unproductive public spending. This narrative recommended that commodity price improvements were only likely to be managed properly in a context of trade and investment liberalization, in other words structural adjustment.

The second of these narratives was enthusiastically embraced by the Bretton Woods institutions, as well as the EU. In the cases of the IMF and the EU, there were practical motives for this embrace. Sharply falling commodity prices could lead to major resource drains from these institutions, through the Compensatory Finance Facility and STABEX, as a result both of increased eligibility for assistance and lower repayment rates. STABEX in particular threatened to distort EU lending generally. In 1990-91 the EU found itself committed to disburse €1.38 billion to eligible applicants, three times more than had been reserved for the purpose, with the consequence that it was able to pay out only 42 per cent of the sum due during the next three years. Even so, STABEX disbursements rose to 13 per cent of all EU aid under Lomé IV.[11] At the same time, repayment rates collapsed. The EU responded in the short term by converting existing STABEX loans to grants, but at the same time both it and the IMF linked further access to adjustment-style conditionalities.

Donors nonetheless continued to directly support commodity production in devel-

---

9. Cf. Sapsford & Singer (1998).
10. Corden & Neary (1982).
11. European Commission (1997), Page & Hewitt (2001). According to Collier *et al* (1998) STABEX transfers accounted for almost a quarter of total government revenue in Ethiopia and Uganda during some years of this period.

oping countries, in the context of adjustment programmes where attention was paid to diversification. According to Morgan & Sapsford[12] the multilateral development banks committed as much as 5 per cent of their loans in the second half of the 1980s to diversification projects, mostly from coffee, cocoa, rubber and palm oil. In Africa, 'good' adjusters such as Ghana and later Zimbabwe, Tanzania and Uganda were major beneficiaries of direct support to commodity production.[13] In some cases, notably cocoa in Ghana, support was so great that worries about possible 'adding-up problems' were voiced.[14]

Precipitous price decline has had particularly severe effects in countries characterized by smallholder production. In many of them, and against the expectations of the architects of market reform, costs to producers have risen with the liberalization of national input markets. Inputs are no longer purchased and distributed in bulk and public subsidies have been removed from their local prices. Meanwhile, smallholders' marketing costs have risen dramatically, with the abolition or disintegration of parastatal or large-scale co-operative export marketing organizations.

By the mid- to late-1990s a renewed policy debate on commodity prices had arisen. On one hand, most of the contributors to a special edition of *World Development*[15] favoured a revival of inter-governmental arrangements – if not a new generation of ICAs, then a uniform export tax levied by producing countries.[16] On the other, some World Bank economists advanced the notion of market-based 'price risk management' in developing countries.[17] Efforts by some producing countries to revive export quota-type arrangements have recurred, notably in the case of coffee,[18] but in the contemporary context it was fairly predictable that PRM would gain more favourable attention from donors.

## 3. Macro-economic effects

It is noteworthy that the countries most dependent on agro-commodities for export revenues are virtually all smallholder-based. In the late 1990s there were nine developing countries for which coffee represented 23 per cent or more of export earnings,[19] and five for which cotton represented 34 per cent or more.[20] In all but one of these 14, smallholder production dominates. At the same time, most of the largest exporters of

---

12. Morgan & Sapsford (1994).
13. Cf. Engberg-Pedersen *et al* (1996).
14. E.g. Toye (1991). 'Adding-up problems' refer to the impact of heavily supported agricultural export market liberalization on the terms of trade for primary commodities, when it occurs in several countries simultaneously.
15. Vol. 22, No. 11 (November 1994).
16. Cf., for example, Maizels (1994) and Schiff (1995). The idea seems to have been that such a tax would eliminate marginal producers and hence restrict global supply, pushing up prices.
17. Varangis & Larson (1996).
18. See Section 6.1 below.
19. Lewin *et al.* (2004).
20. Gillson *et al.* (2004).

these crops – particularly coffee – have been much less exposed to price decline. The share of coffee in total export earnings is only around 3 per cent in both Brazil and Vietnam, for example. In 1998-2002, 19 coffee-exporting countries were more macro-economically exposed to price declines than Vietnam, and 20 more exposed than Brazil.[21]

Humphrey points out that, as a result of their higher levels of commodity dependence, low-income (mostly smallholder-based) commodity-exporting countries are more likely than middle-income ones to experience price and terms-of-trade shocks.[22] Over the period 1981-2001, low-income countries were 13 per cent more likely to experience a price shock than other developing countries, but 60 per cent more likely to experience a terms-of-trade shock. Price-shock effects bear directly on GDP, while terms–of-trade effects bear on the balance of payments. Kruger et al. have calculated that for the five main coffee-producing countries of Central America as a group, the coffee price decline of 1999-2001 alone led to a 1.2 per cent drop in GDP, without taking into account multiplier effects.[23] Given the large size of the populations directly involved in agro-commodity production in low-income countries, the large proportion of these populations falling below the poverty line and the large multiplier effects of changes in income from these sources, it is clear that the price trends described have very substantial poverty impacts.[24]

## 4. Oligopoly and the distribution of rewards from the market

As noted earlier, there is a widespread awareness of oligopoly at the downstream end of agro-commodity chains. Sometimes this is loosely linked to the (declining) share of final prices going to producing countries or producers. Certain schools of thought seek to link these observations theoretically – notably 'global value chain' analysis, through the notion of 'buyer-drivenness.'[25]

Discussion of these issues is almost entirely absent in the case of cotton, however. Indeed, cotton is sometimes cited[26] as an exception to the rule. Levels of downstream industrial concentration in cotton spinning (and beyond) are very low and even the international trader segment exhibits only limited concentration. In 1995, as many as 19 international trading companies handled 200,000 tons of lint or more, jointly accounting for 35 per cent of the global trade. By 2004 the share of the leading 21 companies had increased, but not spectacularly, to 43 per cent.[27] Other dimensions of buyer-drivenness, such as changes in the division of labour along the chain and new definitions of quality, are only faintly evident. No studies of shares of final prices going to producers

---

21. Lewin *et al.* (2004).
22. Humphrey (2004), citing IMF data.
23. Kruger *et al.* (2003).
24. Deininger & Okidi (2003); Kruger *et al.* (2003); Minot & Daniels (2002).
25. E.g. Gibbon & Ponte (2005).
26. Including by Gibbon & Ponte (2005).
27. Larsen (2004); ICAC (2005).

appear to have been carried out, presumably because of the difficulty in deciding what constitutes the final product.

In more buyer-driven commodity chains, rewards have become skewed towards lead agents. Coffee seems to have witnessed the most radical change. Osorio[28] states that in 1992, producing countries' sales were worth $10 billion, in relation to global retail sales of coffee worth $30 billion. In 2002 the respective figures were around $5.5 billion and $70 billion.[29] Besides buyer power, this redistribution reflected market saturation (production during the period increased by 3.6 per cent per year and demand by only 1.0 to 1.5 per cent[30]) and new forms of product differentiation – the 'latte revolution.'

Up-to-date information is hard to come buy, but in 1998 the largest five coffee roasters (Philip Morris, Nestlé, Sara Lee, Proctor & Gamble and Tchibo) controlled 69 per cent of the world market, while the largest eight international trading companies (Neumann, Volcafé, Cargill, Esteve, Aron, Man, Dreyfus and Mitsubishi) controlled 56 per cent.[31] More recent studies of western European markets suggest even higher levels of roaster concentration in several countries.[32] Studies of shares of retail prices of roasted coffee going to producing countries are also quite common. The observations are widely dispersed but the trend they depict is consistent, namely a sharp decline since the 1990s. The median value for all observations from 1989-98 is 35 per cent, while that for the period since 1999 is 19 per cent. A much smaller number of observations for farmgate price-retail ratios also show a declining trend since the 1990s.[33]

While these observations give anecdotal support to the hypothesis of oligopoly power, most leave open the question whether this power is located with roasters or downstream of them. Daviron & Ponte's detailed price data suggest that both roasters and coffee-house chains (though not retailers) possess the power to inflate their mark-ups. Gross mark-ups by roasters over the c.i.f. price are in a range of 81 to 89 per cent of the ex-roaster price, whether they are selling on to retailers or to coffee houses. Gross mark-ups by retailers are in a range of 20 to 25 per cent of the retail price, which is low in comparison with other food product lines. Gross mark-ups by coffee houses are in a range of 70 to 80 per cent of the coffee house price.[34] This seems counter-intuitive since levels of concentration in the food retail sector tend to be on a par with the roaster sector, while ownership of coffee houses is much more dispersed. Part of the answer may lie in retailers' use of coffee as a loss leader.[35]

At least eight econometric studies of the coffee sector have been published in the last 20 years.[36] Only three of these studies provide support for the proposition of oligop-

---

28. Osorio (2002).
29. Oxfam (2002) gives the same figures for 1992 and figures of $6 billion and $60 billion for 2002.
30. Osorio (2002).
31. Van Dijk *et al.* (1998). In 2001 Philip Morris spun off Kraft Foods, which was the vehicle for its coffee interests.
32. Durevall (2003).
33. Talbot (1997); Fitter & Kaplinsky (2001); Strunning (2001); Lewin *et al.* (2004); Pelupessy (1999); Daviron & Ponte (2005).
34. Daviron & Ponte (2005).
35. Cf. Lewin *et al.* (2004).

olistic behaviour. Even these provide no analysis of how oligopoly power is used. In fact, perhaps the most promising argument in this regard is suggested in one of the more sceptical studies, which argues that green coffee price rises provide incentives to roasters to substitute coffee by type.[37] Thereby, margins remain constant as the spread between input and retail prices does not increase. By implication, if green coffee prices fall while revisions to blends are retained, margins can then increase.[38]

Lewin et al. disaggregate roasters' use of specific varieties of coffee, showing a steep decline between 1993 and 2002 in global consumption of the highest premium variety, Colombia milds. Consumption of the other variety historically commanding a premium, other milds, also fell. By contrast, robusta and natural (unwashed) arabica consumption increased. These changes indeed reflect roasters' substitution of inferior for superior varieties, made possible by the adoption of technologies such as steam cleaning.[39] This trend can be understood as roasters capturing some of the quality-based rent formerly extracted by producers.

While not excluding the possibility that active horizontal collusion or simultaneous but uncoordinated imposition of vertical pressures may have occurred, the process described above does not depend on them having done so. Furthermore, it points as much in the direction of recognizing the indirect effects of the demise of supply management as it does in that of demonstrating the effects of oligopoly. Substituting good- by poor-quality coffee while holding price levels steady or even increasing them was not simply 'technologically-led'. It would not have been possible without the end of the International Coffee Agreement's market intervention clauses, under which producing countries could control which varieties could appear in what volumes on the world market.

Meanwhile, amongst the producers, rewards have been redistributed in two ways. The first has occurred within the bulk or 'commercial' market, mainly for robustas and hard arabicas. According to Rabobank,[40] a division has opened up between 'anonymous' and 'non-anonymous' sales. The latter are mainly from large or very large grower-exporters, which can consistently supply high volumes, meet basic quality requirements or better, guarantee proper handling and provide efficient logistics. They can achieve reference prices and obtain medium- and longer-term purchasing commitments from traders. Because of their size and efficiency, their marketing costs are typically low. These producers typically achieve very high yields (around 300 per cent higher than under low-input systems, according to the World Bank[41]), from high-input, irrigated and mechanized farms in frost-free areas. By contrast, producers in the anonymous market

---

36. Roberts (1984), Bhuyan & Lopez (1997), Morriset, J. (1998), Bettendorf & Verhoven (2000), Feuerstein (2002), Koerner (2002), Durevall (2003) and Shepherd, B. (2004).
37. Koerner (2002).
38. This argument was suggested to me by Stefano Ponte.
39. Steam cleaning (subjecting the unroasted coffee bean to high-pressure steam) generates not only less harshness in robustas, but can eliminate some acidity from natural arabicas, to produce a milder taste.
40. Rabobank (2002).
41. World Bank (2002).

typically sell smaller volumes of somewhat inferior product through a series of intermediaries. Their production is lower-input and more weather-dependent, and has lower productivity. The prices they receive are below reference levels.

The new bifurcation between anonymous and non-anonymous sales rests also on national government interventions. Qualifying for the non-anonymous commercial and specialty markets is quite costly, and some subsidization by developing countries' governments is evident. This includes support for land clearing and infrastructure, as well as public research into tree varieties and pest control. Both Brazil and Vietnam subsidized the opening up of new production zones which today form the backbones of the national industries. According to Lewin *et al.*, the Brazilian government granted soft loans to coffee operators worth Real 800 million (ca. $260 million) in 2002/03 and 2003/04 alone, to finance stock retention, farm maintenance and crop husbandry.[42] These loans were rolled over in the wake of falling international prices, despite the fact that much Brazilian production is profitable at these levels. In addition, the Brazilian government absorbed the losses from a put-option scheme it had offered to large operators, when international prices fell below the value of the options.

Secondly, rewards have also been redistributed in the mild arabica market. Roasters and coffee houses have added new, largely immaterial, dimensions of quality, e.g. gourmet-ship, social and environmental welfare content and – in the case of coffee houses – new service dimensions including 'ambience.'[43] These designations are process-based rather than referring to physical characteristics of the crop. In the US the specialty market has grown annually by around 30 per cent since 1999; today it accounts for roughly 17 per cent of imports by value and 40 per cent of retail sales.[44] Since liberalization has led to an across-the-board decline in quality supply, the premiums available are considerable – especially as most sales into this market are direct ones, to specialized roasters lacking 'big buyer' bargaining power. Among coffees certified as conforming with the new private parameters of quality, Ponte cites average 2001-02 prices 100-120 per cent above the reference price for shade-grown, organic and fair-trade coffees.[45] Besides high premiums, this part of the market makes use of long-term contracts or understandings, in a few cases with multi-season prices.

To the extent that some producers supply both 'commercial' and specialty markets, participation in the latter is subsidized in the same way. But most exclusively specialty producers, if they are subsidized, only receive support from donors or NGOs to meet certification costs. What is not clear is the extent to which participation in the latter market would be possible without subsidies. In view of the costs of certification, quality monitoring and marketing, Ponte has questioned whether such markets can be remunerative for groups of smallholders that are not supported by wider programmes.[46]

---

42. Lewin *et al.* (2005).
43. Daviron & Ponte (2005).
44. Ponte (2002).
45. Ponte (2002).
46. Ponte (2002).

## 5. Present donor approaches

The most frequently encountered current policy approaches to the 'commodity problem' amongst OECD countries are *compensatory financing* mechanisms, assistance for *diversification, price risk management* instruments, and private or public-private commodity-specific initiatives, including those directed at promoting 'fairer', more responsible or simply more remunerative trade.

However, *compensatory finance* has been fully integrated into (conditionality-based) general contingency financing in the case of the IMF, and eliminated in the case of EU's STABEX. While it could clearly play a positive role in mitigating the effects of falling commodity prices, the levels paid out will have to be increased sharply if they are to have any impact.

The difficulties of agro-export *diversification*, particularly for many of the most commonly recommended products, are often underestimated. Smallholders' ability to diversify is often constrained by agro-ecological conditions and transaction costs. A further issue is that of 'adding up,' i.e. the terms-of-trade implications when several countries increase exports simultaneously. This may lead to a combination of increasing demand with stagnant prices, or falling prices if demand becomes stagnant.

*Price Risk Management* is only likely to be much use to very large producers. The World Bank launched in 1999 a (public-private) International Task Force on Commodity Risk Management in Developing Countries (ITF).[47] Its initial aim was to assist producing countries – particularly LDCs – to use futures markets. Futures markets have existed since the early 20th century for many commodities.[48] Historically they have been used mainly by international traders and some large producers to hedge risk. Speculators have always played a role in these markets, which has accentuated price movement but assured their liquidity.[49] Futures are legally binding contracts to buy (sell) specific volumes of specific commodities at a fixed price on a given day. A producer can use them to hedge his price risk over a season. Besides the removal of risk from adverse price changes, the main advantage to the producer is that he can sell his own physical crop as and when he pleases.

For reasons that have not been explicitly stated, conventional futures contracts have been displaced as the ITF's PRM instrument of choice by put options, price-insurance transactions and warehouse receipt-based finance – or rather, by a combination of these.[50] A put option is a type of contract similar to a futures one, but in this case the seller – instead of having an obligation to close the contract on day Y – can close it at *any time* prior to day Y. Opening a put option contract entails payment of a premium

---
47. This followed interest awoken by Varangis & Larson (1996).
48. See Cronon (1991) for an excellent discussion of the birth of these markets in the US.
49. A debate exists about how much the rise since 1980 of new classes of speculators (e.g. hedge funds) has contributed to price volatility in commodity futures markets. Mitchell & Gilbert (1997) concluded from a fairly detailed empirical study that the main impact of hedge fund activity has been to accelerate price movements, rather than add greater volatility. Pressures towards greater volatility have arisen too, but mainly smaller speculators' investment strategies.
50. Cf. the International Task Force's website, www.itf-commrisk.org.

by the seller to the buyer, over and above the cost of a conventional futures contract. Price-insurance transactions involve a speculative dimension mainly for the insurer. Warehouse-receipt credit is issued by a financial institution against the collateral of a given magnitude of crop stored in a supervised warehouse, or in some circumstances against the promise of delivery to a warehouse.

In the current thinking of the International Task Force, developing-country producers can engage in PRM through combining these three types of instrument, on the basis of interlocking arrangements with international traders and local credit institutions. As far as is known, after four years of preparation, the International Task Force was able to set up only two schemes of this kind, on a pilot basis and covering a total of a few thousand coffee producers in Uganda and Tanzania.[51]

Limitations associated with PRM in developing countries' agro-commodities have been widely noted,[52] but have not much dampened enthusiasm. They include the facts that not all commodities have derivative financial markets and that, in some cases such as cotton where they do, the contracts are only for one national variety;[53] that such markets only cater for price and not volume risk (which is arguably as great); that the maximum period they cover is rather short (a maximum of two years); that they cannot be used to hedge premiums and discounts on standard prices; that the costs of using them (in brokers' fees, collateral and – where applicable – premiums for non-standard contracts such as put options) are high and in most cases subject to very considerable economies of scale; that users need to be in daily contact with financial markets to make best use of them; and that they require high liquidity. Probably only very large, volume-secure, creditworthy and globally oriented producers will be able to make much use of such markets, in the absence of subsidies, technical assistance, donor-brokered financial intermediation or all three. Even players of this sort will benefit only by price discovery and reducing spot-market losses, rather than price increases. As for commodity price behaviour as such, these instruments are broadly neutral. Their role is to reduce the effects of price volatility for individual actors, rather than reduce volatility in aggregate.

Presumably, it was considerations concerning entry barriers and economies of scale, that led the World Bank in the direction of sold-on price insurance rather than first-hand futures trading when it came to smallholders. But whether even this model can work without subsidies to traders and credit institutions is unclear. Certainly, the transaction costs will be high and there seems no incentive for international traders or credit institutions to assume them for third parties without a subsidy. Moreover, the logical basis of price-risk insurance or put options for producers is not obvious. In a Rabobank study, carried out only a few months before this company became the executing agent for the World Bank's pilot schemes, smallholder price insurance was discussed with outright derision:

---

51. Rabobank (2003).
52. E.g. Maizels (1994 and 2000), UNCTAD (1998), Page & Hewitt (2001), Murphy (2002).
53. Only US cotton can be delivered against the New York futures contract. Some international traders have taken to hedging their non-US cottons by taking positions in the futures market, but this is a very imperfect hedge.

## Chapter 7 | Agricultural Commodities, Trade and Sustainable Development

'*Price risk insurance for producers is not an option. This...was done earlier by governments of some coffee producing countries, but in reality this was a subsidy when the price fell...one cannot insure a market price because one cannot guarantee a market price. No...mutual insurance can give such a guarantee without making the insurance premium equal to the insured deficit.*'[54]

That leaves initiatives aimed at the operation of private-sector trade. Although donors' recent support for *Private Sector Development* (PSD) and *Public-Private Partnership* (PPP) interventions in agriculture have been directed mainly towards higher value-added products, they have also increased for agro-commodities, including the promotion of more responsible and sometimes more remunerative trade. The latter are found particularly in relation to coffee. These interventions are divided more or less evenly between those initiated by private actors alone, and those backed by public agencies. The German bilateral technical assistance organization GTZ has been at the forefront of the latter.

Bilateral donors' PSD programmes have tended to promote links between enterprises and business associations in donor countries and others in partner countries, without any clear relation to overcoming structural problems in recipients' private sectors or reducing poverty. As for multilateral donors, PSD lending mainly takes the form of concessionary equity finance for enterprises, selected on commercial criteria, and conditionality-based adjustment lending to governments. Until very recently, the development – as opposed to business – outcomes were not used as a criterion for direct lending by bilaterals or by any of the development banks. Even the latter's internal evaluations have pointed out that their adjustment lending in support of PSD has been focused almost exclusively on privatization and legal reforms rather than institutional capacity or regulatory frameworks; frameworks for understanding or formulating 'pro-poor' enterprise reform have been generally absent.

Interventions directly bearing on agro-commodities, particularly by multilateral donors, have been afflicted by similar problems. There now appears to be a consensus, even within the World Bank's Rural Development Department, that, for all their defects, export marketing monopolies offered solutions to problems of input credit recovery and quality control which private market systems do not normally provide. Direct lending to private operators appears in some cases to have been associated with a heightening of competition. While this tends to give producers a higher share of the export price, in contexts of weak post-reform institutional development it also leads to a scramble for the crop and a degradation of quality, in turn leading to discounts on world prices. The only multilateral exception to this pattern is the Common Fund for Commodities, which has recently financed 'market development' projects in cocoa and cotton, presumably made necessary by post-adjustment market failure. Indeed such interventions account for the bulk of the CFC's current lending.[55]

During the 1980s and most of the 1990s, bilateral interventions were mainly in support of multilateral donors' efforts at privatization. Bilateral programmes with an

---

54. Rabobank (2002).
55. CFC (2003).

agro-commodity firm-level focus have been rare, but when they have occurred they sometimes departed in interesting ways from more typical bilateral activities. One such is Danida's Private Agricultural Sector Support programme in Tanzania,[56] aimed at supporting the growth of commercial farming and agribusinesses, typically of a size and capability below that eligible for funding from multilaterals.[57] A second is a series of PPPs initiated by GTZ, in the Nicaraguan cocoa and Vietnamese and Peruvian coffee sectors.[58] All three involve Northern companies, but not only German-owned ones. In Nicaragua and Vietnam, production quality is being upgraded with the direct involvement of roaster companies, through specialized extension provision and quality control. Kraft's German subsidiary, Jacobs, is developing (though not itself implementing) new quality standards and instruments for coffee. These three projects in some respects resemble CSR-type initiatives adopted elsewhere by certain lead firms in the coffee sector, usually in collaboration with NGOs. Amongst these are a similar project to the Vietnam one described above, undertaken by Douwe Egberts in Uganda, and projects in Guatemala, Bolivia, Peru and Honduras by Ahold Coffee Company that focus on product quality, labour conditions, social infrastructure and nature conservation.[59]

Interventions of this kind are unusual not only in their involvement of 'chain driver' firms, but in that they imply a level of supply-chain integration between lead firms and primary producers that is rather untypical in these sectors. However, how far the firms themselves see them as instruments for establishing relations with suppliers, as opposed to public relations exercises, is open to doubt. Ackermann, describing Jacobs' Peruvian project in the GTZ house journal Akzente Focus, writes:

*'Fair Trade (initiatives do) ... not offer ... much commercial competition (but) they do considerably tarnish the image of large traditional coffee importers and distributors like Jacobs who are vulnerable to being stigmatized as proponents of unfair trade structures... Is it only a coincidence that, at Jacobs ... PPP concepts are developed in the PR department? Other departments are far less concerned with them.'*[60]

The broad background to all such interventions is the rise over the last decade of new 'immaterial' conventions of coffee quality, already referred to. Amongst these is a sub-convention for 'sustainable' coffee. On the environment side, the two main dimensions originally stressed were the 'organic' and 'shade-grown'. Both were defined by the environmental movement. On the social side, the dimension initially stressed was 'fair trade' – as defined by international movements for social justice in explicitly anti-market terms, in terms of obligations on producers to be members of co-operatives and on buyers to supply credit and pay producers above-market prices.

Roasters, roaster/retailers and roaster/coffee-house chains have devised alternative sustainability standards, aimed more or less explicitly at deflecting these initiatives.

---

56. Danida (2003).
57. The programme mainly takes the form of assisting enterprises to develop feasibility studies, providing credit guarantees in support of commercial borrowing, and some minor participatory loans.
58. GTZ (2003a,b); Ackermann (2001).
59. See Rabobank (2002) for further details.
60. Ackermann (2001).

## Chapter 7 | Agricultural Commodities, Trade and Sustainable Development

Amongst the best known is Starbucks' proprietary 'Coffee and Farmer Equity Programme.' This grants certain suppliers 'strategic' status if they achieve a given level of performance, within a points system that rewards social responsibility, environmentally responsible coffee growing, and processing systems that conserve water and energy and recycle waste. This status gives purchasing priority over other offers at the same price, and (for those achieving especially high scores) a premium over the market price.[61] Other procurement-related schemes include that of Nestlé, in collaboration with the Sustainable Agriculture Initiative, an organization also backed by other large agro-processing companies including Danone and Unilever. SAI has called for a gradual internalization of environmental, social and infrastructure costs into the coffee commodity price.

A somewhat different proprietary scheme is 'Utz Kapeh,' devised by the Dutch roaster/retailer Ahold.[62] It focuses upon 'appropriate' use of pesticides, labour rights, education and health. Utz Kapeh is also subscribed to by other large European retailers, including Casino (France) and Safeway (UK – recently bought by Morrisons). It has a schedule of premiums over market price to reward conformity,[63] although they are only advisory and seem to be applied only in designated projects. The widest such initiative to date is the Common Code for the Coffee Community, supported by GTZ with Nestlé, Sara Lee, Tchibo, Kraft Foods, a number of NGOs and the IUF. Preparations for this Code began in 2002 and it was finalized in October 2004. It covers minimum wages, child labour, trade union rights and environmental standards on pesticides and water.[64]

Proprietary schemes such as these took off only after – and arguably in reaction to – initiatives like fair trade, which threatened non-subscribers with the reputation of *unfair* trade. Where such schemes entail real actions, most of them fall as obligations on producers, who get little in return beyond a somewhat greater security of contract. In most cases, they also have to bear certification costs. These initiatives are skewed heavily towards estate production, with little attention to smallholders. They also extend the general trend towards standards proliferation, which leaves producers facing escalating conformity costs and can leave consumers confused.

In summary, over the last half-century donor thinking and activity on commodities has broadly followed the pattern set by development aid generally. For a long period, Northern countries technically – and to some extent financially – underwrote the agro-commodity economy. Then they became disillusioned and directly contributed to its collapse. This has given way in the most recent period to a more pragmatic and varie-

---

61. In a pilot scheme this premium was $0.10 per pound, but later it was lowered to $0.01 per pound. For more details see Ponte (2004).
62. Ahold later began describing the scheme as a product of Guatemalan farmer organizations as well as itself. The enrolment of farmer organizations is a common feature of recent proprietary initiatives (Daviron & Ponte 2005).
63. $0.07 per pound for washed arabicas, but only when the average arabica price falls below $0.70 per pound. The recommended robusta premium is $60 per ton unwashed and $100 per ton washed, but again only when the market falls below $650 per ton.
64. *International Herald Tribune* (Paris: 11 September 2004).

gated approach, standing on three legs. Respectively, these point towards abandoning the ruins of the commodity economy (diversification), mitigating risk for some of its actors (PRM) and drawing corporate actors in to upgrade pockets of it (PSD/PPP). At first sight this resembles a coherent strategy – more coherent indeed than its predecessors. Further examination however reveals the first two of its legs as less promising, and the third as being undertaken for reasons that cast doubt on its generalizability. At the same time the third leg is potentially interesting because of the actors it involves and some of the issues it deals with.

## 6. An alternative agenda?

Renewed ICAs, global regulation of oligopolistic behaviour through competition law, elimination of subsidies to Northern producers of tropical crops, support to market coordination in producing countries and action on the demand side in the North are five of the main proposals for dealing with the commodity questions that have circulated in recent years on the fringes of the donor community, and amongst NGOs and more heterodox policy researchers. Given the unpromising nature of much of the mainstream agenda, and of the funding for its more promising components, it is important to evaluate these alternatives.

### 6.1 Renewed international commodity agreements

A proposal to revive the ICAs that governed trade in coffee, cocoa, sugar, tin and natural rubber between the 1960s and the 1980s has been made by Oxfam, amongst others.[65] These Agreements arose originally against the background of a broad (though not universal[66]) consensus that action was necessary in relation to the long-term decline in the barter terms of trade of primary commodities relative to manufactures. GATT waivers for such agreements were obtained in the mid-1950s and their establishment was UNCTAD's *cause célèbre* for the first two decades of its existence.[67]

Two questions raised by the proposal to revive ICAs are whether consuming countries would sign up to them, and whether producing countries still could operate export quotas. A third question concerns the relationship today between export-quota schemes and the coffee price. Consuming countries have evinced little interest in the proposal, since the grounds have largely disappeared on which they accepted the original ICAs. These rested in the short term on fears about vulnerability to economic blackmail by 'strategic commodity producers,' against the background of concerns about the finite nature of global supplies. In the longer term, they reflected fears of a link between this

---
65. Oxfam (2002).
66. The IMF never accepted that there were grounds for their existence, even though it created a finance facility to help member governments pay their subscriptions.
67. In 1980 agreement was finally reached on creating the Common Fund for Commodities, whose main task was envisaged as acting as a central financing facility for further ICAs (although it never acted as this).

possibility and a political realignment of developing countries behind the USSR.[68] Today, only hydrocarbons are considered of strategic significance or subject to concerns about finite supply; developed countries' concerns about other commodities have been undermined by substitution. At the same time, with the end of the Cold War, no systematic political realignment of developing countries is considered likely.

As for producing countries, a revolution has occurred in the wake of structural adjustment. The national marketing boards and export monopolies that previously coordinated input credit and distribution, quality control and export sales, have been liquidated or privatized. Most national supply markets are relatively competitive and some are extremely so. Except in a handful of cases, little or no coordination exists or – in the absence of a strong policy initiative in this direction – even seems possible. If there is no national market coordination, then there can be no meaningful national commitments to action in the context of new ICAs.

These problems are clearly visible in recent attempts in the coffee sector to re-launch looser or more indirect forms of international agreement. The Association of Coffee Producing Countries, formed in 1990, introduced a voluntary quota programme. This had some apparent initial success but in 1999 had to be renegotiated as Brazil radically exceeded its quota. It was later abandoned. In 2001-02 the ICO introduced the Coffee Quality Improvement Programme, aimed at taking very low-quality coffee out of the international market. Nevertheless, by 2003, 23 countries had taken steps to implement the programme. Of a total of 127.5m bags on the market that year (97.3 m new production and 30.2m in opening stocks) – and in a context of a demand level of 110.7m bags – the CQP managed to retire 3.5m to 4m bags. This represented 21 to 24 per cent of surplus production, and prices began to rise.[69] The extent to which the CQP contributed to this is unclear. Certainly, its achievements did not convince the ICO's members that the benefits of its continuation outweighed securing the US's readmission to the organization, when the latter insisted upon the voluntarization of the CQP as a condition of its joining.

## 6.2 Global regulation of oligopolistic behaviour

Over the last few years both development NGOs and policy researchers have raised the possibility of using competition/antitrust regulation to address certain trade problems facing developing countries. This has encompassed claims that multilateral competition regulation could and should be used to tackle 'the exercise of monopsony power by multinational buyers' of agricultural commodities such as coffee and cocoa.[70] Hoekman & Mavroidis's contribution to this debate is broadly typical: insofar as the modalities of such a use of competition regulation are specified at all, it is in terms of institutional and political prerequisites rather than economic and legal ones. These authors focus on

---

68. Krasner (1973); Payer (1975).
69. ICO (2003).
70. Hoekman & Mavroidis (2002).

what changes to secure within the WTO in order to advance an international antitrust agenda, rather than developing economic criteria for identifying the exercise of monopsony power or exploring legal reasoning that could serve as a basis for action in relation to it. Until this occurs it is likely that this attractive proposal will remain a non-starter.

Economic criteria (and measurement methods) are available to identify the exercise of monopoly/monopsony power.[71] The use of these in relation to agro-commodity monopsonies is hampered by the absence of critical data series, but this is not an insuperable obstacle. A wider question is the relation between demonstrating anti-competitive outcomes and winning legal judgements over them. This may be less of an issue if the WTO were to administer global antitrust regulation, since it has recently taken to using econometric evidence within the dispute settlement mechanism. But such evidence is used only infrequently in national antitrust laws, which appear to be based mainly on observed evidence about actions by individual firms, rather than the structural characteristics of markets – particularly in the EU. Asymmetry of power between product suppliers and processors, with behaviour by processors that is more opportunistic than collusive, is difficult to frame as an issue within these legal traditions.

Papadopoulou-Zavalis lists the main provisions of EU competition law as prohibitions against a menu of actions undertaken on the basis of collusion between firms, against a similar range of actions taken by a single firm enjoying a 'dominant market position', and against mergers likely to lead to the creation of a dominant market position by a single firm.[72] In the first two cases, the main actions prohibited in relation to suppliers are fixing purchasing prices, fixing physical quotas for specific suppliers, fixing price disparities between different supply markets and fixing trading conditions, including payment and credit terms. The frame of reference is national or regional consumption markets. To be relevant to global agro-commodity trade, this would have to be widened to the global market (raising the issue of how this might occur). Once this is done, there remains the issue of evidence of abuse. While there is widespread anecdotal evidence of the presence of at least some of these actions in global agro-commodity markets, legally firm evidence of them is hard to come by. Even if it is produced, it has to be demonstrated that the action was exceptional in relation to existing market norms. As for actions undertaken by firms acting alone, they can only be considered if there is clear evidence that a dominant market position is occupied. In EU law this is deemed a reasonable 'presumption' only where the firm's market share is 75 per cent or higher. A share of 40-50 per cent is 'strong evidence', but needs complementary data.

Under the 'rule of reason' doctrine, US law can also consider levels of competition in relation to consumer interest and wider welfare outcomes. However, this doctrine appears to be employed more frequently to permit certain types of action that might otherwise be considered anti-competitive, than to widen the range of actions that could be considered illegal.

---
71. Price transmission trends, levels of entry and exit within a given sector, and degree of own-label market penetration.
72. Papadopoulou-Zavalis (2004).

A final problem concerns remedies. The most usual under existing law are fines collected by national authorities from companies found to have acted abusively. In the case of proposed mergers that can lead to a dominant market position, the most usual remedy is prohibition of the merger or (more frequently) actions ordered to dilute its effects. While there are possibilities to order restitution or compensation for collusion between firms and abuse of dominant market position, these have been employed only rarely. The question is how developing countries' producers could benefit from these remedies, other than through deterrent effects.

Given this range of difficulties, it is worth asking whether some of the desired outcomes of global competition law might be achieved by other means. If the problem is not market concentration as such, but opportunistic behaviour in situations of market concentration, then another option may be to directly regulate opportunism. One way would be via corporate transparency requirements. In coffee, opportunism takes the form of substitution of coffee varieties, disguised through steam cleaning; roasters could be obliged to label the final blend with its precise varietal composition and declare whether any coffee in the blend was steam-cleaned. Legally, these requirements would have a similar status to those in the EU requiring labelling of products with GM ingredients. Of course, this is unlikely to have the same implications for processors as requirements for GM labelling, at least in the short term. This is a result of low public awareness of differences between types of coffee. Product differentiation in the coffee-house segment has been largely on the basis of different types of coffee drink (espresso, latte, macchiato etc) rather than bean variety.[73] For transparency requirements to have any impact, they must be linked to actions on the demand side.

## 6.3 Elimination of subsidies to Northern producers of tropical crops

In April 2004 Brazil won a landmark case on cotton subsidies against the US at the WTO. This will hopefully open the door for a case against the EU, where subsidies on a unit basis are around three times those of the US, although the US's aggregate subsidy was $2.3 billion in 2001/02 as opposed to $700 million in the EU.[74] Gillson et al. reviewed six studies carried out between 2001 and 2003, estimating the effects of the removal of all cotton subsidies on world prices.[75] All predict increases in world prices, at a median level of around 13 per cent. Gillson *et al*'s own estimation is an increase of 28 per cent. The range of estimates is equivalent to an increase of income for all developing-country suppliers between $600 million and $3.3 billion, and for West and Central African countries alone between $90 million and $400 million. This represents an increase in income from cotton of between 9.8 per cent and 37.4 per cent of their 2002 export earnings.

Cotton is a unique case, both because of the high level of Northern subsidies and

---
73. As Daviron & Ponte (2005) point out, these drinks all use commodity robusta as a base.
74. ICAC (2000).
75. Gillson et al. (2004).

because (unlike sugar) no developing countries benefit indirectly from those subsidies. Since it is significant for the livelihoods of so many developing-country producers, particularly in Africa, the elimination of subsidies for this crop must be stressed in any policy agenda for agro-commodities. In their 2003 proposal to the WTO for an initiative on cotton, 16 West and Central African countries described the elimination of cotton subsidies as their 'only specific interest' in the Doha Round. Because the removal of subsidies is likely to make virtually all EU and much US cotton unviable, there will be a political temptation to re-introduce support in new guises. Arguably therefore, long-term conformity to the WTO rulings is best secured by accompanying them with other, more radical measures. If interim compensation of developing-country cotton producers is accepted as part of an eventual Doha Round agreement (as under the West and Central African initiative), then a parallel scheme to buy Northern producers of cotton out of cotton production once and for all could represent the long-term remedy most easily saleable in the North.

It is also important to address subsidies to Southern producers. The bulk of these are paid out in better-off developing countries and result in loss of export earnings in low-income countries. China is a major user of cotton subsidies and Mexico a significant one. Direct support to producers is also provided by Brazil and Egypt.[76] As we have seen, a similar picture applies in the case of coffee.

## 6.4 Market coordination and smallholders' compliance with product standards

Three public goods are significant for smallholder production of coffee and cotton: input credit, quality control and producer payment systems reflecting quality. Prior to liberalization, most public marketing institutions supplied at least the first two, though usually in costly, inefficient and often corrupt ways. Where the third was not provided, typically another public good (e.g. inter-seasonal price stabilization) was provided instead. Input credit is critical because smallholders typically lack the means to purchase the inputs necessary for good quality, at the stage of production when they are needed. Quality-control systems were (and usually remain) critical because crop is marketed according to reputation. Producer payment systems reflecting quality are critical because they provide incentives to internalize quality needs in production processes. There are good reasons why such public goods often cease to be supplied in liberalized markets. Input credit is not supplied because smallholders have the freedom to sell to whom they please, regardless of who gave them credit. Quality control breaks down because private operators believe that, if they reject crop on quality grounds, smallholders will sell to those operators making no such demands. Payment systems reflecting quality also break down in consequence.

In reaction to the breakdown of quality-conformity systems in producing countries, international traders have often turned to tighter vertical integration. In the case

---

76. Valderrama (1999).

of coffee this typically means buying from estates, which can be considered insulated from the prevailing market chaos and enjoy economies of scale in meeting new quality conventions. In the case of cotton, where large producers are often absent, it takes the form of outgrower schemes. Both trends pose the issue of keeping smallholders 'in the system,' but in different ways. In the case of cotton, smallholders will be kept in the system provided that buyers can find ways of competing, which provide producers with incentives to increase acreages and improve yields and quality. The alternative is decline of national reputation and marginalization in the global market. In the case of coffee, smallholders will only *get back into* the system if ways can be found to reduce their costs of quality conformity.

Both Larsen and Poulton *et al.* argue that cotton systems with the characteristics described emerge most clearly after liberalization where the market is dominated by a handful of relatively large players who agree to compete on the basis of a near-formal set of rules.[77] They identify such systems as present in Zimbabwe (prior to 2002) and Zambia, but absent in four other southern and eastern African countries. Donors' technical assistance can help such forms of market coordination to emerge, although a problem is to develop institutional mechanisms, which will be credible with private stakeholders. This has not been the case with a number of the initiatives sponsored by the multilateral CFC, which appear to be mainly dedicated to reviving state-led sector coordination.

In the coffee sector the most notable initiatives to simplify smallholder conformity with new product standards are found in organic certification. Here the international organic movement's umbrella body, IFOAM, has designed certification process based on internal control systems. These involve the training and use of these organizations' internal auditors and inspection of their members by international certifiers on a sample basis. Recognition of the equivalence of such certification processes is still patchy amongst Northern import authorities; however, and more importantly, their implementation assumes the existence of well functioning and well resourced smallholder organizations (or a new producer organization put in place by an exporter). This suggests that assisting smallholder organizations to become better organized is a condition of other actions. The central issue is whether it can be done without donor support. Meanwhile, outside the organic sub-sector there are few or no generic systems providing alternative mechanisms for attaining conformity, only disconnected projects. This reflects the often proprietary nature of the quality conventions they refer to.

### 6.5 Actions on the demand side in Northern countries

The importance of action on the demand side in the North has been emphasized by Daviron & Ponte in the case of coffee. As already noted, effective action requires the transparency of roasters' descriptions of the final product. According to these authors,

---

77. Larsen (2004); Poulton *et al.* (2004).

> 'The most problematic aspect (of the current situation) is that consumers do not know how to assess coffee quality. They simply do not have the knowledge and language to discern the many characteristics of coffee…(whereas) a consumer who knows how to discern the intrinsic qualities of coffee will look for particular kinds of coffee and be willing to pay more for them.'[78]

This resembles the situation in the wine sector in most Anglophone countries as recently as 20 years ago. Here, a 'wine bar culture' (which has now vanished in favour of a coffee-house one) provided the foundation for a generalization of knowledge concerning regional appellations and their properties, varieties of grape, the components of wine appearance and taste and which wines are best to drink with which foods – or without food. With support from the ICO, international NGOs and governments of producing countries, initiatives to 'deepen' coffee consumption offer promise.

On the other hand, initiatives to broaden coffee consumption appear to be also necessary. Overall consumption is declining in mature markets, especially amongst the young and in favour of soft drinks that require no preparation. Alcoholic drinks have become more popular amongst this age-group on the basis of a cross-over with soft drinks ('alco-pops') and there may be some mileage for the coffee industry exploring similar directions.

## 7. Conclusions and recommendations to donors

The conceptual formulation of the commodity question has changed somewhat in recent years, as have the policy instruments proposed to deal with it. The issue of oligopoly, once seen as a problem of producing countries (and their marketing boards), is now seen as a problem for them. The new elements of the mainstream policy agenda, PRM and PPPs, simply do not address this. Nor, it must be said, do they address another element of the question, which is more and more about smallholders. Large-estate commodity production has fared much better than smallholder production since structural adjustment, partly because estates alone now enjoy economies of scale. Also, many of the sources of advantage that smallholders once enjoyed – such as conventions of quality that rewarded land husbandry based on hand-cultivation and mixed cropping, as well as ability to exercise detailed control over labour – have evaporated. At the same time, countries with smallholder-based systems, because they are poorer and less economically diversified, have been more exposed to the commodity crisis than ones where large estates play the leading role.

Those elements of the mainstream agenda carried over from earlier periods, namely compensatory finance and support for diversification, remain relevant although there is room for improvement in their funding, focus and design. At the same time, there are some elements of the 'alternative' agenda, which are impractical and unrealistic. New ICAs and global competition law fall into this category. While new ways of regulating market power must be found, better places to look for them are interventions that scale-up the competitiveness and bargaining power of smallholders, target the market distor-

---

78. Daviron & Ponte (2005), Chapter 7.

Chapter 7 | **Agricultural Commodities, Trade and Sustainable Development**

tions which bolster the position of large-scale (including Northern) producers, and impose new obligations of transparency on global oligopolists.

New interventions on commodities would benefit from taking into account the following five issues.

1. Rebuilding local economies of scale is becoming a strategic issue because of the increasingly buyer-driven nature of global markets on one hand, and the fragmentation that has frequently followed market liberalization on the other. The central question is that of assuring forms of sector-wide organization that can balance producer incentives with the enhancement of public goods such as national quality reputations.

2. Analysis of coffee and cotton indicates that the recent emphasis on encouraging production for niche markets has been probably excessive. In the cotton-to-spinning chain there are no niche markets in the conventional sense of the word. Niche markets certainly exist in coffee but entry barriers are high and, because of this, smaller-scale production does not command an intrinsic competitive advantage in them. In any event, it is possible that the current steep rise in demand for specialty coffee in the North will flatten out, unless the 'latte revolution' is deepened in ways similar to those evident in the wine market between 1980 and 2000.[79]

3. Both co-operatives and large outgrower schemes embody dynamics of economic differentiation and therefore internal marginalization. Zimbabwe's highly praised Cottco input credit scheme, for example, has been shown to squeeze out smaller farmers over time.[80] If donors wish to remove constraints to credit, raise smallholder incomes, disseminate cropping technologies and market information, then they need to mitigate the differentiation dynamic in their assistance.

4. There is a need not only for donor coordination within producing countries but also for wider coordination, in relation to choice of partner countries. It seems probable that some traditional partner countries have too low levels of production or too irretrievably fragmented domestic supply markets to remain in the game, with or without interventions. Rehabilitating the coffee/cotton sectors of all current LDC suppliers, for example, would significantly increase market saturation, push down prices and place buyers in an even more powerful position than today.

5. Attention needs to be paid to international as well as national interventions. International interventions could include support for more marginal countries to withdraw altogether from the production of certain tropical export crops, in order to bring supply and demand closer. Other issues include action in relation to some recent Northern-derived entry barriers, principally the new generation of standards for specialty markets, and the cotton subsidies of developed countries which force otherwise competitive developing-country producers off the market.

It is also possible to address some mechanisms for developing countries to advance in coffee and cotton. In each case, both producing-country and international interven-

---

79. See Ponte (2002).
80. Larsen (2002).

tions will be sketched. We do not exclude possible relevance to other chains not discussed in this chapter.

*'Commercial' coffee*: **National interventions** should promote large-scale, efficient and productive smallholder organizations rather than large-scale farming. However, recent experience with smallholder co-operatives in Africa suggests that many governments are unable to resist using them for wider objectives (such as buying crop that private buyers cannot or will not buy). Thus, for such organizations to function in genuinely commercial ways it is necessary for their ownership to be partially privatized. Ideally, such partial privatization should involve a large local private player that has a track record of responsible behaviour with respect to issues like crop quality control, input credit and actions to improve output. Donors could provide technical assistance but there are no strong reasons why they should finance this (and even some why they should not). They could make their successful restructuring a condition of access to other kinds of support, such as:

- soft loans for input credit, financing of crop purchase and rehabilitation of processing or transport equipment;
- provision or rehabilitation, together with the national government, of roads and infrastructure;
- technical assistance for international marketing and development of research and extension.

Such interventions must be accompanied by **actions at the international level**, in particular ones aimed at addressing global market saturation. Donors could usefully consider a global fund to compensate countries for withdrawing from the coffee market. The criteria of eligibility could include likely future role in the world coffee market (degree of centrality/marginality), importance of coffee in the national economy, and national income level.

*Cotton*: **The national-level actions** described above for commercial coffee are also relevant to cotton. For cotton however volume and *national* reputation, rather than volume and basic quality, are key to triggering rewards. The actions described should be accompanied by others aimed at supporting sectoral coordination and, where necessary, rationalization. These could take the form of technical assistance to set up national coordinating mechanisms, with a minimum aim of properly enforcing traditional grading systems. They could borrow best practices from Zimbabwe or Zambia. However, Tanzania's unsuccessful attempts to replicate such experiences indicate that effective coordination is almost impossible where there are a large number of players, including many who are under-capitalized and have little long-term commitment to the sector. In such cases donors should consider supporting rationalization, offering smaller players compensation to withdraw in favour of other activities. Such a programme would entail donors contributing to a rationalization fund, as well as introducing minimum licensing requirements for new market entrants.

The international cotton market operates in a rather different way to coffee, with a more intermittent pattern of supply and lower ability on the part of buyers to take advantage of oversupply. A critical factor is that the world's largest exporter is a developed country granting high subsidies to its producers. **Action at the international level** should therefore pressure the US (and the EU) to eliminate their subsidies, via the WTO and other forums.

*Specialty coffee*: Again, **national interventions** should promote large-scale, efficient and productive smallholder organizations. Support to private outgrower schemes and contract farming should also be considered, since the unit resources required for this trade are much higher than in the case of commercial coffee, and some countries may only be able to enter it through such schemes. Support should include technical assistance for certification. Donors should consider contracting major global first-tier suppliers to provide 'supplier development' assistance. It would be useful if this could be provided through national organizations covering all producers in the sub-sector.

The most important **international action** by donors for specialty coffee is to simplify and rationalize standards. Donors could encourage standard setters to think of how their objectives could be met in less demanding ways, and encourage research to find less costly and more user-friendly methods for their verification. At the same time they could encourage the consolidation of proprietary standards (and accompanying supplier certification), so that producers could use satisfaction of one standard to access several clients. A second area of action could be of a 'market-deepening' kind, aimed at stimulating demand for specialty coffees in the North, especially Europe. This could include support to coffee competitions, with winners being provided with support for marketing, and support to training of journalists as 'coffee correspondents', who would be able to educate public taste in specialty coffee.

## References

Ackermann, U., 'A Bitter Business', *Akzente Fokus* at
  www.gtz.de/dokumenter/de/AKZ_2001_PPP/peru.pdf (2001).
Bates, R., Open-Economy Politics: The political economy of the world coffee trade (Princeton:
  University Press, 1997).
Bettendorf, L., & Verhoven, F., 'Incomplete Transmission of Coffee Bean Prices: Evidence from the
  Netherlands,' *European Review of Agricultural Economics*, Vol. 27, No. 1, pp. 1-16 (2000).
Bhuyen, S. & Lopez, R., 'Oligopoly Power in the Food and Tobacco Industries', *American Journal
  of Agricultural Economics*, Vol. 79, pp. 1035-43 (1997).
CFC, *Annual Report*, at www.cfc.org (Amsterdam: 2003).
Collier, P., Guillaumont, R., Guillaumont, S. & Gunning, J. 'Reforming the Stabex system,'
  CERDI, Université d'Auverge (1998).
Corden, W. & Neary, J.P., 'Booming sector and de-industrialisation in a small open economy', *The
  Economic Journal* 92 (December 1982).
Cronon, W., Nature's metropolis (New York: W.W. Norton, 1991).
Danida, 'Private Agricultural Sector Support in Tanzania,' at www.urval.dk/danida (Copenhagen:
  2003).
Daviron, B., & Ponte, S., *The Coffee Paradox: Commodity trade and the elusive promise of development*
  (London: Zed Press, 2005).
Deininger, K. and Okidi, J., 'Growth and Poverty Reduction in Uganda 1992-2000: Panel data
  evidence', *Development Policy Review* Vol. 21, No. 4, pp. 481-510 (2003).
Durevall, D., 'Competition and Pricing: An analysis of the market for roasted coffee', in Swedish
  Competition Authority, *High Prices in Sweden – A result of poor competition?*, pp. 99-164
  (Stockholm, 2003).

Engberg-Pedersen, P., Gibbon, P., Raikes, P. & Udsholt, L. (eds), *Limits of adjustment in Africa* (Oxford: James Currey, 1996).

European Commission 'EU Action Plan on agricultural commodities, dependence and poverty and a specific plan for cotton' (Brussels: 2004).

European Commission, *The Stabex system and export revenues in the ACP countries*, at www.acpsec.org/gb/trade/stabex.htm (1997).

Feuerstein, S., 'Do Coffee Roasters Benefit from High Prices of Green Beans?,' *International Journal of Industrial Organisation*, Vol. 20, pp. 89-118 (2002).

Fitter, R. & Kaplinsky, R. (2001) 'Who gains from product rents as the coffee market becomes more differentiated?', *IDS Bulletin* 32 (3), 69-82.

Gibbon, P., & Ponte, S., *Trading Down: Africa, value-chains and the global economy* (Philadelphia, Temple UP, 2005).

Gibbon, P., & Schulpen, L., 'Comparative Appraisals of Multilateral and Bilateral Approaches to Financing Private Sector Development', in Odedokum, M. (ed.) *External Finance for Private Sector Development* (Basingstoke: Palgrave, 2004).

Gilbert, C., 'International Commodity Agreements: An obituary', *World Development*, Vol. 24, No. 1, pp. 1-19 (1996).

Gillson, I., Poulton, C., Balcombe, K., & Page, S., 'Understanding the Impact of Cotton Subsidies in Developing Countries, ODI Working Paper (2004).

GTZ, 'Ecological Cocoa Growing in Nicaragua,' project description at www.gtz.de/ppp/english/praxisreport (2003a).

GTZ, 'Improvement of Coffee Quality and Sustainability of Coffee Production in Vietnam,' project description, at www.gtz.de/vietnam/ppp/ppp_coffee_eng.htm (2003b).

Hermann, R., Burger, K. and Smit, H-P. (1993) *International commodity policy: a quantitative analysis*, (London, Routledge).

Hoekman, B. (1997) Competition policy and the global trading system: a developing country perspective. World bank Policy Research Working paper 1735, Washington DC.

Hoekman, B. and Mavroidis, P. (2002) Economic development, competition policy and the WTO. World Bank Policy Research Working Paper 2,917, Washington DC.

Humphrey, J. (2004) 'Commodities, diversification and poverty reduction', paper presented to FAO Symposium on the state of agricultural commodity market research, Rome, 15-16 December 2003.

International Coffee Organization, *Annual Report*, 2002-03 (London: ICO, 2003).

International Coffee Organization, Statement by Mr. Néstor Osorio, 24 May, available at www.ico.org/ed/icc90.htm (London: ICO, 2004).

International Cotton Advisory Committee, 'Review of the World Situation,' Vol. 54, No. 1, September-October, (2000).

International Cotton Advisory Committee, 'The Structure of World Trade', document no. SC-N-476 (2005).

Koerner, J., 'The Dark Side of Coffee: Price war in the German market for roasted coffee,' Dept. of Food Economics & Consumption Studies, University of Kiel, Working Paper EWP 0204 (2002).

Krasner, S. (1973) 'Business-government relations: the case of the International Coffee Agreement', *International Organization* 27 (4).

Kruger, D., Mason, A. and Vakis, R. (2003) 'The coffee crisis in Central America', *Spectrum* (3), 16-19 (World Bank, Washington).

Larsen, M. N., 'Governing Post-liberalized Markets: National market coordination and the global cotton chain,' PhD thesis, Department of Geography, University of Copenhagen (2004).

Lewin, B., Giovannucci, D. and Varangis, P. 'Coffee Markets: New paradigms in global supply and demand,' Agricultural & Rural Development Internal Report (Washington: World Bank, 2004).

Maizels, A., 'Economic dependence on commodities', paper given to UNCTAD X High-level Round Table on 'Trade & Development: Directions for the 21st Century', Bangkok, Document no. TD(X/RT.1/6) (2000).

Maizels, A., 'The Continuing Commodity Crisis of Developing Countries', *World Development*, Vol. 22, No. 11, pp. 1,685-95 (1994).

Minot, D., & Daniels, L. (2002) 'Impact of global cotton markets on rural poverty in Benin', Markets & Structural Studies Division, IFPRI, MSSD Discussion Paper 48.

Mitchell, D., & Gilbert, C., 'Do Hedge Funds and Commodity Funds Affect Commodity Prices?', *Development Economics Notes* No. 29 (Washington: World Bank, 1997).

Morgan, W., & Sapsford, D., 'Commodities and Development: Some issues', *World Development*, Vol. 22, No. 11, pp. 1,681-84 (1994).

Morriset, J., 'Unfair Trade? The increasing gap between world and domestic prices in commodity markets during the past 25 years', *World Bank Economic Review*, Vol. 12, No. 3, pp. 503-526 (Washington: 1998).

Mshomba, R., *Africa in the global economy* (Boulder, Co.: Lynn Reiner, (2000).

Murphy, S., 'Managing the Invisible Hand: Markets, farmers and international trade (Minneapolis: Institute for Agriculture & Trade Policy, 2002).

Osorio, N., 'The Global Coffee Crisis: A threat to sustainable development,' presentation to the ICO World Coffee Conference, at www.eldis.org/csr/coffee.htm (2002).

Oxfam, *Mugged: Poverty in your cup* (Oxford, 2002).

Page, S., & Hewitt, A., 'World Commodity Prices: Still a problem for developing countries?' (London: Overseas Development Institute, 2001).

Papadopoulou-Zavalis, C., 'Legal Regulation of Monopsony in EU and US Competition Rules' (mimeo) (2004).

Payer, C. (1975) 'Coffee', in Payer, C. (ed.) *Commodity trade of the Third World* (London: Macmillan), 154-68.

Pelupessy, W., 'Coffee in Côte d'Ivoire and Costa Rica: National and Global Aspects of Competitiveness', in H.L. van der Laan, T. Dijkstra and A. van Tilburg (eds.), *Agricultural Marketing in Tropical Africa: Contributions from the Netherlands*, Leiden, African Studies Centre Research Series 15 (Ashgate: Aldershot, 1999).

Ponte, S., 'Standards, trade and equity: lessons of the specialty coffee industry,' Centre for Development Research Working Paper 02.13 (Copenhagen: 2002).

Poulton, C., Gibbon, P., Hanyani-Mlambo, B., Kydd, J., Maro, W., Larsen, M.L., Osorio, A., Tschirley, D. & Zulu, B., 'Competition and Coordination in Liberalized African Cotton Marketing Systems', *World Development* (forthcoming).

Prebisch, R., *The Economic Development of Latin America and its Principal Problem* (Santiago: UN Economic Commission for Latin America, 1950).

Rabobank, 'Identification and Assessment of Proposals by the International Coffee Sector Regarding the Poor Income Situation of Coffee Farmers,' report commissioned by DGIS, at www.minbuza.nl/default.asp?CMS_ITEM=MB2455065#P127-2959 (2002).

Rabobank, 'Rabobank Pioneers Hedging Tools for Smaller Commodity Producers in Developing Countries,' International press release, at www.rabobankgroep.nl/persberichten (14 January, 2003).

Roberts, N., 'Testing Oligopolitic Behaviour', *International Journal of Industrial Organisation*, Vol. 2, pp. 367-83 (1984).

Sapsford, D. & Singer, H. 'The IMF, the World Bank and Commodity Prices: A case of shifting sands?', *World Development*, Vol. 26, No. 9, pp. 1,653-60 (1998).

Schiff, M., 'Commodity exports and the adding-up problem in LDCs: trade, investment and lending policy', *World Development*, Vol. 23, No. 4, 603-16 (1995).

Shepherd, B., 'Market Power in International Commodity Processing Chains: Preliminary results from the coffee market' (mimeo), Groupe d'Economie Mondiale, Institut d'Etudes Politiques de Paris (2004).

Singer, H., 'The Distribution of Gains between Investing and Borrowing Countries', *American Economic Review*, Vol. 40, pp. 473-85 (1950).

Strunning, W., 'Green Coffee Prices and the USA Consumer', F.O. *Licht International Coffee Report*, 17 (14) (2001).

Talbot, J., 'Where Does Your Coffee Dollar Go? The division of income and surplus along the coffee commodity chain,' *Studies in Comparative International Development,* Vol. 32, No. 1, pp. 56-91 (1997).

Toye, J., 'Ghana', in Mosley, P., Harrigan, J. & Toye, J., *Aid and Power: The World Bank and policy-based lending* (London: Routledge, 1991).

UNCTAD, *Examination of the Effectiveness and Usefulness for Commodity-Dependent Countries of New Tools in Commodity Markets: Risk management and collateralised finance,* Report by UNCTAD Secretariat, document no. TD./B/COM.1/EM.5/2 (Geneva: 1998).

Valderrama, C. (1999) 'Direct assistance to production on the rise again', *World Cotton Trade,* ICAC (Washington DC).

Van Dijk, J., van Doesburg, D., Heibroek, A. Wazir, M & de Wolf, G. (1998) *The world coffee market.* (Utrecht: Rabobank).

Varangis, P. & Larson, D., 'Dealing with commodity price uncertainty,' Working Paper No. 1,667 (Washington: World Bank, 1996).

World Bank, Study on coffee reported in *Agriculture Technical Notes,* No. 30, June, Rural Development Department (Washington: 2002).

# Chapter 7 | Agricultural Commodities, Trade and Sustainable Development

# Chapter 8

# Where There's a Will There's a Way: Supply Management for Supporting the Prices of Tropical Export Crops

Niek Koning and Peter Robbins[1]

## 1. Introduction

Since 1980, the prices of tropical export crops have decreased sharply (Table 1). The ensuing impoverishment of farmers in the producing countries has stimulated violent conflict, flight into narcotic crops and increased emigration. Ecological damage, such as deforestation due to the decline of shade tree systems and the trend towards less sustainable farming patterns, has also been linked to declining returns from tropical agriculture.

---

1. This chapter is an edited version of a paper presented at the Barcelona dialogue in 2005. The authors thank Floor Verdenius, Hugo de Vos and Gerrit Walstra for comments and suggestions that helped us in writing the paper.

## Chapter 8 | Agricultural Commodities, Trade and Sustainable Development

**Table 1: Commodity price changes since 1980 taking inflation into account**

| Commodity | 1980 | 1980 (adjusted for inflation) in US dollars | 2005 | 2005 (per cent of adjusted per metric ton 1980 prices) |
|---|---|---|---|---|
| Copra | 415 | 984 | 395 | 40.1 |
| Coconut oil | 660 | 1,564 | 625 | 39.9 |
| Palm oil | 617 | 1,462 | 625 | 42.7 |
| Sugar | 254 | 602 | 190 | 31.5 |
| Cocoa | 2,832 | 6,712 | 1,506 | 22.4 |
| Coffee | 3,989 | 9,454 | 2,248 | 23.7 |
| Tea | 1,863 | 4,415 | 1,970 | 44.6 |
| Pepper | 1,974 | 4,678 | 1,550 | 33.1 |
| Jute | 369 | 875 | 400 | 45.7 |
| Cotton | 1,675 | 3,970 | 1,146 | 28.8 |
| Rubber | 1,430 | 3,389 | 1,210 | 35.7 |

(Goods bought for $1 in 1980 would cost $2.37 in 2005 = Federal Reserve Bank of Minneapolis)
Price data – *The Public Ledger*
N.B. The value of the US $ has fallen by 30 per cent against the euro in the last three years. For those countries purchasing imported goods in euros, therefore, the price fall has been greater by this factor.

Many policymakers have conceded that 'something should be done' about the tropical export crop disaster, but they have failed to come up with effective solutions. International commodity agreements for coffee, cocoa and sugar collapsed in the 1980s. Although the main cause was the opposition by OECD countries,[2] many western economists see it as proof that commodity controls cannot work.[3] Also, they may hide behind the recent small recovery in the prices of some crops (in 2002 prices were even lower than in 2005) to argue that such controls are unnecessary. However, with the possible exception of sugar prices, which are influenced by the rise in oil prices, this recovery is due to incidental events, like war in Côte d'Ivoire (cocoa) and harvest failure in Brazil (coffee), which are not likely to change the longer-term trend.

In recent years we have argued that new international commodity controls are needed.[4] These should include supply management to avoid the shortcomings of earlier schemes that did not control the underlying problem of overproduction. They should not rely on the co-operation of importing countries' governments, which have proven to be unreliable partners in past efforts designed to support tropical export crop prices.

---
2. Koning *et al.* (2004).
3. Hallam (2003).
4. Robbins (2003), Koning *et al.* (2004).

In theory, the solution is simple: producer countries could form a cartel, choose a desired price level, and limit their production to what demand absorbs at this price. Koning et al.[5] proposed an arrangement based on individual farmer quotas and a temporary export tax which would be used to buy surpluses and quotas on the market. Several commentators remarked that this would involve problems of free-riding, rent-seeking, abuse and evasion. Some contended that this would make supply management unfeasible.[6] In this chapter, we argue that there are no other solutions. We suggest countermeasures to control the problems that may arise from supply management arrangements and we discuss how broader support could be mobilized for such arrangements that would also improve quality, provide ecological sustainability and improve social conditions for workers.

## 2. Why tropical export crop prices declined

Between 1980 and 2003, the prices of most tropical export crops fell to less than a half, in some cases less than a quarter of their initial value. This was due partly to productivity increases, and partly to exchange rate devaluation in some countries which lowered their export prices in dollar terms. However, these factors probably explain no more than half of the decline in prices.[7] The falling price trend was largely caused by supply increasing faster than demand.

Oversupply means a supply level that depresses prices below the costs of the typical producer.[8] To some extent, it is a general problem of agricultural markets.[9] Since the late 19th century, new techniques have boosted the global supply of farm products. Farmers, as atomized producers, cannot adjust their supply to demand as large companies do, and labour mobility is not perfect enough to compensate for this. Individual farmers can only defend their incomes by adopting innovations, but these increase their production and reinforce the aggregate oversupply.[10]

In the case of tropical export crops, these general causes of oversupply are exacerbated by more specific conditions. These include the reaction by developed countries to low international prices. These countries protect their farmers without combining this with adequate supply management. Where such protection extends to export crops that both developed and developing countries can produce (sugar, for example), this encourages developed-country farmers to increase production. The ensuing dumping and import substitution further depress the world market prices of crops. The policies of the Bretton Woods institutions are another contributing factor. Since the 1980s, these institutions have pressured countries to expand the production of tropical export crops.

---

5. Koning *et al.* (2004).
6. *E.g.* Burger & Ruben (2005).
7. See *e.g.* Gilbert & Zant (2001) for coffee.
8. These costs include a normal remuneration of labour. Mainstream economists who deny the existence of chronic oversupply have a tautological conception of labour cost, in which this cost is derived from the remuneration of labour at the market-clearing price and vice versa.
9. Schultz (1945), Koning (1994), Koning *et al.* (2004).
10. Cochrane (1959).

At the same time, they forced them to introduce deflationary policies and to reduce tariffs on imported food, which restricted the markets for their domestic food crop producers. Finally, the demise of the International Commodity Agreements played a role – especially the collapses of the cocoa and coffee agreements which were followed by steep price falls.

Market manipulation and monopsonistic practices by transnational companies exacerbate the depressing effect of oversupply on producer prices. However, they are not the main cause of low and declining prices in international agricultural markets – indeed, the problems of chronic oversupply were already apparent when the trade and processing phases were much less concentrated than they are today.

## 3. Inadequate strategies

Some commentators contend that better strategies than commodity controls should be applied to improve the incomes of tropical export crop producers. Robbins[11] surveys the main approaches:

- **Increase in productivity**. Innovations that increase productivity raise consumer welfare by allowing prices to decrease. However, in the aggregate these innovations do not improve the relative incomes of producers, because they increase production and aggravate the problem of oversupply.
- **Diversification**. Shifting to products with a more elastic demand (vegetables, flowers etc.) is a good solution for well-placed farmers within short reach of airports. Although these markets are expanding, they remain small, however. They have become saturated long before a significant proportion of tropical export crop producers have made this shift.[12]
- **Off-farm employment**. In the longer term, economic development requires a massive shift of labour from farms to other sectors. However, this shift is too slow to compensate the forces that generate agricultural oversupply. Rather, in poor countries, the reallocation of labour is itself dependent on an improvement of farm incomes, because rural poverty, which represses domestic demand, is a major constraint on the growth of industries and services.[13]
- **New chain and marketing approaches**. Many people have great expectations for agro-industrial chains, value-added strategies and niche marketing to relax the squeeze on producer incomes. Indeed, these developments are robust trends in the agri-food sector, and many farmers are obliged to go along with them to remain in business. Yet the history of agricultural co-operatives and vertical integration in developed coun-

---
11. Robbins (2003).
12. In fact, this is an old story. European farmers were already told to shift to livestock when grain prices fell in the late 19th century. The markets for livestock products were glutted after a few well-placed producers like the Dutch and the Danish had increased their livestock production (Bairoch 1976; Koning 1994).
13. Besides, the deflationary policies that the Bretton Woods institutions impose on these countries further reduce the scope for off-farm employment to solve any problem of farm incomes (Patnaik 2004).

tries gives little reason to expect that chain formation will solve problems of chronic overproduction. Chamberlin's classical theory of 'monopolistic competition'[14] already explains why product differentiation and niche marketing cannot improve producer profits. This theory was formulated in a classical equilibrium framework, but we see no empirical evidence in the agri-food economy that suggests otherwise.
- **Fair trade and organic products**. Fair trade and organic chains are important awareness-raising activities, which also help some farmers. However, it is an illusion to think that an extension of these niches could solve the problem of low prices – unless this includes the building of a producer cartel, which is the subject of this paper. In Section 8, we indicate how fair trade and organic chains could contribute to such a new arrangement.
- **Combating monopoly**. Far-reaching concentration has increased the market power of transnational traders and processors. International anti-trust rules, transnational producer associations that negotiate prices and other conditions, and co-operative trade and processing enterprises that increase competition are needed to combat monopsonistic exploitation. However, as with fair trade and organic initiatives, it is a liberal illusion to think that such measures alone could remedy low prices of tropical export crops, which are largely caused by chronic overproduction. In Sections 7 and 8 we discuss what role anti-monopoly measures and transnational companies can play in an international arrangement for supporting the prices of tropical export crops.
- **Trade liberalization**. Reducing OECD tariffs on processed products would allow processing activities to shift to producer countries. This is important for employment, but the effect on crop prices would be limited. Trade liberalization will have very little effect on coffee and cocoa markets, which were effectively liberalized when commodity agreements collapsed. Ending OECD dumping of other crops could improve the alternative production possibilities for coffee or cocoa farmers somewhat, but this may be undone if import tariffs on domestic food crops are also reduced. Ending the open or disguised dumping of products like sugar, oilseeds or cotton may raise their international prices by something like 10 to 15 per cent, but no more.[15] Besides, the reduction of sugar tariffs would lower the prices received by poor countries that have preferential access to OECD markets. In any case, trade liberalization will not end the chronic overproduction of farm products insofar as this is caused by market forces rather than government intervention.

## 4. The historical struggle for supply management

Supply management is the only way to remedy chronic oversupply in agricultural markets. Developed countries have applied supply management schemes since the 1930s, often after farmers had vainly tried to improve prices by producer strikes and withholding actions. Today, the EU has producer quotas for milk and Canada for milk

---
14. Chamberlin (1946).
15. Diao *et al.* (2001), FAPRI (2002).

and poultry. These countries have remedied problems of surpluses while allowing farm-gate prices to remain at remunerative levels.

Supply management allows for the support of farm prices without causing import substitution or dumping. For this reason, the struggle for supply management soon gained an international dimension. The GATT (1947) allowed countries to use various instruments for protecting their farmers, but only if they also controlled their domestic production and export share. The issue of ICAs also became connected with that of supply management. The first buffer stock agreements or export retention agreements that were concluded in the 1930s could not cope with chronic overproduction. The US Department of Agriculture, which advocated commodity agreements at the time, concluded therefore that commodity agreements should involve supply management in order to be effective.[16]

While many farmers accepted supply management as a way to maintain remunerative prices, many traders and processors feared it would limit their turnover or raise the costs of their inputs. Under pressure from these sectors, OECD countries resisted commodity agreements that included supply management measures in the post-war period. By the same token, the US dismantled many of its domestic production controls in the 1950s. In the sugar and dairy sectors, this was in clear violation of the GATT Article 11 because the US had quantitative restrictions on imports of these products. In the following years, the US increased its dumping of grains and soya beans without adhering to the GATT rules which forbade the use of subsidies to acquire more than an equitable share in world markets. In the EU, sugar refineries pressured governments to retain a right to opt out of sugar quotas. A subsequent increase in these quotas undermined the International Sugar Agreement. In the 1980s, the dairy industry resisted the EU's introduction of milk quotas, which led to recurrent attempts to relax or abandon the system.[17] Like the US, the EU increased its dumping of several staples, ignoring GATT guidelines on equitable market shares.

The agro-industrial interests that resisted a multilateral organization of markets were also the main thrust behind the agricultural reforms in the Uruguay Round and the Doha Round. These reforms were called 'liberalization' and the ICAs were the first victims. In the US and the EU, however, 'liberalization' really involved a shift from open to disguised dumping by substituting direct payments for price support. The introduction of 'decoupled' payments allowed the US to abandon the last remnant of domestic supply management (the set-aside programme) and allowed the EU to continue its dumping of grain in spite of the reduction of export subsidies. Direct payments are only feasible for rich countries. The rest of the world is obliged to accept the dismantling of supportive agreements for its export crops and to reduce the protective tariffs that

---

16. Henningson (1981).
17. The Dutch-French research team that informed the European Commission's recent agricultural policy reform identified a small tightening of the quotas as an option that scored favourably on most policy aims. Nevertheless, the European Commission found it politically inopportune to consider this option, and suppressed it in the policy version of the research report.

protect its farmers against cheap imports.[18]

It is often said that supply management involves problems of evasion, free-riding and rent-seeking. Such problems indeed exist. However, the issue is confused because those who oppose supply management for other reasons strongly exaggerate these problems in order to reject the whole approach as impracticable. One author of this chapter remembers being a secretary of a group of Dutch farmers that, in the 1970s, advocated a quota system to control growing dairy surpluses. The dairy industry fiercely resisted the idea, and the group was bombarded with arguments that quotas were entirely unfeasible, that the idea was a bureaucratic nightmare, and that it required placing a policeman behind every farmer. This continued until the mountains of butter and milk powder caused a budgetary crisis in the EU and the system was introduced overnight.

It should also be remembered that, in the 1930s, several developed countries had quota systems that operated with small farms, decentralized trade and processing structures, and with no recourse to modern information technology. Nevertheless there is no denying that multilateral supply management by tropical countries, many of which have sizable small-scale farming sectors, failing infrastructures and weak governance, will pose special problems. Moreover, it will not be easy to bring the many different countries that are producing various tropical crops into line. Below we survey the various associated problems and propose solutions to reduce them to tolerable proportions.

## 5. Achieving co-operation between producer countries

### 5.1 How to discourage free-riding?

For all the larger tropical export crops, production is spread over tens of countries. A cartel of producer countries could therefore raise prices even if one or two middle-sized producers do not choose to participate. Individual countries would be tempted to benefit from the arrangement without curtailing their own supply, however. This leads to what game theorists call a social dilemma: all producer countries would benefit from a general control of production, but because free-riding is attractive to each individual country, it might nevertheless not be achieved.

How could this dilemma be overcome? The first objective would be to ensure that a careful and thorough diplomatic effort is made to convince each country of the interest that all have in an agreement that improves their export earnings and the incomes of their producers. Political scientists have demonstrated the vital significance of face-to-face contact between stakeholders for creating enough trust in each other's commitment to be able to cope with social dilemmas.[19]

To facilitate this diplomatic process, market model-based tools could be made to allow representatives to explore supply-control arrangements. This would both demon-

---

18. Developing countries had lower tariff reduction obligations in the AoA and LDCs were exempted from reduction obligations altogether, but the World Bank and the IMF have pressured many countries to refrain from using this room as a condition for the renewal of loans.
19. Ostrom (1998).

strate the advantages that an arrangement would have for all countries and allow representatives to experiment with modalities for balancing the divergent interests of the countries concerned. Colleagues of ours are currently working on such a tool for the international coffee market.

A next step for creating trust could be an agreement on how to monitor the restriction of production in each country. Geodata infrastructure could play a role in this.[20] For some crops, the cultivated area could be monitored by satellite imaging. There has been rapid progress in this technology and costs are declining significantly. In other crops, such as cocoa and coffee in smallholder shade-tree systems, GIS mapping and spot checks by a supranational secretariat might be more helpful.

Furthermore, the chances of producer countries achieving successful co-operation would increase substantially if the countries that join the arrangement were to get advantages from it that free-riding countries could not. Such *selective incentives* have played a critical role in overcoming social dilemmas in other forms of collective action.[21] (For instance, the growth of farmers' unions was partly due to the exclusive access that their members had to certain marketing and insurance services.)

To some extent, such a selective incentive will arise automatically. Historical experience shows that international commodity controls entailed a segmentation of the world market. Commodities were traded from countries that were members of the arrangement in the main market segment but those commodities from free-rider countries were traded in another segment at a price discount. This discount arose because member countries preferred to deal with international traders that did not trade with free-riders and major consumers did not wish to take the risk of being dependent on potentially unreliable supplies from a limited number of free-rider countries. In addition, the volatility of prices in the free-rider segment was normally higher than in the main segment, where the application of supply quotas led to a certain price stabilization. An example of this phenomenon can be found in the gem diamond market where producers outside the De Beers cartel are obliged to sell in a discounted and unpredictable market. Other examples include the markets of several minor metals (cadmium, selenium, indium and bismuth) during the 1960s when the so-called producer price system was in operation (effectively, a cartel of the major producers).

Both the discount and this greater price volatility in the free-rider segment of the market were incentives that discouraged free-riding. In practice, however, these factors were often outweighed by the benefits that free-riding had for individual countries. Nevertheless, we think that it is possible to enlarge these incentives so that they would make it more attractive for countries to join the agreement. Rather than passively watching those speculative actions by free-riders, which undermine their collective efforts, member countries could adopt a dynamic approach to make the market outcomes less favourable for free-riders. To this purpose, the international secretariat of the control arrangement could establish its own trading company and hire experienced and trust-

---

20. We thank Hugo de Vos for informing us on this subject.
21. Olson (1965).

worthy traders and managers who share the aims of the arrangement. (Such staff members could be recruited from the ranks of traders and managers who have worked with fair trade companies.) This trading company could act as a broker and sales agent for member countries that wish to make use of its services. In addition, it could undertake other trading activities in the markets for the crop and for derivatives based on the crop. The company's relationships with the international secretariat and with several member countries would give it superior market intelligence. Also, it could grant traded options with limited risks because they could be underwritten by member countries. The company could use these advantages for making transactions that were profitable. Trading strategies could be adopted which would also have the effect of increasing the price discount and volatility of the free-rider market. For example, the company, using its advantage in market intelligence, might take the opportunity to unexpectedly buy or sell free-rider coffee, in short-term periods of free-rider market shortages or gluts and sell or buy back these supplies profitably. This would have the effect of increasing the uncertainty in the free-rider market. Several other types of market 'guerrilla' tactics would be available to the company using more sophisticated derivatives strategies to achieve these objectives.

### 5.2 Low-cost and high-cost countries

Contradictions between low- and high-cost producing countries have also often hindered agreement on commodity controls in the past. For a country that can produce a crop at a lower cost, it may be less attractive to participate in an arrangement in which national quotas are fixed. In the absence of quotas, such a country would normally be able to increase its share in the world market. By entering a fixed quota arrangement, it would lose this possibility. This may dissuade low-cost countries from participating in an arrangement, even if this would improve the prices for its producers.

To make participating more attractive for low-cost producing countries, an arrangement could include mechanisms for redistributing quotas from high-cost to low-cost countries.[22] On the other hand, the arrangement would also need to protect the interests of high-cost producers, especially when these are small-scale farmers with limited alternatives. In any case, the freedom of individual producers and the sovereignty of governments should be duly respected.

In Section 9, we sketch an example that we think does justice to these various considerations. Farmers would be allowed to sell and purchase individual quotas on national quota markets within limitations set by national governments to protect and support certain areas and categories of producers. The sale of quotas on these markets would be made by farmers on a completely voluntary basis. Their decision to sell would depend on whether they thought that the proceeds of the sale would compensate them for the loss of production rights and whether these proceeds would provide them with the means to develop more remunerative activities.

---

22. *Cf.* Burger & Smit (1995).

Chapter 8 | **Agricultural Commodities, Trade and Sustainable Development**

The price of quotas that are arrived at in these markets would be a measure for the differences in production costs between countries. In countries with lower production costs, farmers will bid higher prices for quotas, and *vice versa*. This characteristic would be used as guidance for a gradual redistribution of quotas from high-cost to low-cost countries. For this purpose, the international secretariat would buy quotas in countries with low national quota prices for transfer to countries with high quota prices according to a formula that is agreed upon in advance by the participating governments. This procedure would give low-cost countries a guarantee that some redistribution will occur, while assuring high-cost countries that any non-optional redistribution will occur gradually according to a rule to which they themselves have consented. A pre-agreed formula would also prevent the issue of redistribution from causing endless disputes that could threaten the continuity of the arrangement.

## 6. Achieving successful implementation within countries

Careful preparation will be required to ensure the successful implementation of supply controls within countries. All stakeholders need to be informed in detail about the expected benefits of the arrangement and should have a fully participatory role in its implementation. Farmers, especially, need to have a clear perspective that the arrangement will improve the price of the commodity they produce. This preparation could start with a feasibility study to provide a national implementation plan that is adapted to the specific conditions of the country. This should be discussed and modified in an open dialogue with producer organizations, traders, processors and NGOs. Much energy should be invested in explaining the plan to local farmers and in convincing them that there will be no discrimination or abuse by other parties.

### 6.1 The allocation of producer quotas

Effective supply management requires individual producer quotas. The introduction of these would require some system of administrative initial allocation on the basis of individual farmers' historical or current production. Once these allocations had been made some market mechanism for selling and purchasing quotas may be established. However, to protect certain categories of producers and prevent the benefits of improved crop prices from leaking away through the quota price (which raises the costs for new or expanding producers), this should still be combined with some system of administrative redistribution. Both the initial allocation and this administrative redistribution involve a risk of abuse by officials and politicians who demand bribes or favour their own supporters.

To reduce this risk, the local (re)allocation of quotas should be delegated to institutions that are trusted by farmers. Which institutions these are may vary from country to country. This process could, for instance, be undertaken by local government institutions, farmer associations, or farmer-owned local processing plants. In other locations churches, trusted NGOs or even traders may be the appropriate institutions to be involved in the process. In some cases, local farmer organizations might be formed especially for this purpose.

Effective complaint procedures would also be a necessary component of the arrangements. A hierarchy of inter-professional arbitrage committees would be needed to handle normal conflicts and special complaints departments would be needed to deal with complaints about corruption and abuse. To secure an impartial functioning of the latter, they could be supervised by the international secretariat that administers the entire agreement.

A further deterrent against corruption and abuse would be a rule that requires the international secretariat of the arrangement to refund the costs of the local administration of the system, but only after it has found that the (re)allocation of quotas has been done in an orderly way. Supervision of the complaints departments by the international secretariat would give it a means to judge the process. This refunding requires that the international secretariat have its own income, e.g. from contributions from an export tax. (Some might argue that the costs of these bureaucratic systems would be too high. In reality, these costs would pale into insignificance compared with the increased income derived from the sale of the commodities in question in a market which balanced supply and demand at price levels that reflect the costs of an average producer.)

### 6.2 Combating evasion and smuggling

Individual farmers may be tempted to exceed their production quotas and sell their excess production through illegal channels. Corrupt traders and officials might help them by providing false or stolen stamps (production or export licences). Trust and peer pressure would be the most effective measure for combating such abuse. They would be based on a clear perception by farmers that the system can improve their incomes but that the co-operation of all producers would be needed to ensure success.

Measures designed to deter abuse require careful preparation including participation of stakeholders – especially farmers, and the provision to stakeholders of detailed information about the measures. Another prerequisite is that the introduction of the system comes with clear price signals. In fact, it may be necessary to start raising prices by buying and destroying existing stocks and surpluses before the implementation of the next phase of the arrangement, which is to allocate quotas to individual producers. Besides, the reduction of quota rights to limit total production should occur on a voluntary basis, with farmers relinquishing production rights for compensation. It should be noted that an early rise of crop prices and a voluntary reduction of quota rights are conflicting aims. Higher crop prices will raise the compensation that is needed to persuade farmers to sell production rights. Nevertheless, calculations in Koning *et al.*[23] suggest that both aims could be achieved simultaneously when an export tax is used to

---

23. Koning *et al.* (2004).

Chapter 8 | **Agricultural Commodities, Trade and Sustainable Development**

finance both the buying up of quota rights and the elimination of overhanging stocks and current surpluses.

Even when the advantages of the system are made clear to farmers, maintaining trust and peer pressure requires the effective countering of illegal sales. Measures need to be put in place to prevent those who wish to cheat the system from smuggling the commodity out of the country. Tightening customs control at ports is important but may not prevent overland smuggling to adjacent countries. This problem can be more easily addressed if the adjacent country is also a participant in the arrangement, but if they are not, some way of counteracting overland smuggling becomes important. Controlling inland borders is notoriously difficult in tropical countries which often have weak governance and poor infrastructures. Novel techniques for controlling smuggling trails, such as global positioning systems and GIS might help in some cases. However, a more effective approach would be to make within-quota products recognizable by some counterfeit-proof mark, and to forbid any transport of unmarked products. This would enable potential smugglers to be identified long before they have reached the country's borders while at the same time discouraging the selling of illegal surpluses in the domestic market.

Even if counterfeit-proof tags prove to be effective in preventing smuggling and limiting the total supply within a country, corrupt officials might still furnish smugglers with tags or route tags to farmers in return for bribes or political support and deny them to those farmers who are entitled to them. In developing countries with weak governmental structures, large numbers of smallholders, decentralized trade and poor infrastructure the risk of this happening is very high. A system needs to be designed to address this risk. One possibility would be for the international secretariat of the supply management arrangement to open local offices (or contract local banks) where farmers get tags when they produce their quota certificates together with a personal identification number. To preclude fraud, verification machines (possibly coupled to automated teller machines) could be used that are directly connected to the international head office. The personal identification numbers would be given to farmers in sealed envelopes together with their quota certificates.

An even more secure procedure would be to communicate these numbers to farmers by a simple application of public key encryption – the same technology as is used for securing messages over email and the internet.[24] This would require that, during the allocation of quota certificates, each farmer gets brief access to a simple electronic device (a piece of software installed on a notebook or palmtop computer) that he can consult in private. This device would allow him to choose two numbers that bear a specific mathematical relation to each other. He keeps one number secret (his private key), the other is passed on to the international secretariat and everybody may know it (his public key). The international secretariat keeps a list of all farmers and attributes a PIN code to each. While these PIN codes are kept secret in the international head office, the public key of each farmer is used to make an encrypted version of his code. A list of farmers and their encrypted codes is send to the national counters and divulged to

---

24. We thank Floor Verdenius for drawing our attention to this possibility.

the farmers. By using his private key, each farmer can decrypt his own encrypted code and find the PIN code that the international secretariat has attributed to him. In this way, only the international head office and the farmer himself know the PIN code of a farmer.

Special provision needs to be made to allow farmers to deal with harvest fluctuations caused by variation in weather patterns *etc.* without having to resort to illegal sales. Within each country, farmers may be allowed to trade in tags to balance individual shortages and surpluses. Governments should be allowed to rent quota from other governments on a seasonal basis. Besides, governments could operate buffer stocks and in extreme cases even destroy harvest surpluses.

## 6.3 Discouraging rent-seeking by bureaucrats and traders

Government institutions may be tempted to appropriate the benefits of international price supports and use them for their own bureaucratic survival. In part, this can be countered by introducing producer quotas while leaving the trade in the crop in private hands, so that there are no state-controlled intermediaries that could appropriate price improvements. Such measures, however, would not prevent governments from increasing taxation of producers by fiscal means or by manipulating exchange rates. This would be discouraged if the quota prices in national markets are used as a yardstick for an international redistribution of quotas from high-cost to low-cost producer countries (see Section 5.2 above). Any increase in taxation of farmers would reduce the domestic quota prices in a country, which would entail a loss of production rights of the country and make the policy self-defeating.

Besides government institutions, domestic traders and processors may try to appropriate price improvements for themselves, especially in thin markets where they have local monopoly positions. When the arrangement is introduced, they may buy the crop at the old (low) prices from farmers who are short of money and stock it in order to profit from the price improvement that the arrangement achieves. This could be limited by combining the arrangement with the provision of credit to farmers.

In the longer term, saleable farmer quotas will help to combat monopsonistic exploitation by traders. Traders who underpay farmers will see their supply being affected because it would become attractive for these farmers to sell quotas to producers in other areas. Besides, the greater price stability that supply controls provide will strengthen the bargaining position of farmers by improving their price information.

Market information provision for farmers can be further improved by systems that monitor prices in domestic market centres and disseminating this information to farmers using radio or other media to which farmers have access. Bulking (and sometimes primary processing) of crops by local farmer groups will also strengthen the relative bargaining power of farmers vis-à-vis buyers. In some cases, such group activities may arise as a spin-off of farmer initiatives taken to invigilate an orderly allocation of producer quotas.

## 7. Supply management and transnational companies

In the current situation, producers have no influence over international markets for their crops. At present, these market systems are operated by international traders, brokers and processors and this phase of the chain has become increasingly concentrated. For instance, six trading houses control half the world's trade in green coffee beans. Stock holding and the determination of quality criteria and techniques for raising quality have all shifted to these companies.[25] In the retailing phase, market power is increasingly concentrated in the hands of giant supermarket companies.

These large enterprises use their market power to increase their profits in ways that further depress the prices for producers. Their practices include the one-sided bargaining of contracts with atomised suppliers; the use of secretive tax havens that allow transfer pricing abuse and trader collusion; secret deals with state-controlled organizations that are conducive to corruption; and many other forms of short-term price manipulations that appropriate revenue away from producers.[26] The comparative lack of international control over commodity markets has offered the opportunity for abuse. Cases range from the attempted cornering of the copper market in 1996 which cost the Japanese company Sumitomo US$ 2.6 billion, to the under-invoicing of exports of African agricultural products encouraged by the ending of currency controls under structural adjustment programmes.[27]

These monopsonistic and manipulative practices are not curtailed by any countervailing power of producers. The marketing boards and state enterprises that until recently controlled the supply of export crops have been dissolved by liberal reforms imposed by Bretton Woods institutions. These parastatal organizations had often become inefficient bureaucracies that were overtaxing the farmers for their own survival. However, very few mechanisms have been put in their place to counterbalance the power of international buyers. Delegates of producing countries at the WTO have made proposals that, since state trading enterprises are now obliged to publish all the details of their trading activity to comply with WTO rules, then so should multinational trading companies. However, such proposals, despite their appeal to equity, are likely to be resisted by OECD countries.

The existing oversupply of tropical export crops strongly facilitates the exploitative and speculative activities of international buyers. Oversupply puts producers in a desperate position against the buyers and, at the same time, it increases the buyers' room of manoeuvre. Conversely, a supply management arrangement, built around the common interests and solidarity of producers and producing countries, could help to combat monopsonistic and manipulative practices. Self-help farmer groups formed for the implementation of the arrangement could prevent buyers from picking off the most desperate sellers and forcing all others to follow in the race to the bottom. Countries

---

25. Ponte (2002).
26. Murray *et al* (1981).
27. Global Post Harvest Forum (2002). See also Baistrocchi and Tanzi (www.utdt.edu).

that participate in the arrangement could agree to oblige multinational trading companies to reveal their trading details in return for being given permission to trade in their crops. In addition, exporting countries could refuse to do business with companies who base themselves in tax haven countries or engage in other dubious practices. In the longer term, producing countries could demand to be accepted as co-managers of the international markets where their export crops are traded and use this influence to strengthen regulations against insider trading and market manipulation.

## 8. Broadening the support

Poverty in producing countries can be directly linked to an increase in transnational criminality, narcotic drug production, warfare and mass migration, which reverberate in countries that import tropical export crops. Citizens in importing countries are faced with these effects and are demanding that measures be taken to curtail them. Also, the rising per capita incomes of consumers have encouraged them to take more interest in the quality and the ecological and social sustainability aspects of the products they buy. The overproduction crisis leading to collapsed prices in tropical export crops does not fit well with these ethical concerns. The invisible hand of the free market can only remedy this to a small extent. Social and ecological sustainability is a public good. Everybody profits if the world becomes more sustainable, but the purchasing decisions of each individual consumer only have a slight effect. This leads to another social dilemma. Each individual consumer benefits by buying cheaper products while allowing others to pay the price of sustainability. This is why niches for organic and fair trade products are typically smaller than the number of citizens that value sustainability.

Something similar holds for quality. For really discriminating consumers, the production of high or special quality goods can be organized, but a broader improvement in quality requires changes in the conditions for producers that are complicated by a social dilemma faced by traders and processors. Even if a general improvement is favourable to traders and processors as a whole,[28] individual firms are tempted to reap the windfall profits of squeezing prices while letting others take care of the problem of increasing quality.

The traditional idea is that, if markets cannot meet the desires of citizens, governments should step in. However, citizens cannot easily influence their governments on specific issues. Information problems and economies of scale in political markets give party programmes a broad compromise nature and makes casting one's vote a package deal. Elections are fought over broad political concepts like 'small government', 'welfare reform' or 'new morality'. Most specific issues are addressed at another level of government-society interaction – the lobbying process. Here influence is not distributed according to 'one man, one vote' but to lobbying strength. Civil society organizations can exert an influence, but commercial lobbies are usually more powerful. Sometimes, civil society groups can appeal to the dominating political concept to lend force to their argument. This is why in the 1960s and 1970s, when active government and multilat-

---

28. Talbot (2004).

eral reformism were still leading concepts, some politicians could still be convinced that they should endorse international commodity controls. Under the new hegemony of liberal economic concepts, the room for such action is much smaller. Even the Dutch and Norwegian governments, which in the 1970s supported the developing countries' campaign for commodity agreements, no longer do so.

In their own fields, firms are sometimes easier to influence on specific issues than governments. The quality desires and ethical concerns of affluent consumers and new trends in marketing have made large firms more sensitive to changing consumer opinion. As a reaction, many large firms care about their 'licence to produce and to sell' in the citizens' eyes. This gives civil society organizations some leverage to influence their policies. Many NGOs already mount campaigns against companies or trading sectors that have some responsibility for the disastrous situation in tropical export crops. By the same token, they could urge these companies to co-operate with a scheme that would support the prices for farmers or wages for agricultural labourers and lay down minimum norms for quality and ecological sustainability.

Traders and processors have themselves some interest in an arrangement that would help them to meet consumer desires and to secure continuity in their supply. However, the windfall profits from short-term speculation and depressing of prices are attractive enough to prevent each from taking the initiative – another case of social dilemma. Nevertheless, the interest in some settlement that these enterprises have might help to make them consent to the scheme that producers and NGOs propose, even if this scheme would go further than they, themselves, would be willing to do. To be sure, corporate strategies and cultures differ from one company to another. Some may be more open to the proposal, while consumer action may be needed to force others to co-operate. In any case, fair trade and ecological chains could act as a bridgehead of civil society organizations that try to win the major companies over.

Targeting private companies rather than importing countries' governments may also be wise for another reason. Co-operation by these companies could greatly facilitate the management of a control arrangement. They could refuse to accept products from smugglers and free-riders. They might also help to provide storage capacity, help to destroy surpluses of low-quality products, help to monitor the flows of products and of payments, and monitor the product and process characteristics within the scheme. The collaboration by these companies could compensate for the decreased intervention capacity of government institutions in producing countries.

## 9. An example

Just by way of example, in this section we sketch how a control arrangement for a tropical export crop could be achieved and how it could work, elaborating on a model that has already been described in Koning et al.[29]

First, farmers' associations, producer-country governments and civil society organi-

---

29. Koning et al (2004).

zations form an international coalition to create support for the arrangement among other stakeholders. This coalition agrees on the sustainability and quality norms that are to be achieved by the arrangement. It also asks the major trading and processing companies to co-operate with the scheme and applies legitimate pressure to persuade them if needed.

When sufficient support has been created, producer-country governments, in consultation with other stakeholders, specify the range of world market prices that is needed to achieve the norms, and establish an intergovernmental secretariat to manage the arrangement.

Following this, producer countries impose a uniform export tax that raises the world market price to the desired level. The revenue is transferred to the intergovernmental secretariat. The secretariat establishes its own trading company and uses this company to buy existing stocks, plus as much of the current production as would raise world market prices sufficiently to allow a moderate improvement in farmer earnings in spite of the tax. Preferably low-quality products are purchased from the market. Apart from a buffer stock, all purchases are destroyed or denatured to induce expectations of price rises, thereby stimulating private stockholding and moderating the size of the intervention required.[30] The trading company also acts as a broker and trade agent for the member countries on a voluntary basis, and engages in profitable transactions that increase the price discount and the price volatility in the free-rider segment of the international market for the crop.

Meanwhile, quota certificates are allocated to individual producers on the base of their current production. The allocation occurs through national governments assisted by farmers' associations or other local institutions that are trusted by producers. Inter-professional arbitration committees settle any conflicts. Complaints departments supervised by the intergovernmental secretariat handle any complaints about abuse or corruption. The intergovernmental secretariat refunds the costs that national institutions make for administering the allocation process, but only after it has found that the allocation has been done in an orderly way.

During the subsequent few years, the intergovernmental secretariat uses the tax revenue to buy quota rights from producers to achieve a stepwise reduction of production (by equal percentages per country). In addition, a country may choose to buy additional quota rights from its producers and sell these to other countries that can so limit their reduction obligations. Meanwhile, the intergovernmental secretariat continues to buy sufficient parts of the current production to raise prices further and to allow a gradual increase in producer earnings. (Koning *et al.* present a model that illustrates how this could work in the case of coffee.[31])

When the intergovernmental secretariat starts to buy quota rights from producers, a system with tags and personal identification numbers (as indicated in Section 6.2. above) is introduced to control the flows of the crop and payments within each country.

When production capacity has been reduced sufficiently to move prices within the pre-established price band, the export tax is reduced so that farmgate prices come closer

---

30. Gilbert & Zant (2001) and Koning *et al.* (2004) provide examples for coffee that show that these operations may be profitable.
31. Koning *et al* (2004).

to world market levels. The secretariat limits its intervention in the product markets to the management of a buffer stock for short-term price stabilization. Farmers are now allowed to buy and sell quotas in national quota exchanges (with decentralized sales counters to maximise access) that are managed by the international secretariat. National governments may opt to subdivide exchanges in closed departments for separate areas to maintain production in less favoured districts. Meanwhile, the size of individual production quotas is adjusted periodically to keep prices within the price band. The band itself is adjusted so that the weighted average of national quota prices remains at a fixed level. (Increased quota prices are taken as an indication of decreased production costs).

The intergovernmental secretariat uses the remaining export tax revenue to purchase part of the quotas that are sold at the national quota exchanges. It distributes these quotas for free reallocation to farmers according to criteria that have been decided by the national governments. (Again, inter-professional committees and complaint departments settle conflicts and deal with complaints). In addition, the secretariat transfers part of the quotas that it purchases in countries where quota prices are low (indicating high marginal costs) to countries where they are high (indicating comparatively efficient producers). The volume of quota purchases in a country and the part that is transferred to low-cost countries are calculated using a formula that is agreed upon in advance by the participating governments. This formula specifies (i) an average percentage of the global quota turnover that will be purchased by the secretariat, and (ii) a rule that couples quota price differentials to yearly percentage reductions or increases in national quota volumes. (Besides, countries may still choose to buy additional quotas from their producers and sell these to other countries.)

Apart from these sales and purchases of quotas, farmers and, at the international level, countries, may rent quotas on a strictly seasonal basis to cushion fluctuations in production.

We believe that this could be a robust and transparent arrangement. It is self-financing and does not depend on the co-operation of importing countries. The arbitration and complaint committees, and the audit of the allocation process before administration costs are refunded, guarantee fairness to farmers. Although the national quota exchanges encourage efficient reallocation of quotas within countries, the free reallocation of part of the traded quotas prevents the protective effect of the arrangement from leaking away through these markets. The sovereignty of national governments is respected because they structure this free reallocation and the regional reallocation of all traded quotas within their own territories. Meanwhile, the automatic redistribution from high-cost countries to low-cost countries reduces incentives for governments to free-ride. The transactions by the secretariat's trading company further decrease these incentives by raising the market discount on free-rider products.

On the other hand, no government is compelled to do something against its will, since the price band, average recycling of traded quotas and formula for redistribution between countries are established beforehand by joint decision. Governments can be mutually assured that the principles will be fairly applied, since the implementation is left to a supranational organization (the intergovernmental secretariat). Incentives for misuse are limited and minimized. Export taxes are used only for financing the scheme, they are controlled by the intergovernmental secretariat, and they decrease progressively after the first years. Apart from these taxes, the improvement in world market prices benefits producers. The quota purchases by the intergovernmental secretariat will ensure that the national quota exchanges become the effective markets for quotas, which makes it difficult to bribe farmers to bid up quota prices or withhold quotas to improve a country's position in the international quota redistribution.[32] Moreover, this redistribution is controlled by the intergovernmental secretariat, which has the authority to punish misuse.

## 10. Conclusion

Many development economists have expressed scepticism about supply management of tropical agricultural commodities. No alternative strategy has been proposed, however, which addresses the problem of oversupply – the underlying cause of low commodity prices. Conversely, the potential effectiveness of supply management is illustrated by naturally occurring disturbances such as frosts in the case of coffee or witches' broom disease in the case of cocoa, which show that a relatively minor hiatus in production can achieve a disproportionate increase in the price of the product.

Bringing the supply of these commodities once more into balance with demand at a higher price level by introducing supply management arrangements could contribute significantly to the effort of reducing poverty within the rural communities of producing countries. Increased revenue could be invested in desperately needed infrastructure, in diversification and in agro-processing industries, which offer a higher return and more stable economies.

Our model for the establishment of a supply management arrangement may need detailed modification for some commodities and may not be applicable to all agricultural products. Some of these markets are complicated by the number of grades of the product and others by the fact that arrangements for the supply for domestic consumption would need to be disaggregated from those applying to exports. Some commodities are produced in very few countries, and some in many countries, which may mean that some agreements may be easier to establish than others. Our basic model, however, lends itself to a significant measure of modification to accommodate a wide variety of tropical commodity markets.[33]

---

32. Such bribing by non-monopsonistic traders will also be discouraged by free-rider problems.

33. For those who are not convinced that a supply management scheme would be feasible there remains a much simpler option to support the prices of tropical export crops. Producer countries could impose *and maintain* a uniform export tax. This will reduce the supply and raise the world market prices of the crops concerned. Global supply and demand would be balanced without any need for individual quotas. Producer prices would fall, but the tax revenue that is gained by producer county governments would be much higher than their total loss. Governments could use the proceeds for public investment, including roads and other infrastructure that is important for farmers. The weakness of this option is that it opens a vast opportunity for rent-seeking by governments, which could use the tax revenues to expand their bureaucracies rather than for productive investment. We prefer a supply management scheme such as the one sketched out above, because it would really improve the incomes of *farmers*, and thereby also allow improvements in sustainability and quality.

It is important to bear in mind, firstly, that the markets for tropical export crops are not declining markets – demand for these products has increased steadily over this period of price collapse – and, secondly, that arrangements designed to bring more order to these markets and to provide producers with an equitable share of their value were established in the very recent past. Our task is to learn from these experiences and to design arrangements that can be effective in an increasingly liberalized and globalized world market. Now that we have witnessed the devastating effect of the collapse of the market prices of these commodities on the levels of poverty and on economic social and political stability, failure to provide solutions is no longer an option.

## References

Baistrocchi, E., 'The Transfer Pricing Problem: The Argentinian experience 1932-1998,' UTDT, www.utdt.edu.

Benedict, M.R., Farm Policies of the United States, 1790-1950: A study of their origins and development, (New York, 1953).

Burger, K. & R. Ruben, 'Goederenovereenkomsten of brede plattelandsontwikkeling?', Spil no. 209-210, pp. 29-30 (2005).

Burger, K. & H.P. Smit, *Supply Management Through Area Control: Towards an empirical assessment*, (Amsterdam: Economic and Social Institute, Free University, 1995).

Chamberlin, E.H., *The Theory of Monopolistic Competition* (Cambridge, Mass.: Harvard U.P., 1933).

Cochrane, W.W., *Farm Prices – Myth and Reality* (Minneapolis, 1959).

Diao, X., A. Somwaru & T. Roe, 'A global analysis of agricultural reform in WTO member countries', in M.E. Burfisher (ed.), *Agricultural Policy Reform in the WTO – The Road Ahead*, Agricultural Economic Report no. 802 (Washington: ERS-USDA, 2001).

FAPRI, The Doha Round of the World Trade Organization: Liberalization of agricultural markets and its impact on developing economies, Paper presented at the IATRC Winter Meetings, 2002.

Galbraith, J.K., American Capitalism: The concept of countervailing power, Harmondsworth (1963).

Gilbert, C.L., & W. Zant, *Restoring balance by diversion in the world coffee market*, ESI-VU, Amsterdam 2001, http://www.feweb.vu.nl/esi/bin/pdf/559.pdf.

Hallam, D, 'Falling commodity prices and industry responses: Lessons from the international coffee crisis,' Commodity Market Review- 2003-2004, FAO, 2003.

Global Post-Harvest Forum, *A short history of African Trade*, Phaction News No. 5, 2002.

Henningson, B.E., 'United States Agricultural Trade and Development Policy during World War II: The role of the Office of Foreign Agricultural Relations, Ph.D. diss., University of Arkansas (1981).

Koning, N., *The Failure of Agrarian Capitalism: Agrarian politics in the UK, Germany, the Netherlands and the USA, 1846-1919*. (London and New York: Routledge, 1994).

Koning, N., M. Calo & R. Jongeneel, 'Fair trade in tropical crops is possible: ICAs revisited,' North-South Discussion Paper no. 3, Wageningen (2004), www.north-south.nl/files/Debate/Fairtrade.pdf.

Murray, R., et al, *Multinationals beyond the market* (Brighton, UK: The Harvester Press, 1981).

Olson, M., *The logic of collective action* (Cambridge, Mass.: 1965).

Ostrom, E., 'A behavioral approach to the rational choice theory of collective action', American Political Science Review, Vol. 92, No. 1, pp. 1-22 (1998).

Patnaik, U., 'The Republic of Hunger,' Public lecture on the occasion of the 50th birthday of Safdar Hashmi, organized by the Safdar Hashmi Memorial Trust on (New Delhi: 2004).

Ponte, S., 'The 'latte revolution'? Regulation, markets and consumption in the global coffee chain', World Development, vol. 30 nr 7 1099-1122 (2002).

Robbins, P., *Stolen Fruit: The tropical commodities disaster* (London: Zed Books, 2003).

Schultz, Th.W., *Agriculture in an Unstable Society* (New York and London: 1945).

Talbot, J.M., *Grounds for Agreement: The political economy of the coffee commodity chain*, Lanham 2004.

Tanzi, V. *Globalisation and the fiscal termites*, Finance and Development, IMF, 2001

# Chapter 9

# Leverage Points for Encouraging Sustainable Commodities

Jason W. Clay, Annie Dufey and James MacGregor

## 1. Introduction

This chapter explores the potential for fostering production and trade in sustainable commodities. Sustainable commodities are defined as providing greater positive or reduced negative social, environmental and economic impacts along the value chain than conventional commodities. Benefits are either realized through the production, consumption or disposal processes, or accrue to the people involved in production.

Exploring different leverage points on both the demand and supply sides of sustainable commodities and also the incentives for key stakeholders, this chapter provides guidance on increasing gains from production and trade in sustainable commodities. The first section presents the main sustainable development impacts associated with commodity production and introduces the concept of sustainable commodities. The following sections examine leverage points to foster production and trade of sustainable commodities includ-

### Table 1: Key sustainable development impacts associated with selected commodities

| Commodity | Environmental Impacts | Social Impacts |
|---|---|---|
| Cotton | High water consumption. High use of agro-chemicals. Decline in soil health. Water pollution. Discharge of untreated effluents during manufacturing. | Worker poisoning and illness. Poor working conditions. Child labour. Gender issues.[1] Contamination of drinking water. |
| Palm Oil | Forest conversion and species loss. Loss of eco-system functions. Burning during clearing. Soil erosion and loss of fertility. Use of agro-chemicals. Palm oil mill effluent. | Conflicts over tenure and land claims. Change of land use. Large-scale social transformation. Terms of trade for smallholders. Social justice/grievance procedures. Workers rights and conditions. |
| Soya | Natural habitat conversion and species loss. Loss of eco-system functions. Burning during clearing. Soil erosion and loss of fertility. Effluents. Use of agro-chemicals. | Change of land use. Land tenure conflicts. Loss of rural labour opportunities and rural-to-urban migration. Large-scale production required to be viable financially. |
| Sugar | Loss of wetlands. Water take and reduced water flow. Soil erosion and loss of fertility. Water pollution. Pollution from burning cane fields. Air pollution and solid waste from processing cane. | Subsidies and market barriers in some countries hurt those in other countries. Scale required to feed mills reduces other forms of land use. Poor working conditions. Child labour and indentured labour. |

Sources: Clay (2004) and ProForest and IIED (2003)

ing better management practices (BMPs), labelling, trade policy, government support, and strategic alliances and partnerships. The last section draws conclusions and presents some recommendations.

## 2. The concept of sustainable commodities

### 2.1 Sustainable development impacts of commodities

In many cases expansion and intensification of agricultural commodity production implies mono-crop production, land degradation, deforestation and elimination of wildlife habi-

---

1. There are several claims about women's lack of access and use of cotton revenues, e.g. in Chad and other Sahelian countries. See for instance OECD (2005).

tats as well as pressure on water resources. Environmental and health problems may be caused by the use of agro-chemicals. Expanded production of agricultural commodities, in particular tropical commodities, has been linked with deterioration in labour conditions. In Latin America, it has been associated with the marginalization of small producers and rural-to-urban migration. In other regions, such as Africa and Asia, it has been linked with the marginalization of women and child labour. Table 1 summarizes key environmental and social impacts associated with production of four commodities.

For 99 per cent of human history, people obtained their food by hunting, fishing and gathering. Over the past 7,000 years that has changed. Today only two per cent of human food energy and seven per cent of protein is captured from the wild. The rest is produced by agriculture, animal husbandry and aquaculture. Agriculture is the largest industry on the planet. It employs an estimated 1.3 billion people and each year produces $1.3 trillion worth of goods at the farm gate. In developing countries, however, the poor can spend as much as 75 per cent of their income on food and still be malnourished.[2] Not only has the percentage of income spent on food in developed countries tended to decline, but the money that makes it to farmers, in real terms, has declined as well. Globally, agribusiness produced $420 billion in 1950 and producers received one-third of it. By 2028, researchers estimate that the global market for agricultural production will be $10 trillion and farmers will receive about 10 per cent of it.[3]

Agriculture is a key issue in many countries for employment, food security and export earnings. As population increases and as consumption of animal-based proteins increases as well, it will be a key challenge to expand agricultural production while minimizing its adverse environmental and social impacts. This issue is complicated by the fact that increasingly value is added to agricultural commodities as they move along the value chain, further and further from the farms. In addition, increasing production efficiency and scale and reducing costs does not necessarily make commodities more sustainable. The key questions for this chapter, then, are what are the ways to provide incentives to produce sustainable commodities, under which circumstances, and what can be done to encourage them.

## 2.2 The concept of sustainable commodities

Sustainable commodities involve a wide range of commodities distinguishable by their reduced environmental, social or ethical impacts. UNCTAD defines 'Environmentally Preferable Products' as 'industrial or consumer goods whose production, end-use and/or disposal have reduced negative, or potentially positive, environmental impacts relative to a substitute good providing similar function and utility.'[4] By applying social concerns to the former definition, for the purposes of this chapter we define sustainable commodities as those that generate greater positive or reduced negative social, environmental and economic impacts along the value chain from producer to end-user than conventional

---
2. Clay (2004).
3. Clay (2004).
4. UNCTAD (1995).

commodities. Benefits are realized through the production, consumption and disposal processes and can accrue throughout the chain.

Defining what counts as sustainable under this definition is complex and inevitably subjective as there can be conflict between environmental and social goals and between different types of environmental goals. For example, smallholder production and export of agricultural crops to developed countries can generate social benefits but imply greater 'food miles' and consequent transport emissions. There can also be conflicting equity issues as well. Improved practices are not always fully paid for by consumers, while quite often a disproportionate amount of the price consumers pay for a 'better' product is appropriated before it reaches the producer.

There are a number of voluntary certification and labelling programmes that define social, economic and environmental standards for different commodities, each emphasizing certain aspects more than others: fair trade focuses on the prices paid to growers, organic on the use of pesticides, etc. There are also a number of private-sector initiatives where individual companies are attempting to reduce the environmental and social impacts associated with specific commodities without necessarily any link to a third-party certification programme. Motivations may include financial opportunity, corporate responsibility, market position, consumer demand or a combination of all of the above.[5] This chapter addresses commodity production in this broad sense and explores leverage points for reducing or improving the social, environmental and financial impacts of commodity production.

## 3. Leverage Point 1: Incentives for adoption of better management practices

As competition in the global economy increases, the producers that survive are going to be those that are the most efficient. They will be defined by their ability to invent, identify or adapt 'better' practices that reduce input use as well as waste and pollution. Such producers will be more profitable, or at least will remain competitive, in the face of globally declining prices.

Better management practices exist for both small and large producers, but they will be different. The BMPs for any given producer will probably be those that are adapted from the lessons learned by other producers. BMPs are about continuous improvement – today's better practice is tomorrow's norm and the day after that the practice to be eliminated. BMPs encompass a broad range of environmental, social and labour practices that allow agricultural producers to maintain or improve their on-farm assets (e.g. soil, water, biodiversity), optimize resource-use efficiency, create marketable by-products, reduce waste, increase employees' skills and incomes, encourage employees' loyalty, assure market access and reduce the risk of adverse relations locally. They are largely market-driven and work best where buyers and investors have incentives to reduce risk by encouraging the adoption of BMPs as well. Some examples are when certification

---

5. See Chapter 6.

programmes, buyers or investors require improved performance against a baseline for key agricultural impacts, in energy, water, pesticide or fertilizer inputs; soil health; biodiversity; cumulative environmental impacts; workers' conditions or income; producers' income; or conflicts with neighbours.

Most farmers learned to farm from their parents, who in turn were taught by their parents and so on. But in a world of global markets, limited resources and increased demand, those producers who survive will complement these traditional practices with new lessons, approaches and technology from others. Because of their importance to the overall sustainability of agriculture, the adoption of BMPs cannot be left entirely to producers. Most producers will not make the transition without support or encouragement. Government subsidies can, in the short term, provide incentives. Government regulatory and permitting systems can also encourage this, but for political reasons are likely to stop with the encouragement of 'good' rather than 'better' practices.

There is increasing interest on the part of investors, insurers, and major purchasers to look to BMP-based screens to reduce their risk from exposure to the environmental and social impacts of agricultural production. Investors already evaluate management as a condition of investment in commercial operations. The adoption of BMP-based screens is little more than a more precise way of evaluating a business's management practices as they relate to critical impacts. The intent may not be to reduce impacts but, rather, to reduce liability, costs and wastes, and to increase efficiency as well as profits and returns on investment. In the end, the two issues can be one and the same.

For insurers, the identification and adoption of BMP-based screens can reduce risks by determining whether producers have adopted practices that reduce overall risk and liability. The risk or liability could include such items as crop failure, personal liability or worker injury, downstream liabilities from soil erosion, smoke or runoff, or issues of chemical residues that pose consumer health concerns.

With increasing concerns about food quality and safety, a number of food manufacturers and retailers are developing BMP-based screens to guide their purchases and reduce their liability resulting from pesticide residues in food, for example. Another issue is to be able to trace products back to their source if any problems are found with the product. Self-developed programmes, whether by producers, manufacturers, retailers, investors or insurers, however comprehensive and well intentioned, have limited credibility with consumers. At the same time, many NGO-developed certification and eco-label programmes either do not address or do not measure the improved impact of their programme on the environment and society. Over time, credibility with consumers will most likely be based on third-party certification, multi-stakeholder and transparent standards development processes, and measurable standards.

### 3.1 Motivations to introduce BMPs

BMPs often carry business benefits. They work best where businesses and investors have medium- or long-term horizons. Research suggests that most of the better practices pay for themselves, often within two to three years.[6] Producer-level financial incentives to implement BMPs are key. Some BMPs will increase costs, at least in the short run. However, if they are presented as part of an overall package whose net financial impacts are positive, then a convincing case can still be made to producers for their adoption. Some BMPs give strong financial incentives for adoption – e.g. integrated pest management can minimize inputs. Against a backdrop of intense competition and declining prices, growers are less likely to adopt BMPs without evident financial benefits.

There appear to be links between financing and the adoption of BMPs, although so far the evidence on the efficacy of such arrangements is patchy. Clearly, it is in a financial institution's best interests to reduce the risk of its loans. In part this can be done by ensuring that producers are using BMPs. The potential for financial actors to influence change, however, will depend on the context. Increasing interest among investors in the agricultural commodities sector suggests that BMP-based investment screens may become more common in the future. Rabobank, the IFC, ABN Amro and HSBC are beginning to look at this strategy as a way to reduce their risks in commodity finance.

Similar approaches are being explored by buyers as well. Unilever, GAP, Nike, Tate & Lyle, Mars, COOP (Switzerland), Migros, Adidas, H&M, IKEA, Cadbury-Schweppes, SAB Miller and Wal-Mart are all involved to differing degrees in multi-stakeholder groups in the development of BMP-based purchase screens for food and fibre commodities. BMPs can be leveraged even more when buyers and investors work in tandem to encourage producer adoption. WWF has helped to convene a series of multi-stakeholder commodity round tables intended to create standards for sustainable commodities such as cotton, soya, sugar, palm oil, shrimp and salmon. Each of these includes buyers, investors, producer groups, NGOs and researchers. From these individual efforts to reduce the impact of commodity production, The Sustainable Food Lab is now developing 'meta-standards' against which to evaluate certification and eco-label programmes: it is exploring how the standards were created, whether any claims can be backed up by a measurement of impacts against a baseline, and how the systems are verified.

Developing-country institutions and companies are, with the help of government policies, increasing the applicability of financial instruments to rural contexts. A good example lies in India's recent expansion in access to insurance in rural areas owing to macro-level policy directives coupled with the e-chopal system pioneered by ITC (one of India's premier companies), which helps to streamline supply chains and deliver greater net benefits to rural producers.[7]

Insight Investment has recently been raising with retailers issues related to their sourcing of cotton and shrimp. In addition, the UK Social Investment Forum is examining the impact of food retailers and processors in emerging markets and developing countries, with a view to identifying management approaches and tools that are most

---

6. Clay (2004).
7. Development Alternatives (2004); FDCF(2004).

likely to result in international development outcomes and financial benefits.[8] These programmes are all voluntary. However, it is increasingly common for investors and buyers to require producers to comply with particular policies. Still, the programmes work best when they are win-win, i.e. when the BMPs allow producers to obtain higher net earnings and when buyers and investors are able to reduce their risk.

**Limits of a BMP approach**: Some problems cannot be solved by a BMP approach alone and will require flanking measures. This is particularly the case with impacts associated with environmental issues such as the expansion of agricultural frontiers (e.g. habitat loss) and the cumulative impacts from many agricultural producers in one area. BMPs do not address such economic issues as terms of trade, subsidies and structural oversupply.

Moreover, there can be conflicts between environmental and social goals. The most efficient BMPs for large-scale, efficient market-oriented producers are not the same as BMPs for small farmers attempting to produce on more marginal lands on scales that are less competitive. Too little attention has been focused on this issue since much evidence suggests that most environmental impacts per hectare of production of commodities come from small-scale producers. While these producers cannot afford to change their land, it is not clear that they cannot afford or would not adopt BMPs if they had information about them. Since some commodities are dominated by small-scale producers, the identification of appropriate BMPs and the barriers to their adoption need to be explored. Solutions regarding access to technical knowledge and finance for investing in BMPs will need to be identified and supported in a concerted way. For small producers, proving the business case of BMPs that are tailored for them will probably be insufficient to ensure their adoption. But an even bigger issue will be to identify the BMPs that are appropriate to the assets and skills of small producers. BMPs associated with mechanized production systems are the easiest to develop, but they are not appropriate for labour-intensive systems. Appropriate BMPs for different production systems, as well as dissemination efforts and technical support, will be necessary for commodities where these are significant issues (e.g. coffee, cocoa, palm oil, cotton and sugar in parts of the world where small producers dominate production). Experience with developing private-sector channels for providing extension and other services to small-scale growers has had mixed results, but this work needs to be better documented so that lessons can be learned.

**Traceability**: Relationships between growers and buyers include direct business-to-business relationships, outgrower and contract farming, informal arrangements with small producers, and commodity exchanges. In the case of commodity exchanges and informal buying relationships, there is little scope for traceability and market signals for the implementation of BMPs. In order to establish recognition in the market for a commodity grown according to BMPs, certification and segregated chains for sustainable commodities may be necessary. If these systems are to tip entire industries, BMP initiatives will need to address mainstream commodity markets rather than investing solely in

---

8. IIED and ProForest (2004); UKSIF (2004).

alternative supply-chain structures. In fact, GMO soya and other crops have proven that it is possible to ensure full traceability within mainstream commodity trading systems.

## 4. Leverage Point 2: Labelling of sustainable commodities[9]

Another point of leverage is the use of labelling systems to differentiate sustainable commodities from conventional ones. Inevitably this means smaller but selected and dynamic markets. In some cases, buyers appear to be able to pay premiums which they can then pass on to consumers.

### 4.1 Some statistics on market potential for labelled sustainable commodities

The global market for organic produce was estimated at $25 billion in 2004, with growth rates of 5 to 40 per cent depending on the country. After aquaculture, organic is generally considered the fastest growing segment within the food industry. The final market is concentrated in industrialized countries. In terms of market participation, the organic market in OECD countries in 2000 was less than two per cent of fresh food sales on average[10] Specific products in specific markets, however, can easily surpass a 20 per cent market share.[11] In the case of fair trade products, market sales of products officially labelled as fair trade passed from 25,972 metric tons in 1997 to 83,480 tons in 2003 - an increase of 221 per cent in six years. Though consumption is still confined to industrialized countries, especially the EU and USA, there are interesting growth prospects in some developing countries. However, there are serious concerns as to whether either organic or fair trade will ever achieve 10 per cent of total food market share.

A key driver for such products is the demand from industrialized countries that provides incentives (often tangible premiums) delivered through market mechanisms in the supply chain. In many industrialized countries the increase in demand is higher than the increase in supply – e.g. 40 per cent versus 25 per cent respectively in the UK – meaning those countries have to rely on imports.[12] On the other hand, the UK has a policy to increase domestic organic production to 70 per cent of domestic consumption by 2010.[13] Several EU countries are now subsidizing organic production at two to four times the rates for conventional agriculture. It is not clear if these programmes could withstand a WTO challenge. In developing countries, local markets for organic and fair trade products are still small, but there is growth potential. For instance, in Latin America 10 per cent of the organic produce is sold within the region; sales of organic

---

9. Due to limited availability of information this section focuses on organic and fair trade labels. However, there are many other labels that would need to be analyzed, such as those from Rainforest Alliance, Protected Harvest, IPM, ICM, CCC Coffee among others.
10. Willer and Yusseffi (2004).
11. FAO (2003).
12. UNCTAD (2004).
13. Mason (2004).

food and drink were estimated at $100 million in 2002 and they are expected to increase, especially in big cities in Brazil and Argentina.[14] In China the market for 'green' products has increased dramatically and countries like Malaysia, Thailand and India are expected to show growing markets for organic products as organic farmers step up production in these countries.[15]

An important factor contributing to the growth of the organic and fair trade sectors is the increasing participation of large retailers and grocery chains in their distribution. This trend is likely to continue. On the whole, the market for sustainable products has displayed significant growth over the last decade. If these rates can be maintained, such markets may be an important opportunity for commodity producers all over the world, if they can get access.[16]

## 4.2 Problems and limitations of certification and labelling

There are concerns that certification and labelling are increasingly being seen as market-access requirements or 'entry tickets' set by the private sector rather than tools for differentiation and value added, constituting unintentional but costly barriers, especially for small producers in developing countries. Particular concerns prevail due to:

- **Cost**: The complex procedures and high costs involved in the processes. Since many of the costs are fixed, the impact on producers depends a lot on how much of the product that was certified is actually sold. Many fair trade and organic producers in developing countries do not sell more than 25 to 35 per cent of their certified production at the pertinent premium rate. Where producers have to pay for certification, or the production costs are higher than for conventional produce (e.g. in organic crops), this sharply lowers the 'premium' rate of return.
- **Suitability of the programmes to different contexts**: The 'one-size-fits-all' approach of many international certification schemes leaves little space for country-specific differences in terms of absorption capacities or different environmental and social priorities. This often discriminates against developing countries. In addition, few of these programmes are intended to be applicable to large-scale commercial commodities.[17]
- **Proliferation and lack of transparency**: The international proliferation of eco-labelling programmes and the lack of progress towards harmonization or mutual recognition have reduced transparency and increased confusion to consumers, especially of schemes elaborated by developing countries, and increased costs to producers.

The evidence of reduced environmental and social impacts resulting from certified or eco-labelled commodity production is just beginning to be researched. However, most certification and eco-label programmes certify against prescriptive

---

14. Willer and Yussefi (2004).
15. Willer and Yussefi (2004).
16. Borregaard N (2001).
17. Clay (2004).

standards. They do not measure results. As a result, there are increasing concerns about how sustainable certified production is. The concerns include:
- Fair trade – claims that their social criteria are not as fair or as pro-poor as advertized and that because producers can only sell a small amount of their product at fair trade prices they often have to sell the remainder at prices below commercial rates.
- Organic – environmental impacts in terms of erosion, use of water and nutrient loading or effluents can be equal or worse than those from conventional production of some commodities.[18]
- Eco-label and certification programmes tend to be prescriptive. If they instead told producers what results are expected or acceptable and let producers achieve them in different ways, they would encourage innovation.
- Most programmes do not identify and address in a measurable way the most significant impacts of the commodity being produced.
- Contrary to what is often portrayed, few certification programmes involve a wide stakeholder group in a consultative standards-setting process and they are not particularly transparent.

Buyer groups can exert pressure on the value chain to support specific certification or eco-labelling programmes. However, consumers can be confused by attributes signalled by price premiums for sustainable commodities. For instance, in the UK, supermarkets report that most of the complaints about fresh produce relate to organic products: consumers mistakenly believe that the quality is inherently better because of the extra cost. Marine Stewardship Council (MSC) fish has suffered similar problems.

### 4.3 Need for market intelligence and information

The marketing channels for fair trade, organic and eco-label products are different from their conventional counterparts. Some market segments have found that commercialization in specialized shops or through direct marketing, specialized fairs or the internet are significant.[19] The proliferation of certification schemes does not help the producer in his/her marketing efforts. Rather they make the task of selling more complex. The transaction costs can be high. They have to adapt to different certification criteria for selling to different markets. Producers can organize themselves to reduce some of their certification and marketing costs.

## 5. Leverage Point 3: Trade preferences for labelled sustainable commodities

The development of sustainable trading systems for commodities[20] includes not only addressing environmental and social impacts, but ensuring that both producers and the trading systems are financially viable. Currently, commodity prices fail to include many

---

18. Vetterli, W. et al (2003).
19. See for example, Borregaard, Dufey and Ladron de Guevara (2002) for the case of organic wine.
20. See von Moltke, K. (2002).

environmental and social costs and this is likely to persist if there are no markets for these 'externalities.' Policy action is required to internalize these costs. However, when measures to address externalities have an impact on competitiveness with producers that are not subject to them, trade is distorted in favour of less sustainable producers.[21] Policy tools such as trade preferences for sustainable commodities have been identified as possible mechanisms to help address such externalities and prevent producers that choose more sustainable methods being out-competed.[22] Any such preferences must be compatible with WTO rules. This section looks at the position under these rules.

### 5.1 Relevant WTO rules

According to the rules of the multilateral system of trade, a system of tariff differentiation must be in accordance with the non-discrimination provisions of the GATT, such as Articles 1 ('Most Favoured Nation') and 3 ('Like Products'). Otherwise it must fall within the exceptions outlined in Article 20. Although these rules are to prevent discrimination on a geographical basis, in many cases they also prevent products being treated differently because of the way they have been produced, such as sustainable commodities.

It is generally agreed that product differentiation based on production, process and manufacturing methods is only allowed if the PPM affects the final characteristics of the product. Differentiation on the basis of the way the product was produced, the so-called non-product related PPMs, is not allowed under GATT rules. However, Article 20 of GATT might justify exceptions (see section 5.1.1). In addition, there are two WTO agreements - the agreement on Technical Barriers to Trade and the Agreement on Government Procurement - that contain derogations to the rules on PPMs. Developing countries are opposed to product differentiation based on PPMs because they regard them as a new means of discriminating against developing countries' exports.[23]

#### 5.1.1 Article 20 of GATT

There are two relevant exceptions in Article 20 of GATT regarding environmental and social concerns. The first is Article 20(a), which refers to the protection of public morals. Several commentators agree that this applies to violations of human rights,[24] in particular to the 'core' or 'fundamental' labour rights outlined in the 1999 ILO Declaration on Fundamental Principles and Rights at Work.[25] At the moment, however, there is no jurisprudence from dispute settlements about Article 20(a) over the extent that 'protection of public morals' includes other social rights. Consumer scares relating to trade are

---

21. Hardstaff (2002).
22. Hardstaff (2002). Von Moltke (2002) suggests a rural development fund for sustainable commodities producers in developing countries
23. See Wiers (2002).
24. See Parker et al (2004).
25. These are: freedom of association and the right to collective bargaining; the elimination of all forms of forced or compulsory labour; the abolition of child labour; and the elimination of discrimination in the workplace.

increasing (BSE or 'mad cow' disease for instance), so the 'public morals' exception may gain importance.

The second exception is Article 20(g), which refers to measures related to the conservation of exhaustible natural resources. The meaning of 'exhaustible natural resources' has been interpreted to cover living and non-living resources, including fish, turtles, salmon, gasoline and clean air. Given these interpretations, measures to reduce greenhouse gas emissions and to protect potable water might also be covered by paragraph (g).[26] However, none of this has been tested.

On the whole, trade preferences for sustainable commodities are likely to be accepted at the WTO on a case-by-case basis,[27] as long as the following conditions are met:
- The preferential tariffs apply to all WTO Members and focus on producers, not countries, that comply with the PPM requirements.
- PPM requirements concerning standards, certification and accreditation can be applied with sufficient flexibility, taking into account the conditions prevailing in the exporting country.
- The importing country has made serious efforts to enable exporting-country producers to comply with the PPM requirements.
- Procedural aspects of PPM requirements concerning standards, certification and accreditation are transparent and predictable.

### 5.1.2 The Agreement on Technical Barriers to Trade

In the Agreement on Technical Barriers to Trade only product-related barriers are permitted. The main body of the Agreement covers technical regulations, and the annex contains a Code of Good Practice regarding international voluntary standards such as those elaborated by the International Standards Organization. Thus eco-labelling administered by the private sector and other non-governmental entities falls outside the scope of the WTO rules.

### 5.1.3 The Government Procurement Agreement

The Government Procurement Agreement (GPA) – which does not apply to all WTO members – seems to allow for distinctions to be made on the basis of PPMs. The GPA's rules aim *inter alia* to ensure that members do not discriminate against foreign suppliers covered by the Agreement.[28] Article 6 of the GPA states that technical product specifications (*inter alia*, 'processes and methods of their production') shall not create

---
26. Wiers (2002).
27. Wiers (2002).
28. Currently, there are 27 signatories of the GPA, including Canada, the EU, the UK and the US. The rest of the signatories are predominantly industrialized countries. In addition, not all public procurement of a signatory country is covered by the GPA as many countries place restrictions on both the goods and services covered.

'unnecessary obstacles to international trade.' According to a UK Government report 'This suggests that PPM criteria are allowed in the GP but need to be applied in a non-discriminatory manner.'

Attention is currently being focused on the power of public procurement to stimulate sustainable production. In general government procurement of goods and services accounts for 10 to 15 per cent of industrialized countries' GDP, and so a shift towards sustainable product preferences might have a significant impact. Under EU procurement legislation, a country can list specific criteria to be met but may not specify one certification scheme exclusively. At present, many EU governments are elaborating or implementing guidelines for government procurement in the forestry sector (e.g. Sweden, Denmark, the Netherlands, Germany and UK), whose criteria are based on those of the FSC.[29] This could be taken as a precedent for extending preferences in government procurement to other sustainable commodities, including agricultural commodities.

At present, there is little evidence regarding impacts, although anecdotally the EU says there does seem to be an impact where the public sector has significant presence in a market, e.g. fine paper, timber and IT equipment.[30]

### 5.1.4 The Agreement on Agriculture (AoA)

Currently, the AoA does not allow discrimination based on the sustainability of PPMs. The AoA contains three pillars or areas: market access, domestic support and export competition. On market access the AoA states that measures other than tariffs (e.g. quantitative restrictions, variable import levies etc) are not legitimate, except in extreme circumstances.

Central to the debate over AoA reform are so-called 'non-trade concerns' of agriculture. They can be broadly categorized as the aspects of agriculture that the market does not, or cannot, necessarily provide,[31] including secure supplies of food, rural development, biodiversity conservation, environmental quality, food safety and landscape values. Hardstaff argues that non-trade concerns might provide an opportunity to introduce differentiation based on PPMs. (See section 5.5.2 below for differentiation based on Special Products.)

### 5.1.5 The Doha Mandate on Trade Liberalization in Environmental Goods and Services

At the WTO Ministerial in Doha in November 2001, members agreed to negotiations to liberalize trade in environmental goods and services.[32] Some countries have suggested including products from organic agriculture under these negotiations. However, as noted

---

29. Chaytor and Dufey (2003).
30. Speight P, European Commission (2002).
31. Hardstaff (2002).
32. 'The reduction or, as appropriate, elimination of tariff and non-tariff barriers to environmental goods and services'. (WTO 2001, paragraph 33iii).

above, developing countries are against differentiation and apparently they prefer to lose this opportunity for lowering tariffs and non-tariff measures if it involves opening the PPMs debate. Colombia has proposed different criteria, to include in the negotiations some of the products identified for the country as of special interest, based on the 'benefits that they bring to the in situ conservation'[33] of biodiversity.

### 5.2 Other preferences for sustainable commodities

#### 5.2.1 Generalized Systems of Preferences (GSP)

The GSP is a scheme of tariff preferences for developing countries. These instruments provide an exception to the MFN principle, permitting countries to differentiate between developing and industrialized countries in their tariffs. Most industrialized countries operate a GSP scheme; product coverage and margins of preference vary from scheme to scheme. Industrialized countries are under no obligation to provide tariff preferences to developing countries, but if they do, they must be 'generalised, non-reciprocal and non-discriminatory.'[34]

In the case of the EU's GSP, the appearance of products derived from sustainably managed forests began at the start of this decade. These include sensitive products included in the International Tropical Timber Convention, covering about 50 tariff lines. Regarding social issues, the EU's GSP includes incentives for the protection of international labour standards. In October 2004 the EU adopted a proposal setting out a revised GSP. This includes a new programme called 'GSP+' that covers approximately 7,200 products which can enter the EU duty-free from vulnerable countries that accept the main international conventions on social issues, human rights, environmental protection and governance.[35]

It should be noted that GSP benefits are, in general, granted for only a limited range of raw and processed agricultural products and vary from one preference-giving country to another. In addition, GSP are often subject to frequent changes and short-term and ex-post renewals. This means that specific exporters have no guarantee of the continuation of their benefit, undermining the value of the GSP as the basis for investment decisions on sustainable practices.

#### 5.2.2 Other trade agreements

A new generation of trade agreements[36] is commencing, which include preferences for sustainable products. For instance, the promotion of fair trade is mentioned in the

---

33. Carolina Jaramillo, Ministry of the Environment of Colombia, Expert Meeting on Definitions and Dimensions of Environmental and Goods and Services in Trade and Development, UNCTAD, Geneva 9-11 July.
34. Parker et al (2004).
35. See http://www.dellao.cec.eu.int/en/2004/GSP_2006_2008_en.htm.
36. The first generation only included tariff issues, but the new generation adds issues such as investment, intellectual property rights, labour and the environment.

Cotonou Agreement (Art. 23g). In APEC, Chile has submitted a proposal on Voluntary Initiatives for Sustainable Production as part of an overall initiative to strengthen sustainable development.[37] In Mercosur, one of the four thematic areas of the Framework Agreement on Environment, signed in 2004, consists of 'Environmentally sustainable productive activities,' and mentions sustainable tourism and sustainable forest management.[38] Finally, the Framework Agreement between Mercosur and the Andean Community mentions the promotion of Biotrade as one of its activities.

Thus, international preferences for sustainable commodities exist already on behalf of several countries. So far the interests of developing countries have been safeguarded. Positive discrimination for sustainable commodities can demonstrate to developing countries that industrialized countries' proposals to integrate environmental measures into the trading system do not imply green protectionism through the back door.

### 5.3 Expected benefits of trade preferences for sustainable commodities

The expected benefits from preferential market access for sustainable commodities include:
- They may shift the balance in favour of sustainable commodities and thus set an incentive to switch production towards better environmental and social practices in exporting countries.
- Preferential tariffs may improve the premium that producers receive or reduce the price to consumers.
- Trade preferences may improve developing countries' competitiveness, particularly given that sustainable products in industrialized countries are sometimes heavily subsidized.[39]
- A reduced consumer price may lead to increased demand for sustainable commodities. This will allow producers to sell a greater proportion of their products as sustainable.
- If trade preferences are agreed to within long-term arrangements, producers might perceive a lower risk of investing in sustainable practices. It is still not clear whether the current rate of investment in better practices is due to actual risk or lack of information.
- Trade preferences for sustainable commodities at the WTO will send a strong political signal to consumers, producers and the international community about the importance of sustainable commodities, and highlight the fact that economic issues are not the only important issues.
- Positive discrimination for sustainable commodities can be a way of showing devel-

---

37. See APEC Secretariat (2004). The initiative focuses on the tourism, mining, aquaculture and agriculture sectors.
38. Borregaard and Dufey (2005).
39. Borregaard *et al* (2002) estimated for the case of the EU, subsidies to sustainable produce may easily reach 20 per cent of production costs. To this need to be added other important forms of government support in terms of certification and marketing and also support from the private sector.

oping countries that industrialized countries' proposals to integrate environmental measures into the trading systems is not green protectionism 'through the back door'.
- Trade preferences for sustainable commodities may promote policy coherence. They would be in line, for example, with the pursuit of sustainability by the EU in CAP reform.

### 5.4 Main concerns to be addressed

The benefits associated with better market access for sustainable commodities are not straightforward. In order to realize them several concerns need to be addressed. These include:

- **Winners and losers**

Among producers, there will be winners and losers depending on current levels of trade preferences, prevailing production systems and characteristics, ability to shift towards sustainable production, and ability to cope with the different certification structures or harmonize certification programmes, among other things. Likely main winners will be producers in middle-income developing countries, especially those that have stronger certification and labelling structures, such as some Latin American and East Asian countries. At country level, producers using industrialized methods might be the main winners due to economies of scale. Producers in poorer developing countries will very probably have little to gain. Such countries export only small quantities of material and lack certification structures that would allow them to sell sustainable products to international markets. In addition, most of them already enjoy preferential access to industrialized countries' markets (e.g. under the Everything But Arms and Cotonou initiatives) and with trade preferences to sustainable commodities for all countries, those preferences will be eroded.

Trade preferences for sustainable commodities, such as those certified as organic, may increase competition between domestic producers and those in developing countries. With the UK intending to increase its own organic production, preferential access of organic products from overseas could start a price war. This, obviously, is not a desired result.[40] Verschuur et al suggest the implementation of trade preferences together with mechanisms to support domestic production in importing countries. Given the subsidies that have been available to support EU producers converting to organic production, many developing-country producers would have a hard time competing with them. This is well documented for many conventional agricultural commodities such as cotton and sugar, but it is increasingly the case also for organic production in the EU, where subsidies can be equivalent to 20 per cent of production costs.

---

40. Vershuur et al (2003).

### Leverage Points for Encouraging Sustainable Commodities | Chapter 9

- The mechanics of setting preferences

**Margin of preferences**: In order to provide sufficient incentives to encourage more sustainable production practices, there must be an adequate margin separating conventional and sustainable produce (e.g. the MNF tariff and a preferential tariff).[41]

**Product coverage**: Both raw materials and value-added products must be covered.

**Which policy tool**: While the focus of this discussion has been on preferential tariffs, it is also worth analyzing other policy measures to improve market access for sustainable commodities, e.g. quotas. It has been argued that preferential tariffs are not the best option as in the long term the best solution would be to internalize external costs for conventional production.[42] Parker *et al* suggest, for the case of bananas, to consider having quotas alongside a differentiated tariff on the basis of sustainability.

**Special customs codes**: International customs codes, known as the Harmonized System, are essential for the trading system. They allow authorities to track trade flows and negotiate tariff rates. Currently, both sustainable and conventional commodities share the same HS codes. The HS system is maintained by the World Customs Organization, which at regular intervals updates codes. In January 2002 the WCO for the first time included the social and environmental fields, particularly relating to products under certain Multilateral Environmental Agreements (MEAs).[43] This set a precedent for further differentiation on the basis of social and environmental concerns. A special HS code for sustainable commodities may facilitate the collection of data regarding their production and trade, which is crucial for the design of policies to promote them.

### 5.5 Product differentiation not based on PPMs

Much of the previous discussion focused on commodity differentiation based on production and process methods. In this sub-section we discuss other potential sources of trade differentiation for sustainable commodities.

#### 5.5.1 Geographical Indications

GIs are a type of collective monopoly right provided by the TRIPS Agreement that allows the users of the indication to differentiate their product in the market and provides a barrier to entry to the market.[44] GIs have been used to access niche markets by, for instance, coffee and tea producers (Café de Colombia, Jamaica Blue Mountain

---
41. See Parker *et al* (2004) for an exercise on tariff differentiation on the basis of sustainable criteria on bananas.
42. Verschuur *et al* (2002).
43. See www.wcoomd.org.
44. Rangnekar, D. (2003).

and Darjeeling, among others) and have also been used alongside other initiatives such as organic and fair trade labels. However, few if any GI products can demonstrate that they have any measurable positive impacts on the environment. In addition, such programmes can be easily corrupted. It is estimated, for example, that as much as three times as much Jamaican Blue Mountain and Hawaiian Kona Coffee is sold at premium prices in developed-country markets as is exported from those production areas. In short, it is not clear how much local producers actually benefit from the prices that are paid. More research would be required to understand who along the value chain makes most of the money from the sale of these products.

In this context, it would be important to understand the implications of using GIs to distinguish agricultural products from ecologically sensitive regions such as Amazonia.[45] Origin, by itself, is not sufficient to indicate either positive or negative social or environmental impacts. Producing crops for export in sensitive environmental areas is a very delicate matter. In short, the potential benefits associated with GI protection for sustainable commodities need to be balanced with potential problems. One such is the distribution of benefits through the value chain – rents often lodge with manufacturers and not primary producers. Analyses of European support for banana production in specific developing countries suggest that most of the payments did not leave Europe and that many of the remaining rents were captured by other players along the value chain than producers.[46] In addition, GI commercialization requires adequate certification and traceability structures and all the costs that these imply, especially for small producers.

### 5.5.2 Special products

In response to developing countries' proposals, provisions were made at the WTO Agriculture Special Session of March 2003 to allow developing countries to designate a number of agricultural products 'as being special products with respect to food security, rural development and/or livelihood security concerns.' These products would be subject to minimal tariff reductions. These provisions were later incorporated in the July Framework that established 'modalities' in the AoA.[47] Technical discussions on SPs have concentrated on how those products should be designated and what flexibility of treatment should be accorded to them.[48] Whereas proponents favoured self-designation, meaning each developing country could decide which products to identify as SPs, other WTO members stressed the need for objective criteria that would limit the scope of these products and guarantee such provisions would have a minimal impact on trade.

Overall, SPs might offer an opportunity for developing countries to differentiate their products, which is not based on PPMs. SPs would be those commodities that deliver significant social benefits in terms of subsistence or rural development and livelihoods.

---

45. Trade BioRes (2003).
46. Konrad von Moltke, personal communication.
47. Bernal, L. (2004).
48. See Chapter 2 above.

## 6. Leverage Point 4: Government support for sustainable commodities

Markets do not internalize the environmental and social costs of commodity production. Some form of policy intervention is required. At present, governments have a reduced role in internalizing such externalities, especially in developing countries. But they can only do what is politically possible. They rarely encourage innovation—the norm is to tell people what to do or not to do. In this way, they discourage the worst actors in a sector rather than helping the best actors.

In industrialized countries, the internalization of negative externalities generated through the production of conventional commodities is fairly advanced (e.g. through taxes on the use of pesticides and chemical fertilizers). Support payments to compensate for positive externalities can also be significant. In the case of the EU, support to organic production can reach 20 per cent of production costs.[49] Anecdotal evidence suggests that in the UK levels of support for organic farmers are twice what they are for conventional farmers.

In developing countries, by contrast, governments have tended towards reactive environmental management and there is still only an incipient internalization of negative externalities. Very few developing countries have tax or charge systems for pollutants or the exploitation of natural resources. Although several developing countries' governments are showing interest in sustainable produce and are starting to implement tools to promote production and trade of these products, most initiatives have been limited with regard to the range of products included as well as the financial resources available to them.[50] The lack of government support might be an important drawback for sustainable commodities producers that are targeting markets in industrialized countries where they compete with subsidized production.

In addition, in many cases commercialization of sustainable commodities requires expensive and complex certification procedures and special market information, which often are not easily accessible for small producers in developing countries. Governments can help producers with technical assistance and capacity building. In some cases, governments have started to implement their own national systems of certification. However, these systems must be methodologically credible and harmonized with other systems. Sustainable commodities require interdisciplinary thinking and teamwork to cover the environmental, social, economic and cultural dimensions. This poses a challenge for traditional certification and accreditation institutions.

The marketing channels for sustainable commodities are often different than for conventional products. Export markets usually require certification and monitoring. The proliferation of certification schemes makes marketing complex and at times costly. Moreover, there are no official sustainable commodities trade statistics and market information is scarce. The geographical separation between developing country producers

---

49. Borregaard *et al* (2002).
50. See Borregaarrd and Dufey (2005) for more details on these initiatives.

and industrialized country consumers raises additional issues and costs.

Finally, governments may finance and generate information about the sustainable development impacts associated with sustainable commodities. This information is crucial for the elaboration of policies to promote them – by maximizing their benefits while minimizing their negative impacts.

## 7. Leverage Point 5: Strategic alliances and partnerships

No single stakeholder group or set of government or private sector policies will address all the sustainable development problems associated with commodity production and trade. Commodity markets involve many players, and if the goal is to use the market to make commodity production more sustainable then many different actors in the market chain will need to be involved. In order to do this effectively, it is important that each understand why it is in their best interest to do something different and to make sure that the rules apply to all like players equally.

As mentioned in Chapter 6, several groups are attempting to bring different players together for coffee. There are similar groups working on cotton, palm oil, soya and sugar. Under the auspices of the Sustainable Food Lab Initiative, NGOs, food manufacturers, retailers and investors are beginning a programme of side-by-side comparisons of commodity eco-label and certification programmes with the aim of developing meta-standards against which both the content and the process of creating commodity certification programmes for any commodity could be compared.

In the promotion and trade of certified and labelled sustainable commodities, the most significant multi-sectoral initiatives are the Global Eco-labelling Network and the International Social and Environmental Accreditation and Labelling Alliance, which has taken an important step towards creating voluntary rules for transparency and participation in standard setting, emphasizing the importance of harmonization. GEN has been established to support the eco-labelling of products. At the multilateral level, the ISO's work on standardizing standard-setting procedures; UNCTAD's work in promoting environmentally preferable products (e.g. the BIOTRADE Initiative); and the International Task Force on Harmonization and Equivalence in Organic Agriculture, convened in 2002 by FAO, IFOAM and UNCTAD, should also be recognized for the work they are doing to make certification and eco-labels both better understood and more meaningful.

## 8. Conclusions and recommendations

### Overview

The potential impacts of the leverage points identified in this chapter are not well understood. To have a better understanding of the potential impacts we would need to analyze and where possible quantify key impacts, e.g. on the demand and supply sides of the value chain as well as their overall economic, social and environmental performance. Finally, there are likely to be trade-offs with the use of any of the leverage points identified in this chapter. More research and thinking on this topic will be needed to understand the limits of the tools or the possible impacts of combining two or more of them in a strategy. It does appear to be clear, however, that none of the options outlined here can address the environmental impacts caused by agricultural expansion at the frontier, or the social impacts of changing production systems on those that are not directly involved in commodity production. In general, it would appear that most of the systems tend to impose more burdens on the poorest producers than on the more affluent ones.

It is clear that levers to encourage sustainable commodity production need to be targeted. To be most effective they need to target the biggest impacts and show measurable reduction over time. Few programmes do this. Instead, most rely on prescriptive behaviour, practices and proxies, telling people what to do rather than requiring on-the-ground results. In addition, there is a tendency to overburden sustainable commodities systems with objectives that the market will not support short of better, verifiable information and market intelligence. Agreeing on the basic results desired and impacts to be addressed is key here to each of the leverage points identified.

**BMP approaches** present a great opportunity for combating adverse impacts of commodity production. They can be encouraged by buyers and investors through 'voluntary' schemes as well as through mandatory government programmes. Through these mechanisms and to the extent that BMPs are profitable or at least cost-neutral, they have the potential to tip entire commodity industries. There are some areas of concern about the BMP approach, however. For example, most attention to date has been focused on more capital-intensive, high-input commodity producers rather than small producers in developing countries, including the poorest farmers. **Action:** further commodity-specific research/investigation into BMPs, identification of the main barriers to adoption and research and analysis to assure they do not marginalize small producers.

There is a rapid proliferation of BMP standards. These come from companies, producer groups, NGOs, buyer groups, government agencies etc. Most of these do not address the scale issue and some of them are not truly 'voluntary' as they are required of any producer who wants to sell product to a specific company. **Action:** to foster processes of harmonization (technical equivalence) of standards of diverse groups such as Eurepgap, the Thai Code of Conduct for Responsible Shrimp Aquaculture, Better Cotton etc, side-by-side comparisons need to be undertaken of the standard-setting processes as well as results.

Emerging evidence suggests that **financial incentives** can help reduce social and environmental impacts. This will require further research and analysis. **Action:** encourage the private sector and governments to identify opportunities and tools for encouraging BMP adoption among small producers.

There are growing markets for a number of **eco-labelled products**. To date, however, these have not been able to grow beyond niche markets. Barriers for growth appear to be based on high costs, complex procedures, small volumes, high transaction costs and, perhaps most important, the lack of harmonization and mutual recognition of standards. These represent the main constraints for eco-labelled products. They are even more pronounced for small producers. The overall market share of such production appears to remain small even in large consuming countries like the UK.

- Eco-labelled products need to deliver on their claims. Most eco-labels do not measure what they claim to measure. This is an important issue. Some of the first studies on certification/label systems have documented failures on delivery of social and environmental benefits. **Action:** undertake side-by-side comparisons of claims versus what is measured by different eco-labelling programmes to encourage them to begin to undertake this important work. Research should focus both on environmental and social impacts.
- Consumers care most about the quality of products. Many eco-label programmes have been unable to deliver consistent quality at the retail level. **Action:** undertake direct comparisons of the quality of product that is delivered through different eco-label programmes.
- There is a proliferation of eco-label programmes. It is not clear what most of them mean. Even with organic production, there are not common standards that apply across all countries and producers of specific commodities. **Action:** encourage harmonization of different standards as well as mutual recognition of the different programmes.

**Trade preferences** may offer an opportunity to foster sustainable commodities. It is not clear exactly how the WTO will regard this issue. There are still several obstacles to overcome. These include:

- Trade in sustainable commodities is generally insignificant in terms of overall commodity flows. As a consequence, it has very little impact on overall commodity production practices.
- Poorer countries have little to gain and might see their preferential access to current markets erode through this mechanism. **Action:** explore ways of increasing the benefits to poorer countries, through market access, reduced transaction costs, capacity-building etc.
- Trade barriers can affect the competitiveness of sustainable commodities produced in developing countries. For example, subsidy payments or market protection for sustainable production in industrialized countries might undermine producers in developing countries. **Action:** undertake research to better understand the impact of developed-country producer payments for sustainable commodities on developing-country producers of the same commodities.
- Developing countries oppose product differentiation based on PPMs, which are regarded as a new means of discriminating against developing countries' exports. **Action:** Undertake research on trade preferences to sustainable commodities to ensure that they do not imply unnecessary barriers to trade for developing country producers. Understand which trade arenas represent better opportunities for sustainable

commodities. Identify additional options (not just based on PPM) for differentiation of sustainable commodities.

**Government action** in developing countries is crucial for the development of sustainable commodities. Experience shows that interest and influence in developing countries tends to be insufficient when compared to the role of government in developed countries. **Action:** provide technical assistance and capacity-building regarding certification procedures, health and safety issues, and market intelligence and information. For the most part, small producers do not have access to this kind of information. This information is key to enable governments to develop policies to help producers nurture and sustain their markets.

**Partnerships and strategic alliances** offer great opportunities for sustainable commodities. In fact, some of the most significant progress on understanding and promoting more sustainable commodity production has occurred when transparent processes are created that include a wide range of stakeholders, including producers, private-sector players, NGOs and governments. While the innovations in market structures linking production and consumption are not examined fully in this chapter, they suggest promising avenues for further work. Coordinated action needs to be undertaken commodity by commodity as well as across commodities. The IFC, WWF and others are showing some success in such initiatives for a number of commodities by combining BMP screens, market demand and government regulatory and permitting systems.

## References

APEC Secretariat, Paper for consideration submitted by Chile, document no. 2004/SOMIII/ESC/002 (Asia-Pacific Economic Co-operation, 2004).

Barnes, J.I., Nhuleipo, O., MacGregor, J. Muteyauli, P.I. (2005). Preliminary economic asset and flow accounts for forest resources in Namibia. Environmental Economics Unit, DEA, MET, Windhoek, Namibia. April. Draft.

*BBC News Online*, 'Organic firm set to make job cuts,' news.bbc.co.uk/1/hi/wales/mid/4537945.stm (12 May, 2005).

*BBC News Online*, 'Local food "greener than organic,"' news.bbc.co.uk/1/hi/sci/tech/4312591.stm (2005).

Bernal, L. 'Guidelines for Approaching the Designation of Special Products and SSM Products in Developing Countries,' Paper prepared for ICTSD (2004).

Borregaard and Dufey, 'Confronting Myths and Open Questions around Trade in Sustainable Products and Eco-labelling: towards win-win win for developing countries,' (London: IIED, 2005).

Borregaard and Dufey, 'Sustainable Products and the PPMs Dilemma: How the international community can help in resolving developing countries' concerns,' available at www.iied.org/docs/global_gov/Sustainableroductsandppms.pdf (London: IIED, 2004).

Borregaard, Dufey and Ladron de Guevara, 'Green Markets – Often a lost opportunity for developing countries – the case of Chile and the European Union' (CIPMA-RIDES, 2002).

Borregaard (2001) 'Sustainable trade, value chain, governance, and resource mobilization for sustainable development', Paper prepared for the International Institute for Environment and Development (IIED).

Chaytor and Dufey (2003), 'Liberalizing Trade in Goods from Sustainable Forest Management: Addressing Eco-labelling and PPMs', Draft.

## Chapter 9 | Agricultural Commodities, Trade and Sustainable Development

Clay, J., *World Agriculture and the Environment* (Washington, DC: Island Press, 2004).

Cotton Incorporated (2005). The Classification of Cotton. Cotton Incorporated On-line. http://www.cottoninc.com/ClassificationofCotton/Classification.

Development Alternatives, 'Regoverning Markets – Ensuring Small Producers' Participation in Agri-Food Supply System,' www.regoverningmarkets.org/docs/India_report_sm.pdf (London: IIED, 2004).

FAO, 'Environmental and Social Standards, Certification and Labelling for Cash Crops' (Rome: 2003a).

FAO, 'World Banana Economy 1985-2002,' www.fao.org/es/ESC/common/ecg/47147_en_WBE_1985_2002.pdf (Rome: 2003b).

FDCF (2004). FDCF Support for Development of Pro-Poor Insurance. www.enterplan.co.uk/fdcf/docs/FDCFTheme per cent20Paper2_ per cent20Support per cent20to per cent20the per cent20Insurance per cent20Sector.pdf. DFID / FDCF / Theme Paper No.2, May.

Hardstaff, P. 'Addressing non-trade concerns within the WTO Agreement on Agriculture: The need to regulate market access,' paper to International Conference on Non-Trade Concerns, Paris, available at http://www.rspb.org.uk/Images/non-trade_tcm5-45234.pdf (Sandy, UK: Royal Society for the Protection of Birds, 2002).

ICO (2005). Coffee Market Report – April 2005. International Coffee Organisation. April.

IIED (2003). Trade and Sustainable Forest Management – Impacts and Interaction. Paper prepared for 'Expert Consultation on Trade and Sustainable Forest Management', FAO, Rome, 3/5 February.

Lines, T., (2005). Is an IBA feasible? COLSIBA/ WINFA/ EUROBAN/ IUF/ USLEAP. February.

Mason, J. (2004). British farmers will meet rise in demand for organic food. Financial Times (UK), 3/8/04.

Nautilus Consultants and IIED (2003). Investment Mechanisms for Socially and Environmentally Responsible Shrimp Culture. Nautilus Consultants and IIED. August.

Nyoro, J.K., Ariga, J. and Komo, I., Kenyan case study on fresh fruits, vegetables and dairy products, www.regoverningmarkets.org/docs/Kenya_final_report.pdf (London: IIED, 2004).

OECD, 'Economic and Social Importance of Cotton Production and Trade in West Africa: Role of Cotton in Regional Development, Trade and Livelihoods,' Sahel and West Africa Club Secretariat / OECD, draft paper (2005).

OECD, 'Processes and Production methods (ppms): Conceptual framework and considerations on use of ppm-based trade measures' (Paris: 1997)

Organic Farm Foods, 2005, www.organicfarmfoods.co.uk/

Parker, L. and J. Harrison, 'Bananas: Differentiating Tariffs According to Social, Environmental and/or Economic Criteria', EUROBAN (2004).

ProForest and IIED, 'Feasibility Study for a Generic Supply Chain Initiative for Sustainable Commodity Crops: Findings and Recommendations,' report to the Advisory Committee on Consumer Products and the Environment, which advises the UK Department for Environment, Food and Rural Affairs (Oxford and London: 2003).

Rangnekar D (2003) ' The socio-economics of geographical indications—A review of empirical evidence from Europe' UNCTAD/ICTSD capacity building project on intellectual property rights and sustainable development

Robbins, P., *Stolen Fruit: The Tropical Commodities Disaster* (London: Zed Books, 2003).

Sahota, A. (2004). Overview of the Global Market for Organic Food and Drink. In Willer and Yussefi.

Speight P., European Commission (2002) 'Annexe E:Greening Government Procurement', available at www.number-10.gov.uk/su/waste/report/downloads/ae.pdf.

Tancotton (2005). Cotton grades classification and determination. Tancotton On-line, www.tancotton.co.tz/cotton per cent20grades.htm.

Trade BioRes, 'Special Issue: 18th Global biodiversity Forum', 8 September 2003.

UNCTAD, 'Environmental Preferable Products (EPPs) as a trade opportunity for developing countries,' document no. UNCTAD/COM/70 (Geneva: United Nations, 1995).

UNCTAD, 'Trading Opportunities for Organic Food Products from Developing Countries –Strengthening research and policy-making capacity on trade and environment in developing countries' (New York and Geneva: United Nations, 2004).

UKSIF, 2004: www.uksif.org/J/Z/Z/jp/home/main/index.shtml

USDA (2004). Cotton classification – understanding the data. Cotton Programme, Agricultural Marketing Service, United States Department Of Agriculture, July.

Verschuur G, Hin C. and van der Weidjen (2003) 'Feasibility study on Preferential Tariffs for Sustainable Produce', Centre for Agriculture and Environment, Utrecht.

W. Vetterli, R. Perkins, J. Clay and E. Guttenstein, 'Organic Farming and Nature Conservation,' paper presented in Washington at OECD Workshop on Organic Agriculture (2003).

von Moltke, K. (2002) European/Mercosur Negotiations. The environment and sustainable development dimension', World Wide Fund for Nature, April.

Wiers (2002) 'Trade and Environment in the EC and the WTO. A legal analysis' Europe Law Publishing, Groningen.

Willer and Yussefi, 'The World of Organic Agriculture: Statistics and Emerging Trends,' available at orgprints.org/2555/01/willer-yussefi-2004-world-of-organic.pdf (International Federation of Organic Agriculture, 2004).

WTO, 'Doha Ministerial Declaration,' document no. WT/MIN(01)/DEC/1 (Geneva: 2001).

# Chapter 9 | Agricultural Commodities, Trade and Sustainable Development

# Chapter 10

# Conclusions[1]

## 1. Introduction

This chapter sets out some key points of the discussions that took place at both strategic dialogues, and then lists a series of conclusions drawn by the participants on future policy and research directions.

## 2. Sustainable development, poverty and agricultural trade reform

Agricultural trade reform through the WTO process will not provide all the answers to food security, poverty reduction and sustainable development. Trade policy, though important, is only one element of any successful growth and development strategy. To reduce poverty at the national level, numerous domestic reforms are required in tandem with improvements in international trade. One also needs to be realistic about what the reform of developed-world agricultural policies can achieve. Such reform by itself cannot deliver development, which requires complementary measures to promote

---

1. This chapter is based on reports by Bernice Lee and Bill Vorley, who also drew on inputs from John Audley and Jacob Werksman, the rapporteurs during the Windsor dialogue, as well Ricardo Meléndez-Ortiz and Camilla Toulmin. It was compiled from the reports of the Windsor and Barcelona dialogue meetings by Thomas Lines.

## Chapter 10 | Agricultural Commodities, Trade and Sustainable Development

sustainable livelihoods for poor people. There is also a need to reinforce understanding of different types of agriculture-led growth strategies.

The history of the agricultural negotiations bears witness to the recurring pattern of expectation and disappointment with regard to genuine reform and opportunities for developing countries. The creation of the Cairns group in the late 1980s provided an initial political push for subsidy reduction. The very slow pace of reform of the CAP means that impacts of subsidy removal may not start to be felt until 2015, or later. If the timetable cannot be accelerated, the international community will need to focus on helping the poor and vulnerable adjust to continued sweeping changes in the interim.

Even though the AoA recognized the need to develop trade disciplines for agricultural products, which had been left out of the GATT system, the rules agreed, have often been viewed as imbalanced by developing countries. This is because of the low level of market access achieved through these rules, and the high level of subsidies paid by rich-country governments that continues to be tolerated under the AoA.

Two major tensions continue to shape agricultural trade negotiations at the WTO – one between those concerned with the interests of subsistence and smallholder farmers in developing countries and those seeking continuous support given by Northern governments to their agricultural sector; and the other between the rules-based trading system and the need for developing countries to have the flexibility and the 'policy space' to develop their economies as they see fit.

In the strategic dialogues that form the basis of this book, many participants expressed misgivings about the infant industry argument, and asked whether all countries wanted, or would be able, to climb the same development ladder. The need for progressive and innovative thinkers to **capture and define the 'policy space' debate** at this critical juncture was underlined. In addition, policymakers should ensure that trade rules will not constrain their flexibilities in implementing **domestic policies** that have worked best in delivering poverty reduction in the past. These include investment in health care and education, which can have far-reaching impacts on the welfare of the poor.

With respect to the Doha Round negotiations, participants differed in their expectations. Some felt there had been excessive optimism in the ability of trade to deliver pro-poor, pro-sustainability outcomes, as fundamental reform was unlikely to take place in the near future. This is not least because international trade rules often reflect an agreement not to worsen the status quo rather than achieve significant reform. Reductions in developed-country agricultural protection are likely to bring immediate benefits only to middle- and upper-income developing countries. The likely short-term 'losers' from liberalization will be a number of LDCs, especially net importers of food. Poorer developing countries facing many infrastructural and institutional constraints will struggle to compete with better developed non-OECD economies, such as Brazil and China.

Other shortcomings of the multilateral trading system were also discussed, such as the dominance of mercantilist concerns in trade negotiations and failure to target reductions in subsidies for products of specific interest to developing countries. The system also provides no meaningful special and differential treatment (SDT) for poor countries or regions, nor adjustment measures to ease the pains of sweeping change brought about by liberalization. There has been insufficient technical assistance for poor countries to implement SPS and TBT measures, for example.

Since small farmers often lack organization and political representation both within their own countries and on the international stage, their concerns are frequently not reflected in trade negotiations, whether at multilateral, regional or bilateral level. Participants discussed the need for a new kind of **multi-stakeholder alliance around commodity chains** to give voice to the rural poor, and ensure their concerns are reflected in campaigns to champion poverty reduction and sustainability.

Other issues of relevance to small farmers were also discussed, such as their need for public goods such as infrastructure, transport, technologies, seeds and targeted research as well as access to argue their case with policymakers in their countries.

## 3. WTO negotiations on agriculture

Developing countries are yet to achieve real access for their exports to many to developed country markets, which remain closed due to relatively high, often escalating tariffs, overly burdensome food safety and other technical requirements. Highly subsidised developed country farm products are also often 'dumped' on the world market, creating import surges in developing countries and jeopardising the livelihoods of many farmers. In addition, subsidised exports from OECD countries frequently displace developing country products in third country markets.

Even though developed countries have reduced their overall levels of tariffs and subsidies for agricultural products as a result of the WTO negotiations, they have retained protection for certain 'sensitive' products, which are often also products of interest to developing countries. Developed countries have thus been able to increase production-linked support to specific commodities so long as the aggregate reduction target is met.

Many participants at Windsor agreed on the need to **prevent shifting of support from one AoA 'box' to another**. For example, the reduction in Amber and Blue Box subsidies should not be achieved through slipping these subsidies into the Green Box. If the criteria for Green Box subsidies continue to be loosely defined, countries will be able to maintain subsidies that continue to distort the market and impede the ability of producers in developing countries to compete. As discussed earlier, although some subsidies may be justified as contributing to environmental protection and rural development, there should be **stricter disciplines on the Green Box**. In particular, a distinction needs to be made between public and private goods – where the latter must be strictly time-bound.

**The role of trade liberalization in the commodity crisis:** Trade remains only one of several factors that need attention when looking at how to mitigate commodity price decline. Others include structural change, productivity, technology and competition policy. The EU's white paper, for example, attributed the commodity price decline to productivity increases. Several participants noted that there is no clear understanding of the relationship between declining prices and either poverty or sustainability impacts. In order to get a better understanding of this relationship, it is not enough to analyze impacts at the macro level alone. There is a need for value chain analyses that can identify how the costs and benefits of liberalization will be distributed, in order to determine the effects of price and market changes on the livelihoods and sustainability of small farmers. Liberalization could move domestic prices closer to world prices, which strengthens the case for allowing poor countries to take special safeguard measures.

**State trading enterprises:** Some participants suggested that private and state trading enterprises could serve as instruments to address falling prices, notwithstanding the risk that they engage in unfair trading activities. Agricultural export STEs can assist in combating the market power of processors, wholesalers and traders. Participants agreed that it is necessary to analyze the market behaviour of private and public enterprises in the agricultural sector.

**Domestic support:** Participants concurred that subsidies distort markets for commodities in general and have a strong impact on the trade of products such as wheat, sugar, cotton and rice. Support for farmers in industrialized nations is estimated to be 30 times the amount provided as aid for agricultural development in poor countries. As a result, the 2.5 billion people in the developing world who rely on farming face food insecurity and lack of support. Different countries are impacted in diverse ways, and it is not clear exactly how eliminating subsidies would affect food prices, productivity, poverty elimination and sustainable development.

There is a link between subsidies and the deterioration in developing countries' terms of trade, although how the transmission occurs, and how significant it is, is not known precisely. Nor is it not known yet which subsidies will really be eliminated, and how many existing subsidies will be re-classified into the permissible Green Box. Subsidies to the production of animal feed, for example, are not even addressed by WTO rules. Another issue is whether the trade-off between removing Northern subsidies and reducing tariffs on imports into African countries will end up helping small African farmers or flooding their domestic markets.

There is a need to devise policies that distort trade as little as possible. Whether the Green Box is an appropriate framework through which countries could develop such non-distorting policies needs further analysis. This would include impacts of subsidy elimination on prices, poverty and the environment, as well as the effects of reallocating subsidies into the Green Box.

**Trade preferences:** Participants discussed the links between trade preferences and economic development. Many were sceptical about trade preferences as a driver of development. While African countries have enjoyed important trade preferences, their share of global exports has decreased over the last 30 years. In contrast, many Asian economies have seen a dramatic increase in their global export share. It was noted that preferences can generate over-dependence on a single commodity (e.g. raw sugar in Swaziland).

**The cost of adjustment and preference erosion:** An eventual Doha reform package will generate net gains for some countries, but others may not benefit – particularly those currently benefiting from trade preferences, such as LDCs, some small island economies and countries in the ACP group. The adjustment burden of any new rules will mostly fall on the poor. Complementary reforms will therefore be needed to address economic and social costs. Poorer countries that are unlikely to gain much from a global set of trade reforms in the short term could perhaps gain from increased aid to support multilateral trade. This could soften the negative effects of preference erosion and allay fears regarding the costs of implementing additional rules.

**Special Products (SPs) and a Special Safeguard Mechanisms (SSMs) and the need for a more development-focused AoA:** The July framework's provision on SPs and an SSM was seen as a positive move towards addressing problems faced by resource-poor farmers. Participants agreed that the number of products nominated should be kept to a minimum. However, if products such as rice, sugar, dairy and cotton were designated as 'sensitive products' by industrialized countries, developing countries would risk losing all the benefits.

A number of participants emphasized the need to provide support to develop **analytical and technical capacity** within the G90 countries. This could be done by strengthening existing institutions, such as the South Centre, or the establishment of the equivalent of the OECD Secretariat to provide impartial research and analysis for these countries. Others suggested that NGOs could help through imparting their **media and press skills** to officials in these countries. The need to identify effective and like-minded people and organizations with whom to collaborate in developing countries was also emphasized.

## 4. Trade, agriculture, the environment and development

**Rise of regionalism and shift to protectionism by industrialized countries:** Participants acknowledged the rise of regionalism and argued it could reinforce multilateralism. Where countries have similar economies, a regional agreement can lead to economies of scale and improved governance, and facilitate negotiation within multilateral trade agreements.

It was said that industrialized countries are becoming increasingly protectionist, as shown by decisions of the US Congress. On the other hand, the lobbying that will accompany the 2007 expiry of the US Farm Bill could include some positive pressures, such as the demands of environment groups, the need to cut expenditure, equity issues and the hunger lobby.

**Trade negotiators need to consider poverty and environment dimensions:** Although multilateral trade negotiations can create export opportunities by lowering barriers to trade, developing countries are often unable to take advantage of market access because they lack the supply-side capability and competitiveness. The WTO therefore needs to increase its relevance to developing countries by establishing more linkages to such issues.

# Chapter 10 | Agricultural Commodities, Trade and Sustainable Development

**Need for a commodity approach:** Many participants highlighted the danger of generalizations about trade liberalization. Differences in power structures, institutions, production sectors and national sustainable development goals mean that responses to trade liberalization can be very different, depending on the commodity and country in question. Trade liberalization must be accompanied by institutional reforms, including the rule of law and improved access to markets in practice. While within a country there may be products that simply cannot compete after liberalization, other products might be able to benefit. There might also be a need to protect a sector for food security purposes. Since some commodities can contribute more than others to poverty reduction strategies, they could be analyzed and treated in different ways.

Some participants suggested that compensation payments against price shocks would perpetuate inefficiencies. Others noted the value of **introducing compensation mechanisms into the WTO's Dispute Settlement Understanding (DSU)**. Arrangements are needed to alleviate the problem that weak countries often refrain from retaliating even if they win their case at the WTO due to imbalance in power relations. In this context, for example, the losing party could be required to lower its tariffs on exports from the winning party. This could be compensation for maintaining subsidies and could effectively improve market access for the winning party. Another participant suggested that compensation could be linked to DSU suspension of certain rights including, for example, the right of the losing party to trigger future DSU proceedings. Since the DSU remains open to reform, experts and civil society groups could make use of this opportunity to explore ideas to right the current imbalance against poor countries. Some expressed the hope that the recent case of Brazil against US cotton subsidies would arouse efforts in other developing countries to identify how the DSU could be used as a tool to bring about change. Others, however, felt that too strong a reliance on the dispute settlement system could contribute to an eventual systemic collapse.

Debate on access to medicine has absorbed much of the political energy surrounding intellectual property rights, which means that the nutrition dimension seems to have slipped off the agenda. More work could usefully be done to explore the **links between food security and TRIPS**.

In the WTO, divergences exist not only between developed and developing countries but also within the latter group. This is problematic since current negotiations acknowledge that SDT should be integral to new commitments and disciplines. Even though there are strong arguments for allowing flexibility for some developing countries, rich countries' negotiators will not look favourably on a broad-brush approach that tries to provide sufficient flexibility for all developing countries. Developing countries will have to pay a price for any SDT they wish to include in trade rules, so they need to be sure that SDT will be effective in meeting their development needs. On the other hand, SDT that is too specific and tightly defined will undoubtedly leave some countries exposed.

But while many developing countries expect to benefit from agricultural trade liberalization, LDCs resist the erosion of trade preferences and net food-importing countries do not want prices to increase. The FIPs (Five Interested Parties – the US, EU, Brazil, India and Australia) is a group of countries that brokered among themselves the compromise leading to the 'July framework.' This implies a risk of oligarchic decision-making at the WTO, which may weaken the faith of middling and small countries in its decision-making processes.

While the ability of the current negotiations at the WTO to deliver pro-poor, pro-sustainability outcomes has been questioned by many, participants agreed the need for a two-pronged strategy – working within the current negotiation agenda to argue for pro-poor measures, and pursuing a set of parallel, complementary processes. These include those at the UN's mid-term review of the MDGs, the FAO and UNCTAD, which may be better able to take a broader view, and address questions of poverty and environmental sustainability. The political opportunities raised by trade negotiations can also be used to leverage parallel processes that generate support, for example, for flanking measures.

One participant noted the increase in misuse of environmental justifications as a means of protectionism. For example, in addition to the European Commission, countries like Switzerland, Norway and Japan have all separately emphasized the perceived environmental benefits that their subsidy programmes confer. These include various public good elements, such as limiting soil erosion, maintaining biodiversity and other environmental benefits from traditional rice farming in Japan and ancient traditions of dairy farming in the Swiss Alps. International commitments within and outside the WTO to reduce environmentally harmful subsidies should be a target of research and negotiation, but many of them remain embedded in the Green Box. Fishing subsidies, which had been the focus of early research and negotiation, could be a useful model for future negotiation regarding other products.

Some subsidies can be beneficial for the environment. But it is important to ensure that such subsidies are transparent, contestable and do not distort trade. A number of participants pointed out that many agricultural subsidies often negatively affect both trade and the environment. Unfortunately, there are few reliable estimates of EHS.

## 5. Conspiracy of silence

**The way forward depends on what vision is held of the role of commodities in development.** Comparison of alternative scenarios might be a useful way to shape the debate around trade, subsidies, tariffs, supply management, and the power balance in commodity chains.

**Tough unknowns such as climate change, declining oil reserves and the changing influence of different countries.** Climate change will affect where commodities are produced and where large food companies source materials, and will lead to greater volatility. The consensus is that commodity yields will drop 10 to 20 per cent (in Uganda, a 45 per cent reduction in rainfed coffee production is expected by 2020) and the growing season in the North will be considerably extended. Biofuels are becoming more prominent as an alternative to oil, with Brazil poised to be a major player with up to 20 million ha of sugar cane. This raises important environmental issues.

**Diversification and its risks.** Some participants considered that the long-term decline in commodity prices is inevitable as it reflects structural changes and policy reforms which will not be reversed. It is necessary to look beyond agriculture for solutions, especially for high-cost producers and countries that do not have an obvious comparative advantage. Clearly, there is more at stake in poverty reduction than the commodity issue alone. There are many barriers to diversification out of agriculture. NGOs have given insufficient emphasis to migration and tourism as diversification strategies. But diversification within agriculture is also important, although it does not always bring about quality employment, as demonstrated by the flower sector, where employment is seasonal, casual and low-paid.

**Distinguishing between commodities.** It is important to disaggregate the commodity sector, recognizing specific solutions rather than a one-size-fits-all. The framework of *competing* and *non-competing* products is useful but further differentiation is required within these categories. Domestic consumption should not be forgotten, especially in China where demand for meat is leading to rising demand for imported feedstuffs.

**Drivers of overproduction and commodity dependence.** Many agricultural development projects have the effect of increasing oversupply at the global level. But supply can increase even where there is no development assistance, as in the case of coffee in Brazil. If prices drop, for many small producers the only way to sustain household income for essentials is to *increase* production, thus leading to further oversupply. Aid to agriculture from donor agencies is low and agriculture commodities rarely feature in the PRSPs. Subsidies in the North may contribute to low commodity prices, but even without subsidies there will be continued production growth in areas with comparative advantage in natural resources such as the US, Ukraine, Russia and Brazil. Agricultural markets are caught in a deeper dynamic of overproduction and shifting of production to low-cost locations, which is reinforced by the irresponsible way in which Northern countries attempt to correct for these trends.

**The role of the private sector.** The private sector cannot be expected to fill completely the vacuum left by withdrawal of government support to agriculture and the demise of marketing boards. But it could do more to address gaps in relation to inputs, finance, storage, marketing and processing. Business decisions and livelihoods are closely linked, e.g. Unilever in Indonesia, where procurement of a given weight of soya supports 3,000 to 4,000 farmers, compared to two or three in the US. Moreover, for every job created by Unilever in Indonesia, 100 were created in the wider economy. Alternative financing mechanisms need to be explored; while market risk management approaches have not shown significant progress so far in developing countries, they should not be ruled out yet as a way to make markets work.

**Corporate concentration.** It was suggested that 'market power' is a more useful term than corporate concentration. Concentration exists but it is not well quantified either at the retail or input level, and is exacerbated by technology (e.g. GM, patents). Most food is produced and consumed in local markets, so attributing poverty to global concentrations requires careful analysis. But not all trade is local, especially in tropical commodities. Supermarkets are adopting 'ethical' policies but this appears to be in contradiction with their pricing policy.

**Competition Policy.** Participants discussed the importance of strengthening competition policy at national and international levels, to prevent restrictive business practices such as cartels and anti-competitive behaviour by the major corporations that dominate the agrifood sector. One in three developing countries does not have an adequate competition framework. Competition policy may not always be the best way to tackle market power in the food chain. There was agreement that national competition authorities can help, but most of the major companies in food chains are beyond their reach. Competition policy was put into place to promote economic efficiency, and requires proof of collusion and abuse of dominance. As its emphasis is typically on consumer welfare, there is a lack of clear economic models to deal with impacts of market power on producer welfare. Corporate concentration is not always negative: if corporate activity is concentrated in a few hands, problems can be regulated via only a small number of companies. Even then, market concentration may be used by buyers to depress the share of revenue gained by different actors along a given value chain. It may be worth considering a multilateral competition agreement – in or outside the WTO – to redress the structural shift in the balance of power in value chains.

# 6. Commodity production and trade: public policy issues

The crisis in tropical commodity prices is central to any attempts to reduce poverty. A commodity-specific focus in multilateral agricultural trade negotiations provides a valuable approach, especially when dealing with poverty alleviation. In general, commodity supply chains are changing in major ways, towards saturation in some markets, steeply falling prices, bigger gaps between farm and retail prices, a clear distinction between bulk and origin-specific sales, widening price spreads between premium and discounted grades, and quality premiums now attached to specific processes such as fair trade and shade-grown. The commodity price collapse is not just a supply-demand issue, but also the result of quality, and hence added value, being generated closer to the point of consumption. In the case of coffee, the decline in overall coffee bean quality, with the abolition of marketing boards in producing countries, combined with new processing technology, means that Northern processors can 'add' quality (and therefore more value) to a low-quality bulk commodity.

The governance of international commodity markets is also changing, with major impacts on quality where liberalization has not been managed and coordinated. There is also much greater vertical integration within supply chains, by international trading companies, with buyers exercising greater control through the setting of higher and higher standards. There has been a shift to cut government involvement in trade and

## Chapter 10 | Agricultural Commodities, Trade and Sustainable Development

standard setting, with the private sector driving many of the market changes. Approximately 300 to 400 buyers account for 80 per cent of global trade in the main commodities. These bottlenecks, at which buyer power is highly concentrated, represent leverage points where major change could be effected. Consumer dominance and supermarket power are potential forces for good, including improved production practices. Consumer preferences are determining the standards relevant for market entry, enforced by a combination of contractual and statutory measures.

But it is increasingly difficult for producers and consumers to distinguish between publicly and privately generated standards. Private standards are outside the WTO at the moment, and are being pursued through parallel, industry-led processes. The private sector is pushing environmental practices beyond legislative requirements, but without an increase in the price they are willing to pay. Hence, meeting these new standards has become a cost for producers of doing business. Farmers may be willing to live with higher standards and labelling regimes, but they do not want the extra cost imposed on them without gaining a share of the value. The biggest single challenge from a poverty and environment perspective is this growing differentiation according to distinctions based on process and production methods.

The policy discussion around commodities is quite poorly developed, and focused predominantly on upgrading quality, or technical assistance to help producers diversify away from commodities. As mentioned earlier, it is not well understood which commodities will be most impacted by trade liberalization and changes in subsidy regimes. For example, a cut in subsidy for sugar and cotton is likely to bring an initial increase in the international price, leading to an increase in production and subsequent downward pressure on prices. These developments are likely to have negative impacts on those least able to adjust to such price swings, as open markets favour those with flexibility and the strongest comparative advantage.

There are problems in reinstating ICAs, because the demise of state trading enterprises raises the question of who is supposed to implement these agreements. The private sector is increasingly engaged in SM through forward contracting and inventory management, which means that many companies will be strongly opposed to re-establishing ICAs. But there is also a growing civil society movement in favour of looking again at SM approaches, and the commodity price crisis is now high on the NGO agenda. This has implications for civil society engagement with the WTO agenda. Analyzing commodity supply chains needs to link with an understanding of the complexity of livelihoods at household and community levels, to identify how changes in market governance could bring benefits to poorer producers.

**Standards** and technical regulations were highlighted as important barriers to trade as well as potential opportunities for developing countries to earn a price premium. On the one hand, many of the standards set by importers are beneficial to the exporting country and its consumers, through efficiency gains and improvements in health and environmental quality. However, there is very little empirical evidence to substantiate how standards could support supplier upgrading and development. This is an important area for new research. Traceability "from farm to fork" presents a major challenge for developing countries. For example, DNA traceability will be introduced as the next new EU standard, and will become compulsory for all Codex members, once agreed. This is likely to be followed by microchip traceability, which may impose significant costs on the producer. There is a need for clear and binding commitments for standard setters to enter into mutual recognition agreements with each other and exporting countries. Technical and financial assistance will also be needed by producers and exporters in poor countries to offset incremental costs. It would help greatly if these producers and exporters could participate in standard setting to ensure that their constraints are taken into account.

## 7. Commodity policy in an era of liberalized global markets

Participants pointed out that, in an era of liberalized global markets, commodity policy has to take into account a number of issues:

**The connection between overproduction and the compression of producers' share of retail price.** Overproduction is inherently beneficial to buyers, and there is evidence that there is less price compression in managed markets.

**The concentration in retail and processing sectors, and cost-price squeeze on suppliers.** For instance in coffee roasting, the number of major companies has declined from over 1,000 in the 1950s to only five today. There are new (retail) players in the market: Wal-Mart is organizing its own roasting in competition to roasters, getting low-price beans and making own-brand blends. Price pressure downstream leads to deteriorating working conditions upstream.

**The importance of workers** – estimated at 40 per cent of the agricultural workforce, but often overlooked in discussions on commodities. Contradictory forces are at play – the loss of small farms which puts more people into wage employment, but on the other hand the growth of subcontracting and outsourcing (e.g. in sugar cane), which can increase the size of the small-farm sector. Both trends have significant implications for worker welfare.

**The organization of producers and producer countries,** to (a) accrue countervailing power (price and policy influence), (b) build scale in smallholder production to meet the requirements of modern procurement systems (quality, standards, traceability), and (c) invest in storage and downstream value-adding (while appreciating problems of tariff escalation for value-added products, and also not romanticizing producer ownership of downstream sectors).

**The opportunities and limits of *private* sector power and CSR,** and the balancing role of public policy. While appreciating that corporate incentives can be a powerful lever of more sustainable and ethical production, CSR, voluntary self-regulation and private standards need to be balanced by public policy and international norms.

**Contract farming,** the benefits of which need to be better understood.

**The role of competition policy,** which is limited by design to protect consumers.

## Chapter 10 | Agricultural Commodities, Trade and Sustainable Development

There may be lessons from regulating natural monopolies such as utilities.

**Financing of the commodity sector.** Structured finance mechanisms can generate lower interest rates for poorer producers.

## 8. Where there's a will there's a way

The participants' views on international supply management (SM) could be divided into three categories. Some participants dismissed SM on the grounds of economic efficiency, some were more willing to entertain the idea but felt that the political will was lacking, while others felt these approaches are worth considering because of the lack of viable alternatives. Discussion concentrated on the following aspects of SM:

**Core issues:** In spite of some participants' scepticism of the ICA concept, there was agreement that something must be done to address the decline of commodity prices, and that SM is one possible means. Successful SM schemes exist, such as in Canada's dairy and poultry sectors. One discussant said the key to dealing with oversupply is to encourage high-cost producers to leave production, and the proposed transferable quotas would help to achieve this as they would allow such producers to sell their quotas. Some cited evidence that a predominantly non-interventionist approach can be pro-poor and equitable: trade liberalization would have similar impacts without creating a large bureaucracy.

**International secretariat (including trading company):** There was scepticism that such a secretariat could succeed where the market has failed. Koning and Robbins maintained that the main activity of the trading wing of the secretariat would be risk-free sales agency work, based on superior market intelligence. Yet the validity of this secretariat was questioned, owing to a lack of room for failure of the 'trading wing'. One delegate said the only successful trading companies are privately owned and do not publish their information.

**Existing conditions:** Industrial structures are well entrenched, raising the possibility that large firms could retain the ability to restrict supply in ways that benefit them. Indeed, it is generally believed that commodity price transmission is not linked to the international price. Prices and production are fickle – one weather event can trigger an adjustment process.

**Cooperation:** The issue of cooperation is key to the final outcome, and the obstacles to such cooperation are significant. Strong institutions are needed to make contemporary SM work, yet many such institutions have been dismantled in developing countries as a result of structural adjustment. Rebuilding them would be essential – particularly cooperatives and mixed enterprises. Cooperation in commodity markets is fraught with problems of free-riding and illegal activity, not to mention structural issues such as quality and grades in addition to the changing preferences of consumers.

It appears necessary for large producer countries and companies to be involved. However, one delegate claimed that the private sector is not interested in intervention in the market, since the business case for it is weak. The case for developing political will is stronger. One suggestion was for the commodity SM strategy to be couched in terms of commodities in general rather than an individual commodity.

**The economics of commodity SM:** Participants pointed out potential economic weaknesses. Quota allocations have in-built biases and lead to artificial production structures. Preventing consumers from reaping the benefits of productivity growth cuts out an important stakeholder group. Commodity SM is on a larger scale than domestic SM, and hence inherently risky. The whole supply chain for commodities needs to be appreciated: for instance, many commodities are inputs for other industries – what will be the impact on growth? Some of these industries are in developing countries, but many are owned by developed countries.

Diversification not only counters the argument about oversupply but also affords new opportunities for conventional commodities as technology enables processing for new ends. For instance, in Uganda, an excess supply of milk has generated a focus on new markets and free supply to schools. SM may affect diversification out of agriculture and commodity dependence, which has profound implications for sustainability.

The interim export taxes proposed in the paper were criticized as a means to extract income from agriculture. Similar measures had failed to help cotton production in Pakistan.

**Cooperative agreements in markets and other forms of cartel:** Some national SM schemes have proved successful in delivering a living wage to producers and stable prices for consumers, while not influencing world prices. Tropical crops, however, have little in common with the sectors in which these successful schemes exist. Better understanding of how commodity markets function might reveal the existence of some of the initial conditions for developing viable cartels.

**Tweaking and understanding, not reforming:** Many participants considered the proposal for commodity SM to be too radical, contending that minor changes or 'tweaks' to the current system would be more profitable lines of inquiry. One participant observed that plenty of money continues to be made from commodity supply chains, and that to attempt reform would endanger profitability that could be used to leverage widespread change through gradual sequenced redistribution. This argument was countered by evidence that reform of commodity markets would also achieve this. However, it was said that more time was necessary to understand the effects of private voluntary standards, especially with regard to claims that they promote sustainability, and the extent and transferability of such benefits.

**Political resistance** to change might prove crucial. There were a number of ways to reduce it, such as reducing tariff escalation, revisiting competition policy and translating research findings into powerful arguments. Many participants held the view that 'where there's a will there's a way', and that while SM might appear unlikely, politics will hold the key. Many saw piloting SM on a small and contained commodity market, such as nutmeg, as workable. However, some considered that industry would not take the idea of contemporary SM seriously.

## 9. Leverage points for encouraging sustainable commodity production

**Definitions:** Participants questioned the proposed definition of 'sustainable commodities' (SC), arguing that it could include all agrifood commodities. Equally important is the concern over who defines SC parameters. While there was a general expectation that Northern companies and governments will set standards, this has implications for transferability and the rate of uptake in the South.

**Efficiency and the 'business case':** In some agrifood industries the business case for SC and better management practices (BMPs) does exist. For example, General Mills reduced pesticide use by 70 per cent in 30 years; likewise Coca-Cola reduced sugar; and Gap is working with producers to reduce risk through private voluntary approaches such as EurepGAP. Many participants agreed with the authors that focusing on what is wanted and letting business get there makes good business sense.

**Transparency:** It is becoming increasingly difficult for companies to require chain-of-custody standards in their supply chains, but to claim ignorance of what is going on in the field. This raises liability issues and makes companies more interested in SC.

**Measuring impacts:** Participants considered that impacts of SC need to be measurable and standards should cover the whole supply chain. Measurements should be taken at national, international and local levels, of a range of benefits and costs – social, economic and environmental – some of which are tricky to measure. Decisions will need to be taken over trade-offs between global costs, such as pollution, and local benefits. Few of the current BMPs measure results, rather these have proxies. It was mentioned that the three-way split between social, environmental and economic may need to be explored, to accommodate values such as gender and small-producer participation. Participants agreed that we need to find practical strategies that avoid the 'race to the bottom' and raise standards while ensuring inclusion.

**International trading architecture:** One participant believed that SC should not be a product category for WTO negotiations, even though another participant suggested the Green Box as the place for this discussion on SC. Indeed, it was described as theoretically incorrect to use trade preferences to promote SC owing to unintended consequences – and hence unfair for the WTO to be used for such purposes. SC preferences could be viewed as protectionism in disguise. Several participants mentioned that the agenda at the WTO is already over-complicated, and that since preferences have not helped countries to date, it is unclear how new ones could do so. Several participants raised equity concerns that preferences could create, and recommended a closer look at how trade policy capacity building is designed to deal with such concerns. It was also pointed out that the WTO is not the only trade arena relevant for SC. Other trade agreements give preferential access or provide for cooperation on SC and they need to be further explored.

**The economics of SC:** There was a view that the scale at which impacts accrue to different-sized producers needs to be accounted for. Promoting SC raises access issues based on economies of scale, and participants considered it important not to widen the gap in market power between small and large industry participants. It was said that SC often puts pressure on the weakest and poorest producers. Increased costs for producers are often not outweighed by premium prices. This could affect poorer nations and continents, particularly Africa. Equally, financial instruments are needed to help engineer diversification. BMPs are useful but need flanking measures to help the poorest families. It was mentioned that some large retailers are not interested in eco-labels since they would indicate that some of their produce is less sustainable. The industry requires incentives to promote SC, and the evidence was said to be unclear on how processors, manufacturers and traders might react to BMP initiatives.

**Industry participation in SC:** There is a need to build legitimacy into associated processes through multi-stakeholder engagement. However, smallholders usually lag behind in BMPs. Mechanisms are needed to help them keep up with progress. One potential market-based solution is to focus on getting the largest 15 to 20 per cent of companies and countries committed to a BMP process, to create incentives for others to follow.

**Stakeholder cooperation in SC:** In addition to building industry interest in SC, it is essential to build alliances along the supply chain. It was suggested that a follow-up meeting be organized to which funding institutions, UN agencies (UNDP, UNCTAD, ILO) and others (the Common Fund, donors, banks) should be invited; and to engage with other processes (e.g. the meeting in The Hague on 'Aid for Trade'/trade adjustment). Further thought is needed on how to involve governments, but it was thought that a good start would be in financial architecture, such as a fund for kick-starting regulatory processes, investment and financial instrument design.

**Flanking policies:** There was heated discussion over the most appropriate 'flanking' policies (financial instruments, trade, social and environmental policies and cumulative environmental impacts and their enforcement) and their significance.

**Technological developments:** Most better management practices are the result of producer or buyer innovation. It is likely that new BMPs will also evolve, such as new systems of traceability.

## 10. Conclusions and leverage points

### 10.1 Windsor Conclusions

The main conclusions of the Windsor dialogue were summarized into priority areas with respect to negotiations, policy analysis and research, advocacy, and constituency building. The 'Windsor Initiative' proposed at the dialogue (see Annex 1), would serve as a process of follow-up and monitoring and the mechanism through which the priorities below would be regularly updated.

#### 10.1.1 Issues for immediate and short term action

**In the WTO/Doha Round context:**
• Pro-poor, sustainability definition of

a. *Special Products* and their identification;
  b. *Special Safeguard Mechanisms*;
  c. Criteria for *Green Box* subsidies;
  d. Non-development distortive, essential food aid;
  e. Food security;
- Further explore special and differential treatment possibilities in the Doha Round negotiations on agriculture;
- Technical work to support quest for balance for market opening and pro-development flexibility on market access – better understanding of proposed formulae in Doha talks and their specific impacts from poverty/sustainability perspectives;
- Transparency in allocation and purpose of subsidies in OECD countries and other major providers of such support, including:
  a. Disaggregated public information on allocation of subsidies and other forms of internal support–purpose and destination;
  b. Criteria for blue and amber boxes;
- Dispute settlement review – issues related to enhanced participation of developing countries and use of DSU for pro-poor outcomes;
- TRIPs, particularly the nutrition policy objective (TRIPs para. 8, and the Doha Declaration para. 19 negotiating mandate) and the relationship to the use of genetic resources for food and agriculture.

**On bilateral and regional trade negotiations**
- Agricultural-poverty aspects of the Economic Partnership Agreements (EPAs) currently under negotiation between ACP countries in the context of the Cotonou Agreement;
- Agriculture-related aspects of the Free Trade Area of the Americas (FTAA) process and sub-regional contexts, including US-Andean, US-CAFTA, US-Chile bilateral negotiations, Andean-Mercosur and EU-Mercosur negotiations;
- Development of special and differential treatment schemes in the context of Regional Trade Arrangements (RTAs) and other cooperative schemes among developing countries (including the revived Global System of Trade Preferences -GSTP);
- Competition policy schemes at regional level;
- Adjustment mechanisms at regional level.

**On parallel processes and forums:**
- Harnessing objectives of reform to UN MDG process
  a. Urgent - Effective work on MDG 8 (such as the impacts of developed country policies and connections to agricultural trade reform);
  b. Urgent – input into UN Millennium Project Task Force Reports (Trade; Hunger; Poverty; Environment) and the March 2005 public debate
- Link to work in U.N. Human Rights Commission bodies

**Others:**
- Strengthening analytical capacity for agricultural trade policy formulation in developing countries;

## Conclusions | Chapter 10

- Improving means for providing effective voice to small farmers and poor communities;
- Critical review of agriculture trade policy technical assistance and capacity building, including standard-setting bodies;
- Identify and foster action on specific US/EU initiatives and policies vis-à-vis poorer countries (such as AGOA).

### 10.1.2 Issues for intermediate-term actions

a. Technical work related to disaggregating AMS;
b. Linking trade obligations to adjustment mechanisms;
c. Compensation/remuneration mechanisms for small farmers and their Agro-biodiversity and environmental services;
d. Environmentally harmful subsidies (EHS) – look into lessons from debate on fisheries subsidies and at possible cross-fertilization of negotiations in the two areas;
e. PPMs and standards use and management;
f. Explore idea of a Global Adjustment Facility to assist countries on agriculture reform impacts;
g. Explore using the DDA mandate on environmental goods and services as a win-win-win solution;
h. Review and utilise currently available material on export/import surges;
i. Enhance effectiveness of advocacy and other communication-based agriculture reform-related initiatives through:
    - Promoting use of more comprehensible language to explain outcomes and impacts of agricultural policy on poverty and sustainability;
    - Promoting attention to policy impacts at sub-national levels and among diverse communities;
    - Promoting development of indicators against which to assess performance against a set of pro-poor/SD objectives;
    - Promoting better understanding of what is possible in the Doha Round negotiations;
    - Exploring the roles of state/private actors.

## 10.2 Barcelona Conclusions

The presentations of participants' working groups at the Barcelona dialogue were summarized around three themes: *public policy, private-sector engagement* and *research gaps*. These represent a collection of ideas and divergent views, rather than a consensus statement or a plan for action.

### 10.2.1 Public policy interventions

Recommendations for government action were targeted at both national and multilateral levels, with distinctions made between policy-related and technical interventions, and between short-term and long-term measures.

**Policy – Short-term**
- Keep the WTO agenda simple: don't overload it with commodity concerns, and guard against barriers to market access.
- Fight market barriers that keep the rules unfair. In WTO negotiations, address tariff escalation to make value addition in developing countries attractive.
- Ensure countries can protect themselves against dumping of underpriced commodities.
- Challenge the power balance at the WTO between North and South.
- Shift the power balance in national trade policymaking, to increase producer and farm-worker representation.
- Ensure coherence between WTO, World Bank and development processes, including the MDGs and debt relief.
- Pay attention to what's going on in regional trade agreements.

**Policy – Longer-term**
- Build on, shape and exploit the renewed interest in commodity issues among many governments, some multilateral institutions and a few funders.
- Improve understanding of where resistance to proposals for SM is centred, and the reasons for that resistance.
- Fight the 'race to the bottom' in the externalization of environmental and social costs associated with commodity production.

**Technical – Short-term**
- Ensure better informed national trade positions that take into account the broader policy context – aim for coherence among trade, commodity and other policies.
- Use the trade policy review mechanism to look forward and see what trade policy should be doing.
- Convene a stakeholder dialogue on SM.
- Ensure a better understanding of the uses and limits of subsidies as a tool to promote good practice for sustainable commodities.
- Consider targeted national spending on commodities, e.g. credit, extension and research.

**Technical – Longer-term**
- Re-empower state organizations, including infrastructure, resource management, credit, risk management, oversight of contracts, standards, producer associations, worker health and safety. Revisit the benefits of directed spending on commodities.
- Review competition policy tools and objectives.
- Look at diversifying within commodity production, and identify where exit strategies are needed and what they should be. Diversification can be a complement for additional revenue (e.g. co-planting of black pepper with coffee) rather than an alternative.
- Focus on broader economic growth in the economy.
- Invigorate South-South trade and increase domestic demand for commodities.

### 10.2.2 Private-sector engagement

Sustainable commodity production needs chain-long cooperation. Industry has tremendous interest: if they do not invest in helping farmers to develop a quality product, there may be shortfalls in supply. It is important to know how to develop dialogues with business people.

**Fairness in trading**
- Get producers back to the 'profit zone,' given the evident overall profitability of commodity supply. The answer may not be in producers entering the industrial process, where they become a competitor with their customers. The moment a coffee or cocoa grower association, for example, enters into industrialization and competes on supermarket shelves, it will be forced out by discounting. The required investments are huge; only Brazil and Colombia have succeeded in coffee. The focus should be on how to add value at point of production, through management, through bargaining power, through breaking dependency, without creating the incentive to increase production.
- Redefine CSR to include fair trading relations. It was noted that there are few policy proposals to encourage the private sector to do better at roles where it has an advantage.
- The private sector should prepare itself for greater civil society scrutiny.
- The private sector should both help to build, and work with, producer associations.

**Sustainable commodity programmes**
- Consolidate and improve certification schemes. There is now a huge number of certification programmes, and it is not clear if all have a benefit. For instance, for bananas in Central America there are eight different compliance programmes, and small-scale outgrowers bear the most cost. We need a side-by-side comparison of what they actually deliver on the ground. We need meta-standards in order to know how to implement social and environmental programmes in the right way. We need to re-evaluate BMPs and their impacts in different commodities, moving from 'less bads' to 'more goods.'
- The private sector should acknowledge its role in rural poverty reduction and MDGs, and deal with 'messy' small farms rather than 'tidy' plantation/wage-labour systems.
- The private sector must not be blind to the issues associated with outsourcing.
- Be aware of the impacts of private voluntary standards and traceability requirements.

**Role of the financial sector**
- Introduce financial mechanisms to support sustainable commodities, and smart finance.
- A comparison of financial mechanisms and their impact should be undertaken.

**Links and communication between corporations and government/multilateral level**
- Transparent communication needed.
- Sustainable commodity programmes are generally private sector-driven and mostly avoid governments – we need to avoid a policy failure.

# Chapter 10 | Agricultural Commodities, Trade and Sustainable Development

### 10.2.3 Research gaps

Participants highlighted the need to fill knowledge and research gaps in a crisp, policy-relevant fashion. This included the need for **better mechanisms for generating knowledge** that can reach different stakeholders, especially those in greatest need, such as the rural poor and small-scale farmers. Recommendations focused on price setting and value distribution, and *legislation that works* to reduce risk and improve the profitability and sustainability of commodity production. There was an acknowledged weakness on power analysis and a shortage of policy tools to regulate market power. Global developments like the impact of Chinese growth were also addressed.

Suggested knowledge gaps include:
- Impacts of liberalization policies, particularly import surges on incomes and livelihoods of poor people, both farmers and consumers;
- Assessing policies for their impacts on poverty and environmental sustainability;
- Exploring commodity supply chains that will be particularly affected by removal of subsidies and domestic support;
- Cost-benefit analysis of conforming to rapidly changing agrifood standards;
- The efficacy of trade-related technical assistance e.g. assistance to developing country delegations in strengthening negotiating capacity;
- New forms of SM given the demise of STEs;
- Addressing highly concentrated market power, e.g. via international competition policy;
- Coordinating and democratizing the process of setting new standards e.g. support for participation by developing country farmers, group certification, etc. ;
- Addressing differential impacts at sub-national levels from trade liberalization;
- Improving coherence between parallel negotiations (RTA, Cotonou, FTAA, etc.);
- Investigating how best to tackle environmentally harmful subsidies;
- Lessons from work on fisheries subsidies for tackling similar issues with agricultural support;
- Linking trade rules to adjustment mechanisms;
- Identifying entry points for proactive, targeted work on those WTO rules with greatest implications for poverty and sustainability.

**Basic information for informed decision making**

Timely and relevant information is essential to strengthen governments' negotiating positions in regional and multilateral trade forums. This includes the latest information on (for example) applied tariffs, domestic support and export subsidies, tariff structures, exchange rates and the effects of the choice of baseline period. Broader analysis is needed on: how the WTO and the private sector can address problems faced by the rural poor, (small) farmers etc; how rural strategies relate to international economic and trade policies in agriculture; the policies and interventions needed to enable rural producers and enterprises to benefit from international trade, including the role of local and regional markets; and private-sector input in trade policy.

Some of this information needs to be made available in WTO terminology. For example, the WTO uses the AMS while the OECD uses the PSE to compare support

levels. Although useful, both AMS and PSE are imperfect measures of relative government support. For example:
- Ensure that no newly proposed WTO rules undermine future flexibilities to address food security or undermine obligations under other international agreements. It is important to undertake trade-policy impact assessments of these rules before negotiations start.
- What is the relative importance of domestic support and tariff escalation? A simple methodology is needed to identify and calculate tariff escalation, given the different tariff structures for primary inputs and processed products.
- Will the elimination of tariff escalation lead industry to move to developing countries? Or do other trends dominate, such as the need to produce close to the market?
- What is the impact of existing development projects on commodity production?
- What does the Chinese growth model mean for commodities, trade, poverty and sustainable development?

### Price transmission and the price-sustainability relationship
This is the process through which international price fluctuations affect the farmgate price. The process of price transmission is not well understood in the case of commodities, for example:
- How the transmission mechanism works in different commodity value chains - this can help to determine where interventions are best placed;
- Linkage between retail prices and farmgate prices;
- Links between commodity prices and poverty – if prices go up will poverty be reduced?
- Linkages between commodity prices and environment - if prices go up, will the environment be improved?
- How much difference would sustainable commodities make to improving prices and export earnings of developing countries?

### Policies to reduce risk in commodity production
- What are the best ways to reduce risk to the small-scale commodity producer? Can markets be used to build assets and extend opportunities?
- What financial tools would help small farmers reduce capital costs and price risks?
- What models of intermediate state institutions could take up some of the old functions of marketing boards? These include purchasing and procurement, contract development and administration, negotiations, transport and logistics, storage, distribution, inventory control and management, strategic planning, product development and forecasting.

### Supply management
The coordination of information flows and the reaction of prices are well understood in the manufacturing sector but less so in agriculture. Research is needed on the following:

> **Impact of current programmes.** Better understanding is needed of the connection between supply-chain mastery and marketplace performance and the impact of current SM programmes such as the Canadian system in poultry, dairy and eggs.

## Chapter 10 | Agricultural Commodities, Trade and Sustainable Development

**The private sector and SM.** Which activities in the management supply chain could the private sector undertake and what are the incentives that governments could devise to attract private sector involvement in managing aspects of the SM process?
- Identify the roles that could be implemented by the private sector and other stakeholders such as producers' alliances.
- Testing new approaches – build a demonstration case of a producing-country cartel, with a small commodity such as nutmeg.

### Policy tools to encourage Sustainable Commodities
- Identify success stories and related policies, legislation and private-sector initiatives.
- What are the best policy tools (domestic and international) to encourage sustainable production?
- Is there a developing-country angle? (The concept of sustainable commodities has been driven from the North, and is often interpreted as another barrier to market entry.)
- Are subsidies the only tool or are there other instruments? What size of subsidy and timing is appropriate?
- Where should subsidies be targeted: at the farmer or the bank that supports the farmer?
- Should the subsidy come from government or from foreign assistance?
- Is the business case for sustainability weakening or evolving?
- Increasing domestic demand for commodities.

### Regulating market power
- Assess the literature examining imperfect competition in agricultural markets.
- What should be the economic criteria for identifying the exercise of monopsony power or types of legal reasoning that could serve as a basis for action?
- Review mainstream policy options in relation to oligopoly in commodity trading.
- Review evidence on market concentration and monopsonistic behaviour in order to devise appropriate global competition law.
- What national policies and market structures have succeeded in building countervailing power, protected primary producers' interests and prevented the abuse of market power?
- Compare commodities for degree of value-chain compression – where is compression occurring?

### Financial institutions
- Identify the instruments that financial markets could deploy to reduce risk to the small farmer who produces commodities. In other words, how can financial markets contribute to building assets and extending opportunities to small, resource-poor farmers?
- What arrangements could financial markets and the state introduce to help small farmers reduce capital costs and price-fluctuation risks?
- What other sources of lending could be made available to small farmers (for example buyers are increasingly lending to producers)?

### Price-sustainability relationship
Sustainable and stable pricing at the farm gate would directly affect the incomes of small-scale farmers. It is crucial that a study be undertaken to establish the relationship between fluctuations in commodity prices and the impact on poverty reduction.

**Market information**
Small-scale farmers need up-to-date market information on global production and demand to make decisions about production, storage and processing. In this respect, there is a need to:
• Generate more information about commodity production systems and trade;
• Compare certification programmes and production systems;
• Assess the impact of better practice in different commodities.

## 10.3 Next Steps

The goals of the dialogues were to determine (i) how the Doha Round agricultural negotiations could increase benefits for poor people and nations, (ii) how to link developments in those negotiations to other areas of policy necessary for trade liberalization to realize its potential to improve the lives of the world's poor, and (iii) what are the main leverage points for action and opportunities for collaboration within ongoing negotiations and other processes. The meetings established a platform for individuals and organizations to carry forward the thinking on poverty and promote sustainable development in their respective countries or regions, and to influence the multilateral trading system and other international processes.

Participants agreed that the discussions had helped shape an agenda for reform towards pro-poor, sustainability-oriented agriculture policy reform. Findings and further work can be fed into trade negotiations through a number of well-placed organizations based in Geneva and in the key capitals. Activities to promote greater coherence between agricultural policy and other domestic policies were discussed, as was the need to define clear policy objectives to bring together a range of actors and to link those that understand what is going on in the South with those shaping policy in the WTO and in the North that shape the options for developing countries. To foster pro-poor outcomes, it may be more important for developing countries to be connected to those that influence decisions in Washington and in Brussels than in their own capitals. Concerns were raised that the recommendations emerging from the MDG Task Forces (particularly hunger) appear to be incompatible with existing or emerging trade rules, and we might have a limited window of opportunity to foster pro-poor outcomes at the WTO given the proliferation of regional bilateral agreements. A number of participants emphasized the need to review and improve the effectiveness of current efforts on trade capacity building.

As part of the follow-up process, the Windsor Initiative was proposed by the organizers to provide a set of principles and a process based on an informal network. An annual review of progress will be carried out. While the initiative will focus on the WTO, it will be broad enough to reach into regional and bilateral trade issues that focus on developing countries. The network will be open for other organizations and individuals to join.

ICTSD and IIED will continue to offer this platform to practitioners and academics within a range of disciplines to discuss and generate innovative ideas to maximize trade, improve agriculture outputs, reduce poverty and support sustainable development.

# Chapter 10 | Agricultural Commodities, Trade and Sustainable Development

## Annex 1

## The Windsor Initiative

**Towards Pro-Poor, Sustainability-Oriented Agricultural Policy Reform: Priorities for the Next Five Years**

Why now?
- Pressing need for action: the overall direction and possibilities for policy making in vital areas, such as food security, poverty reduction, sustainable livelihoods, nutrition, rural development, environment, and the use of genetic resources are being determined by the global agricultural trade reform agenda, currently under negotiation at the WTO. Concerns about development, vulnerable social groups, and sustainability are not driving the negotiations and risk being further marginalized.
- Manifest need to respond to the challenges facing societies around the world – particularly small-scale, resource-poor farmers - by impacts from highly dynamic globalisation trends in agricultural trade.
- Overwhelming need to include voices of those most affected: trade debates are dominated by policy analysts, inter-governmental and non-governmental organisations, and advocacy initiatives. But many communities most affected by agricultural trade reform are excluded from policy formulation processes. They are particularly absent from decision-making arenas in which economic integration and trade liberalization is being taken forward. As a result, their aspirations and priorities are rarely articulated or channelled into such processes.
- Need to map-out space for debate and innovation in development policy: the ability of national governments and societies to devise agricultural policies to advance sustainable development goals is increasingly limited by regional and bilateral trade and investment agreements, which provide tight constraints on their room for manoeuvre.

What we will do:
Establish a mechanism to review, facilitate and promote policy debate on rural development and agricultural trade reform, at national and international levels, which offer the prospect for more sustainable development.

More specifically, participants in the Initiative would, collectively and individually, actively engage in information-sharing; promote equity concerns in policy-making and negotiation contexts; initiate innovative problem-solving activities; stimulate further analysis and generation of knowledge to fill research gaps and advance pro-poor, sustainability issues; systematically review outcomes from the negotiations; encourage and support participation by stake-holders who have found it hard to get their voices heard at national and global level.

The format:
Our initiative would consist of an open-ended network of concerned individuals - acting in their personal capacity - as well as civil society organisations (NGOs and

IGOs), policy and academic institutions, campaign groups, media, policy-makers and other.

**Our status would be:**

Flexible, independent, non-partisan and firmly committed to the ultimate objective of ensuring that agricultural trade reform and complementary mechanisms are shaped in favour of more equitable, pro-poor and sustainable development objectives.

**How it would operate:**

By identifying and networking with the many global public policy networks, policy analysis groups, opinion and decision-makers and others active in this field. Linking WTO-focused debate with a range of parallel processes in which jointly to make progress with a pro-poor, sustainable development agenda, such as the MDGs, regional trade negotiations, EPAs, PRSPs, and so on.

**Under collective leadership:**

The initiative would operate under collective leadership, with a steering committee or task-force, made up of participants at the first dialogue on agriculture, trade negotiations, poverty and sustainability in Windsor, who are willing and able to serve. This task-force would define its rules of operation and identify an institution, to serve as a focal point, possibly on a rotating basis. The functioning of this mechanism would be assessed annually at a joint session of partners, to share lessons from the past year's work and identify priorities for the future.

## Annex 2

List of participants at dialogue on Agriculture, Trade Negotiations, Poverty and Sustainability, Windsor, June 2004

| Name | Affiliation/Country |
| --- | --- |
| John Audley | German Marshall Fund (GMF) USA |
| Adriano Campolina | ACTIONAID Americas / Brazil |
| Laura Carlsen | Interhemispheric Resource Center-Americas Program/CECCAM /Mexico |
| Chantal Line Carpentier | NAFTA CEC / Canada |
| Jason Clay | WWF US / USA |
| Ken Cook | Environment Working Group / USA |
| Annie Dufey | International Institute for Environment and Development (IIED) / Chile |
| Christian Friis Bach | Royal Veterinary and Agriculture University / Denmark |
| Peter Gibbon | Danish Institute for International Studies / UK |
| Duncan Green | Department for International Development (DFID) / UK |
| Janet Hall | UN Foundation / USA |

## Chapter 10 | Agricultural Commodities, Trade and Sustainable Development

| | |
|---|---|
| Phil Henderson | German Marshall Fund (GMF) / USA |
| Jürgen Hoffmann | Namibian Agricultural Trade Forum / Namibia |
| Faizel Ismail | South African Delegation to WTO / South Africa |
| Scott Jerbi | Ethical Globalization Initiative / USA |
| Rashid Kaukab | South Centre / Pakistan |
| Gawain Kripke | Oxfam America / USA |
| Bernice Lee | International Centre for Trade and Sustainable Development (ICTSD) / Hong Kong |
| Xavier Maret | Adjustment Programme (WWF-MPO) / France |
| Janet Maughan | Rockefeller Foundation / USA |
| Ricardo Meléndez-Ortiz | International Centre for Trade and Sustainable Development (ICTSD) / Colombia |
| Dominique Njinkeu | International Lawyers and Economists Against Poverty (ILEAP) / Canada |
| Santiago Perry | Foundation for Participatory and Sustainable Development of Small Farmers / Colombia |
| Susan Sechler | German Marshall Fund (GMF) / USA |
| Shweta Siraj-Mehta | William and Flora Hewlett Foundation / USA |
| Smita Singh | William and Flora Hewlett Foundation / USA |
| Camilla Toulmin | International Institute for Environment and Development (IIED) / UK |
| Ann Tutwiler | International Food and Agricultural Trade Policy Council / USA |
| Vangelis Vitalis | Ministry of Foreign Affairs and Trade, New Zealand / New Zealand |
| Bill Vorley | International Institute for Environment and Development (IIED) / UK |
| Jake Werksman | Rockefeller Foundation / USA |
| Jack Wilkinson | International Federation of Agricultural Producers (IFAP) / Canada |
| Alex Werth | International Centre for Trade and Sustainable Development (ICTSD) / Germany |
| Linxiu Zhang | Center for Chinese Agricultural Policy, Chinese Academy of Sciences / China |

## Annex 3

List of participants at dialogue on Commodities, Trade, Poverty and Sustainable Development Barcelona, July 2005

| Name | Affiliation Country |
|---|---|
| Mehmet Arda | UNCTAD / Switzerland |
| Samuel Asfaha | South Centre / Switzerland |
| Constantine Bartel | ICTSD / Switzerland |
| Christophe Bellman | ICTSD / Switzerland |
| Debapriya Bhattacharya | Centre for Policy Dialogue / Bangladesh |
| Adriano Campolina | ActionAid International Americas / Brazil |
| Jason Clay | WWF-US / USA |
| Jonathan Cook | WWF-MPO / USA |
| Daniel De La Torre Ugarte | Agricultural Policy Analysis Centre, University of Tennessee / USA |
| Annie Dufey | IIED / Chile |
| Fernando Frydman | Roundtable on Sustainable Soy / Argentina |
| Duncan Green | OXFAM / UK |
| Roman Grynberg | Commonwealth Secretariat / UK |
| Joe Guinan | German Marshall Fund / USA |
| Udo Höggel | CDE / Switzerland |
| Piet Klop | Ministry of Foreign Affairs / The Netherlands |
| Niek Koning | Wageningen University / The Netherlands |
| Bernice Lee | ICTSD / Hong Kong, China |
| Sue Longley | International Union of Food and Agricultural Workers / Switzerland |
| James MacGregor | IIED / UK |
| Akhtar Mahmood | Consultant / Pakistan |
| Raol Montemayor | Federation of Free Farmers Cooperatives / Philippines |
| Ricardo Meléndez Ortiz | ICTSD / Colombia |
| Sophia Murphy | Institute for Agriculture and Trade policy / Australia |
| Néstor Osorio | International Coffee Organization / UK |
| Peter Robbins | Commodity Market Information Service / UK |
| Anil Sharma | National Council of Applied Economic Research / India |
| Smita Singh | William and Flora Hewlett Foundation / USA |
| Ramón Torrent | University of Barcelona / Spain |
| Camilla Toulmin | IIED / UK |
| Ann Tutwiler | International Food and Agricultural Trade Policy Council / USA |

## Chapter 10 | Agricultural Commodities, Trade and Sustainable Development

Bill Vorley — IIED / UK
Jan Kees Vis — Unilever / The Netherlands
Ajay Vashee — Southern African Confederation of Agriculture Unions / Zambia
Paul Wagubi — Independent Consulting Group / Uganda
Christopher T Wunderlich — IISD / USA